TRUE
HEROISM

TRUE HEROISM

IN A WORLD OF CELEBRITY COUNTERFEITS

DICK KEYES

NAVPRESS
BRINGING TRUTH TO LIFE
NavPress Publishing Group
P.O. Box 35001, Colorado Springs, Colorado 80935

© 1995 by L'Abri Fellowship Foundation
All rights reserved. No part of this publication may be repro-
    duced in any form without written permission from Nav-
    Press, P. O. Box 35001, Colorado Springs, CO 80935.
Library of Congress Catalog Card Number: 95-14407
ISBN 08910-98925

Cover photograph: Photodisk

Some of the anecdotal illustrations in this book are true to life
and are included with the permission of the persons involved.
All other illustrations are composites of real situations, and any
resemblance to people living or dead is coincidental.

Unless otherwise identified, all Scripture quotations in this
publication are taken from the *Revised Standard Version Bible*
(RSV), copyright 1946, 1952, 1971, by the Division of Christian
Education of the National Council of the Churches of Christ in
the USA, used by permission, all rights reserved. Another version used is the *New Revised Standard Version* (NRSV), copyright
1989, by the Division of Christian Education of the National
Council of the Churches of Christ in the USA, used by permission, all rights reserved

Keyes, Dick.
     True heroism in a world of celebrity counterfeits /
Dick Keyes.
        p.   cm.
     Includes bibliographical references.
     ISBN 0-89109-892-5 (hardcover)
     1. Heroes—Religious aspects—Christianity. 2. Jesus
Christ—Person and offices.   3. United States—Moral
conditions.
I. Title.
BV4647.C75K48   1995
261—dc20   95-14407
                                                  CIP

Printed in the United States of America

1 2 3 4 5 6 7 8 9 10 11 12 13 14 15 / 00 99 98 97 96 95

FOR A FREE CATALOG OF
NAVPRESS BOOKS & BIBLE STUDIES,
CALL 1-800-366-7788 (USA)
or 1-416-499-4615 (CANADA)

CONTENTS

❦

PART ONE: HEROES TODAY

1. WHO NEEDS HEROES?   11

2. HEROISM AND CYNICISM   27

3. HEROISM AND TRIVIALITY   57

4. HEROISM AND THE PERSON IN THE STREET   79

▼

PART TWO: A NEW LOOK AT HEROISM

5. A FOUNDATION FOR HEROISM IN THE TWENTIETH CENTURY   99

6. FOOLS AND FOOLWORSHIP: KNOWING THE PSEUDOHERO   119

7. TRUE HEROISM: WHY THE IMITATION OF CHRIST?   139

8. THE IMITATION OF A HUMBLE PERSON   149

9. THE IMITATION OF CHRIST: THE BREADTH OF HEROISM   165

10. HEROES NEW AND USED: IMITATING CHRISTLIKENESS IN OTHERS   187

▼

PART THREE: HEROISM AND THE YOUNGER GENERATION

11. HEROISM AND MORAL LEARNING   209

12. THE INTEGRITY OF THE PARENT GENERATION   221

13. CHILDREN IN SOCIETY   237

NOTES   249

BIBLIOGRAPHY   259

118897

To the living memory of Francis Schaeffer,
whose life and faith inspired aspiration

PART ONE

HEROES TODAY

WHO NEEDS HEROES?

The urge to heroism is natural, and to admit it honest.[1]
ERNEST BECKER

In heroism, we feel, life's supreme mystery is hidden.[2]
WILLIAM JAMES

*It would appear that the modern age denies the desirability
or need of great people.*[3]
RAY BROWNE AND MARSHALL FISHWICK

Philip Hallie, a Jewish professor of ethics, had researched the phenomenon of human cruelty to other human beings for years, the numbing, repetitive pattern of the strong crushing the weak when they had the opportunity. One area of his study was the Nazi era, and his research had imprisoned and exhausted him. On a certain day he happened to be reading, in an anthology of documents from the Holocaust, an account of a small village called Le Chambon in the south of Nazi-occupied France. In reading the simple, factual account of the events there, he was annoyed to discover that he was crying. Disgusted at himself for letting his emotions intrude into his scholarship, he left his college office and went home.

That night, as he lay in bed, he found himself visualizing the story he had read. He saw two large, empty buses and twenty gendarmes arrive at Le Chambon to take away the Jews they knew to be hiding there. Then he saw the Huguenot pastor of the village, Andre Trocme, face-to-face with the police captain. At the risk of his life and the lives of his parishioners, the pastor quietly but defiantly refused to give up a single one of the Jews who had come there for refuge (the Nazis had sometimes massacred entire villages for lesser crimes). The story went on to tell of the four years in which Le Chambon rescued between two and three thousand Jews, many of them children, of how the villagers had given permanent haven to some and a temporary hiding place to others on their flight to neutral Switzerland. Although several of the villagers were arrested, and some lost their lives, there was no record of them betraying a single one of their dangerous guests during the entire occupation. As he let the story run through his mind, again he found himself crying.

Professor Hallie got up in the middle of the night, got dressed, and went back to his office to reread the account. He began to realize that the depth of his emotional response was itself something significant. He decided to investigate Le Chambon to try to understand moral excellence more deeply. This decision eventually led him to interview those still living in Le Chambon. He later wrote an account of the village and its pastor in the book *Lest Innocent Blood Be Shed*, from which this account was taken.[4] It tells a story of human excellence in our time, played out not on battlefields nor by famous statesmen but in kitchens and bedrooms by poor farmers, shopkeepers, and their wives and children.

My concern in this book is not with the story of Le Chambon. That story has been told well already. Rather it is to understand moral excellence and our relationship to it. Why would a grown man cry while reading that story? If we shed tears when we hear such a story, what does it mean? Do we just need to get some rest and snap out of it? Professor Hallie thought so at first but then changed his mind, realizing that his involuntary tears were an "expression of moral praise, praise pressed out of my whole personality like the juice of a grape."[5] Having been overwhelmed by accounts of cruelty and degradation to the point of exhaustion, he was confronted with human excellence rising against all odds from the midst of that very depravity. He found it disturbing and painful, but also healing and inspiring. A moral consciousness deep within him was responding to a story of excellence and was demanding to be recognized.

It seems extremely difficult today to get a grip on a solid and believable vision of human excellence. Could it be that we are starved for such a vision? On the one hand we are pinched and narrowed by our own cynicism and the cynicism of those from whom we learn about the world. On the other, we are disgusted by overexposure to the high-visibility vanity and mediocrity of the celebrity world. Could it be that we have let these influences so trivialize us that we have ignored or suppressed our need for a vision of human excellence? If so, we have lost a source of meaning, motivation, healing, and growth.

We are good at talking about excellence in sports, the corporate world, education, music, and hundreds of other activities demanding skill and dedication. Thinking about excellence in these areas is easy because the standards of excellence are for the most part agreed upon and measurable, and those who excel are recognizable. They are the visible winners of our society. But it is as if there is a taboo against enlarging the scale, daring to ask, what is excellence, not in playing the guitar or managing a corporation but in a whole human life? What is it to live a good life? These questions have to do with human greatness— or heroism.

The reasons for this taboo are not very mysterious because the nature of human excellence is not universally agreed upon, is usually not obvious at first sight, and is virtually impossible to measure in any quantifiable way. True heroes are not necessarily the visible winners in our society.

Jonathan Swift once wrote, "Whoe'er excels in what we prize, appears a hero in our eyes."[6] If this is true, and it seems a good place to start, a hero is a person who lives out the things that we prize or value most, enough so that we want to emulate that person. Of course, people prize very different things—many of them mutually exclusive. This should not surprise us since we are surrounded by such a vast diversity of views of the world and of the human place in it. But it does guarantee that a discussion of heroism will be lively and controversial.

WHAT IS A HERO?—SOME NECESSARY DISTINCTIONS

Let me begin with some distinctions to help us map out the territory. We use a number of categories to describe exceptional or notable people. Three of the most common are the talent, the celebrity, and the hero. If we are able to clarify what a hero is by contrasting him or her with these unusual people, we will save ourselves a good deal of confusion.

Talent

A talent is someone who can do something well. He or she has a skill. It could be a natural talent or one perfected by years of discipline and training.

Almost any human activity can be done badly or extremely well—playing the piano or playing the stock market, writing poetry or designing airplanes, throwing a football or throwing a party, leading a nation or leading a classroom, making people cry or making people laugh.

Talents are often uniquely gifted to help others learn their skills either by direct instruction or by being a distant source of inspiration. They often function as examples or models to others even hundreds of years after their deaths, as we have seen in the history of philosophy, literature, visual art, and music.

However, most people with great talents are not particularly well known simply because relatively few talents attract great public attention—even after the communication revolution. Also, someone who is a magnificent talent might have no moral stature but could be a public nuisance—and plenty of them are. G. K. Chesterton illustrated this well. He wrote, "The word 'good' has many meanings. For example, if a man were to shoot his grandmother at a range of 500 yards I should call him a good shot, but not necessarily a good man."[7]

Celebrity

A celebrity is someone who, according to historian Daniel Boorstin, is well known for being well known.[8] Actually, this definition is a little too uncharitable, because most celebrities became well known by having at least one talent that pushed them from obscurity into the public eye.

A celebrity is one who is famous and well publicized. He or she is a celebrity apart from how that publicity came about or how long it might last. One can be both talented and famous but still be a thoroughly obnoxious person and a menace. A great baseball player like Pete Rose was talented enough to be a celebrity and deserved to be in the Baseball Hall of Fame. But he also deserved to go to prison.

Celebrity itself is indifferent to moral character and only indirectly related to talent. It is possible that Mother Teresa and a serial killer could share top celebrity billing on any given day, in that they might receive the same level of name recognition in a poll taken after the evening news. It is also possible, though uncommon, to be a celebrity with no talent. It can happen when one hangs around with the rich and famous enough to be seen in the same frame of the camera with them, or if one has inherited enough money to buy publicity.

Hero
We have started with the idea that a hero is someone who excels in what we prize. But a hero goes beyond that. Heroism involves not just admiration for valued qualities, but aspiration for them. A hero not only defines or embodies something of value to us, but he or she engages our imagination and motivates us to try to make that virtue our own. The hero, as I will be using the word, is someone we want to emulate—male or female.

It is helpful to think of the hero in two steps. First, the hero is the focal point of your aspiration. That is, if you call a man your hero, you mean that he excels in what you happen to prize so that you shape yourself after him. This is to define "hero" in terms of the response of others to him. Although true as far as it goes, this definition leaves out a crucial factor. Some of the most effective generators of their own admiration and emulation in this century have been Lenin, Hitler, and Mao Tse-Tung. They certainly qualify as heroes by the definition just given— what they represented was prized and striven for by many. But this first step sees them in only a value-neutral way, as people who were highly revered by others. It ignores a moral evaluation of what they actually did with their lives.

Many of us, at least, would want to say that these men do not qualify as heroes. Despite their extraordinary leadership talents and great fame, they were not worthy of the admiration heaped on them— because of their vanity and cruelty and the millions that lie dead at their feet. Perhaps we would want to call them "pseudoheroes" or "counterfeit heroes" or even "heroes of evil," illustrations of the hero-making capacity gone astray.

Unhappily, there is nothing in human nature or society that ensures that those who excite and captivate people's imaginations are necessarily morally good. There is no guarantee that power, wisdom, and virtue always come in the same package.

To distinguish heroes from other kinds of revered people, we have to move on to a second step and call a hero a man, woman, or child who shows qualities of moral character that are excellent and worthy of our aspiration. To get at the meaning of greatness implicit in "hero," we may even need to dust off and rehabilitate words like *honor* and *glory*.

As soon as we make this distinction between true heroes and pseudoheroes, we have added a new dimension. We are moving beyond "hero" as a value-neutral description of a person based on the number of his or her aspirants. We are introducing moral judgments about whether he or she is worthy of that respect. We are therefore also appealing, at least implicitly, to some yardstick of human moral excellence that is above our individual preferences, and even transcends the norms of our society.

Of course, introducing this moral perspective raises the largest questions of human life. What are true moral/heroic values, and what are skewed ones or counterfeits? How do we know? Who, if anyone, gets to say? Because there are different viewpoints, is any one person's view as valid as any other's?

We can easily anticipate the controversial nature of this discussion if we think about the diverse reactions to Oliver North in the aftermath of the Iran-Contra fiasco. He was, for moral reasons, simultaneously both hero and villain in the eyes of different segments of the American population. We could give many examples of the interaction between worldview, morality, and heroism in the pluralistic modern world. Think of the polarizing effect such diverse heroes as Rush Limbaugh and Hillary Rodham Clinton have had in the popular mind. As we shall see, it is difficult to come to grips with these questions without appeal to a larger system of meaning.

If we center heroism in moral character, that means human greatness is not *in its deepest essence* tied either to talent or fame, although it may coexist with either. Heroism becomes less a question of a person's ability to lead a talented or dramatic life, and more a question of virtue as a whole human being. By "virtue" we mean not just a single morally good act but the habit, tendency, or disposition to do good in some important aspect of life.

Some will disagree with the idea of linking heroism to moral character. But it is worth noting that the only people who are almost universally accepted as heroic are seen as such not for their high performance skills or renown but for their moral qualities. One need only to think again of Mother Teresa, or of the rescuers of Jews in the Nazi era, such as Oskar Schindler or the villagers of Le Chambon.

Having seen the differences between the talent, the celebrity, and the hero, we must say that they could all be found in one person. There is no reason why someone could not at the same time be talented, famous, and also heroic. It might be that celebrity status forced heroic choices on a person, or that heroic actions led to celebrity. But these categories of exceptional people can also be quite independent in the ways that I have already outlined. The differences between them stand, even when in certain individuals the categories overlap. It is important to see that one can have heroic qualities without necessarily having extraordinary talents and without appearing to be heroic in the eyes of the wider public.

A LOVE/HATE RELATIONSHIP TO HEROES
The current ambivalence about heroes is captured well by Elizabeth Kastor of the *Washington Post*. She puts it this way:

> Ask any adults about heroes today and the very word elicits a
> surprised smile and an extended struggle to come up with some
> name, any name. Although they want their children to have
> figures to look up to, for themselves the concept has become
> irrelevant. Behind their skepticism there is often a certainty
> that . . . they should believe—if only they could—a nostalgia
> for the time when that was possible.[9]

There are many good reasons for skepticism about heroes. We might have seen a good number of them let us down. Some have shown themselves to be corrupt, perverted, or cynically selfish behind carefully managed images of virtue. Others, in all sincerity, have led stampedes into misguided and destructive causes. In either case, the landscape is littered with followers who have been left disillusioned, cynical, and often broke as well. It is easy to understand the view that heroes are dangerous.

But on the other side of the ledger, there is the great hunger to have heroes, to recognize and emulate those who live out excellence as we understand it. There is an awareness that we are approaching a moral crisis in our country. We see the moral disasters in politics, media, business, law, sports, religion, education, and throughout all the structures of society associated with them. We see educational institutions, from the early grades through graduate professional schools, scrambling to put together ethics or values curricula. Through it all, people wonder, where are the heroes to show us something to look up to?

I agree that it is certainly unsafe to have the wrong heroes. It is unsafe even to have the right heroes with the wrong attitudes toward them. But it is also unsafe to have no heroes at all. Think again about Jonathan Swift's view that a hero for us is one who "excels in what we prize." What does it mean, then, if we have none?

It means that we have searched far and wide and can find *no one* who is actually putting into practice the things that we value and prize, and doing it really well! What, then, becomes of the "prized" values themselves? They become disembodied, abstract, and associated with nostalgia or impotent idealism. They become window dressing, but they never quite touch ground in this rough and tumble, cracked and broken world. They are not a source of serious motivation for us.

In other words, if we can think of no one who does put flesh and blood into them, what realistic chance do we have of ever living them out in our own flesh and blood? They become values and ideals that we ourselves believe in only halfheartedly, for the sake of appearances or with our fingers crossed.

Another way to put this is to say that people with no heroes disconnect their imaginations from their futures. The power of heroes in people's lives comes from the motivating force of their imaginations to seize hold of human excellence and realize that that excellence might someday actually become their own. Since heroism implies emulation, to have a hero means, by definition, to want to be heroic — to want to be excellent as our hero is excellent. This is not the same as wanting to be seen or acknowledged as a hero by other people. If that is our only desire, we have restricted heroism to celebrity. The hunger for approval becomes more a vice than a virtue. The pursuit and achievement of excellence can be its own reward, as something beyond accolades.

So, our fascination with heroes and with stories (which are the theaters for heroes to work in) is not a mere academic interest. Our fascination with heroes comes from a hunger for excellence. Without heroes the whole source of imaginative motivation is disengaged from life. Without heroes, what will inspire us to go beyond mediocrity and cynicism? What will keep us from becoming bored and boring?

THE POWER OF THE HERO

Having touched on the theme of the imagination, let us see how hero-ism actually functions in our imaginations. I first realized the impor-tance of heroes when I started doing counseling. I began to see that we can be so motivated by our heroes that those heroes are sometimes a stronger influence than almost everything else in life, including our con-sciously held moral principles. Our heroes can be strong enough to lead any of us to make choices that we know to be morally wrong.

This happens because we are not motivated only by abstract prin-ciples or rules of right and wrong or by rational incentives and disin-centives. We are motivated also by stories, images, and accounts of flesh-and-blood people — and fictional characters — who have lived in ways that we find exciting, challenging, and admirable. By hooking our imaginations, heroes exert a gravitational pull on the shape of our lives, like the effect of the moon on the tides.

Reflect for a moment on the formidable power of the imagination in a trivial area. Imagine yourself late at night trying to do some not-so-thrilling task such as filling out your income tax forms or bal-ancing your checkbook. You begin to nod off and finally give up and say to yourself, "Forget it, I'm going to bed." But suppose you have been unwise enough to leave a good novel beside your bed, and you pick it up just to read a few pages before going to sleep. Perhaps an hour later you are quite alert and might be thinking of reading one more chapter, just to see what happens. Physiological changes have taken place, of blood pressure and pulse rate. Why has this happened? A story has engaged your imagination and fired your flagging body and mind. Of course, you don't get something for nothing — you pay for it the next day — but as you read you feel like a different person.

Take another example that comes closer to our area of concern. Why do you suppose perfectly normal and otherwise sensible people give away millions of dollars to the state lotteries? Of all the money that the lotteries take in, less than half goes back to the winners. I am told that your chances of winning are statistically worse than your chances of getting struck by lightning. By anybody's definition it is a ripoff. What has happened to outweigh the economic common sense that people were born with? Again, it is the power of the story capturing the imag-ination. It is the success stories of the few people who did strike it rich and went from rags to riches, quitting their jobs and buying expensive cars and boats.

Heroes—For Childhood and Beyond

Through history, most generations have passed their values on to their children not by giving them lists of rules and laws to follow, but principally by telling them stories that embody the values of their culture. It is intriguing that children have heroes long before they can understand moral principles. Look at the hats they wear—of the nurse, the fire chief, the soldier, the police officer. These are people that children identify with, and they want not only to wear their hats but to walk in their shoes when they grow up.

The role of heroes in the lives of children is easily seen, but a common misconception is that only children have heroes. It is true that children are very open and unashamed about those they admire. We are apt to associate heroic fantasies with early childhood, followed by a slightly more realistic shaping of life around "role models" in adolescence. But do we really outgrow heroes in late adolescence? Or, more likely, are we embarrassed with some of our heroes and try to push them into the closet? Perhaps we suspect that we ought to be growing more self-sufficient and self-contained as adults, not needing to look up to anybody. In fact, we usually retain a high level of motivation from heroes even as adults, although our heroes are now better hidden from ourselves and others.

Mark Gerzon, the author of one of the more popular recent books about heroism called *A Choice of Heroes*, wrote about the hero's significance beyond adolescence. From many interviews with Vietnam veterans he concluded that the main reason many of them had gone to fight in Vietnam was not patriotism, anticommunism, or commitment to self-determination in Southeast Asia. It was John Wayne—and especially his film *The Sands of Iwo Jima*. Again and again John Wayne's name would come up in his interviews with veterans, representing the heroic model that had inspired them to want to go to war. They wanted to walk in his World War II footsteps.[10]

The business world, more than other parts of modern life, is usually considered to be "down to earth" and "no nonsense," free from mythology and fantasy. One naturally associates heroes and mythology with literature, music, and the arts, but certainly not with the stock market, banking, manufacturing, or sales. Yet only a little reflection shows that heroes exert immense power in this part of life also. Lawrence Shames, in *Hunger for More*, studied New York's money culture of the 1980s. He determined that it was driven not only by the crude incentive of greed but by the mythic stories and heroics of the

"big timers" (entrepreneurs or bond salesmen) in an age with boundless horizons. He found the highly touted "logic" of the business world
very deceptive:

> Business rationality is, as it were, an overlay, a distillation of
> the seething broth of ambitions, aggressions, yearning, and ter-
> rors that define the American tribe. . . . The stock tables are a
> Delphic code, the want ads a blueprint of destiny. Alongside
> the endless series of mundane and routinized business func-
> tions there exists a masked and poignant ardor for the exalted,
> the heroic.[11]

Peters and Waterman, in their best-selling book *In Search of Excellence*, recount with admiration how some of their favorite corporations
have exploited this need to feel heroic. They describe how the manager
of a sales force rented a football stadium and had each salesman run
onto the field through the players' tunnel.

> As each emerged, the electronic scoreboard beamed his name
> to the assembled crowd. Executives from corporate headquar-
> ters, employees from other offices, and family and friends were
> present, cheering loudly. . . . The company is IBM. With one act
> (most nonexcellent companies would write it off as too corny,
> too lavish, or both), IBM simultaneously reaffirmed its heroic
> dimension (satisfying the individual's need to be part of some-
> thing great) and its concern for individual self-expression (the
> need to stick out).[12]

The point here is that if we think heroism is only significant for those
under the age of eighteen or in arts-related vocations, we will hopelessly
misunderstand ourselves, others, and our society. In fact, a study called
The Hero's Farewell[13] charts CEOs' activities when they retire and chron-
icles their attempts to retain heroic stature in and after retirement. It
tells of one executive, so unable to part with his heroic role, that after
years of overstaying his usefulness finally appointed a successor—who
was known to have terminal cancer. Predictably, in six months the successor died and the "retired" CEO came back to the rescue.

I have emphasized heroism within the business world because the
stereotype is that commerce has nothing to do with myth or heroism
but works along strictly rational and functional lines. If heroes pack

enough force to fire the imagination in the corporate world, are they not likely to do so in all walks of life?

The Leverage of Heroism

One of the best ways to see heroism in action, and to appreciate its power, is to observe the interaction between heroism and moral principle. Let me illustrate with a story from the New Testament, in the sixth chapter of the Gospel of Mark.

King Herod, the Roman tetrarch over Galilee when Jesus was alive, had divorced his wife to marry his half brother's wife, Herodias. John the Baptist, an influential Jewish prophet with a large following in Palestine, denounced Herod's marriage, according to God's law. For this impertinence, Herodias bore John a grudge and wanted him killed. Her husband had him arrested and imprisoned to keep him quiet, but was afraid to kill him because he knew he was a righteous man who was widely respected.

One day Herod had a birthday party. Herodias's daughter danced to entertain the guests. She so captivated them all that Herod, in a magnificent gesture of power and goodwill in front of all the guests, vowed to give her anything she wanted, "even half of my kingdom." She realized the career opportunities of such an offer, but not knowing what to ask for, withdrew to get some advice. After some hasty coaching from her mother, she rushed back into the banquet hall and said, "I want you to give me at once the head of John the Baptist on a platter." We can only imagine the scene from Mark's understated account. He wrote that Herod was "exceedingly sorry; but because of his oaths and his guests he did not want to break his word to her."

Herod was caught in an extreme form of a common human dilemma. On one side he held moral principles that told him it was wrong to kill John and thus faced his own guilt if he went through with John's murder. But on the other side, he had just made this heroic vow in front of people whose respect he obviously valued. What would happen if he retracted his vow to spare John's life? He would have forfeited his heroic stature in their eyes and been shamed as a coward and buffoon in front of them all.

If he chose one way, he would bring on guilt. If he chose the other, it would be shame—the experience of extreme unheroism or negative heroism. It is losing honor and self-respect, being reduced as a whole person to the dimensions of your own failure to live up to your heroic ideal.[14] Of course it is magnified if it comes with public discovery of the unhero-

ism, but its main disintegrating force is that it smashes your own preferred image of yourself. It breaks your favorite version of who you are.

King Herod's sense of the heroic "out-pulled" his moral principles.
He ordered John's head to be delivered as requested because his own
desire to be a hero had more leverage over his choices than did his convictions about right and wrong. In the story you can recognize the two
yardsticks by which Herod was measuring himself, the moral and the
heroic, because in his case they were pulling in opposite directions. You
can also see the formidable power of heroic desire to brush aside the
moral scruples that lay in its path.

Aspiration and Aversion

The story of Herod and John the Baptist not only illustrates the power of
heroism but also introduces us to the way each hero has a powerful opposite number. Every heroic virtue is attended by its own unheroic vice. For
example, if courage is considered heroic, then cowardice will be shameful; if wealth is heroic, poverty will cause shame and self-loathing; if power
is heroic, then weakness will be dishonorable; and so on.

Every hero who inspires a goal for aspiration also suggests an opposing focus for aversion. The power of heroism is that it can give us enormous rewards and punishments. The rewards of heroism attract our
aspiration while the punishments of shame inspire aversion. Remember that heroism (by definition) deals with what we prize and value
most, so it touches our lives in areas that we care most about. Anticipated shame, similarly, has enormous leverage on us in the other direction. Through aspiration, having a hero might inspire us to kick down
boundaries and limitations in the spirit of "maybe I can do it too."
Through aversion, having an unhero might motivate us to jump back
for fear that we might walk into some ambush of shame and humiliation. Think of the literature of Alcoholics Anonymous, aimed at inspiring motivation in people crushed in the degradation of alcoholism. It is
for the most part made up of the stories of men and women who have
been able to gain and maintain sobriety, clearly laying out the difference between virtue and vice and the consequences of each in their life
stories. The purpose is to engage the imagination powerfully in the right
aspirations and aversions.

The leverage of our sense of the heroic is powerful because ideas,
images, and stories mediate to us either the reward of heroic success or
the anguish of unheroic shame and dishonor. That is why it matters so

much who our heroes are and how they correspond to what we believe to be ultimately good and important in the world.

HEROISM AND MORALITY

It is useful to think of the three ways that heroism and morals can relate to each other in any one person. First, our heroes can correspond to or reflect our moral values. Heroes are then heroic for moral reasons, and those who live truly moral lives are seen as heroic. In this case the two yardsticks of self-measurement—of morality and heroism—are in focus and reinforce each other. A person is integrated, at least in terms of his or her own standards of self-evaluation. If I betrayed a friend, I might feel guilty for having done something I believe to be morally wrong, but I might also feel ashamed, having behaved unheroically. I would be shocked to realize that I was such a coward, that I had been afraid to stand up for him.

Second, morality and heroism can be quite independent of each other. That is to say, our heroes can be heroic for reasons that have little to do with moral categories. This is true of us, for example, if we treat talents like power, the ability to earn a lot of money, or beauty as heroic. These things in themselves are neither good nor bad in moral terms. But if these are the central things we prize in ourselves and look up to in others, they will distract and confuse our efforts to live a moral life. We will also spend a good deal of time being ashamed of ourselves for all sorts of things that are not wrong according to our moral standards and probably not wrong before God either.

For example, to the extent that physical beauty is heroic to me, I am likely to feel ashamed of my body—the shape of my nose or the size of my ears, having the wrong clothes on for the right occasion. If wealth is heroic to me, and if I am not very wealthy, I will feel ashamed of my home, of my clothes, of my collection of consumer products, and of my inability to spend weekends in the Caribbean. In no sense are these things moral problems, and yet shame about them can bring crushing feelings of self-hatred, disgust, and failure.

The third kind of interaction is the *opposition* of heroism and morality. This happens when people are heroic to us for reasons that we ourselves consider immoral. Then our morality and our sense of the heroic are in the tug of war that we observed in King Herod. His need to be heroic in arrogant power put him at loggerheads with what he knew to be morally right. Likewise, many heroes of the modern world are heroic for their power to exploit and misuse other people—physically, psychologically, sexually, economically. If our heroes oppose our moral values, then we are deeply divided against ourselves. Not only do our goals diverge dramatically, but we face the punishment of either shame or guilt whatever choices and actions we take. It will be impossible not to offend one or the other standard of self-evaluation.

A conflict might arise in which someone wrongs me. If power is heroic to me, I will have a strong motivation to get even, to use what power I have to make the other person suffer humiliation, at least. I would feel ashamed of myself for being a wimp if I did not retaliate. On the other hand, my moral values might say that I should forgo revenge. I am in a crossfire. If I retaliate, I feel guilty. If I forgive, I feel ashamed of myself.

For simplicity's sake, I have so far described any one person's heroes as if they existed in coherent and consistent clusters around certain heroic virtues. But in fact, a typical person's heroes can be very scattered, representing different, conflicting values, with some heroes stronger and others weaker. In the mind of the person who holds strong immoral heroes (are any of us entirely free from them?), there will still be some moral heroes. Therefore, the opposition between morality and heroism is seldom as clear-cut as I have implied. We usually have heroes pulling against other heroes from opposite sides of internal battle lines, although their weight may be overwhelming on one side, as we saw in the example of Herod.

It's likely that there is a confusion of heroic voices within us. If so, that may shed some light on an earlier question. We mentioned those who claimed that, for whatever reason, they had no heroes. To be sure, some people really claim to have no heroes. We will devote the next chapter to their important ideas. But just as certainly, many of us have heroes that we are loath to even recognize ourselves, let alone acknowledge in public. They are underground, in-closet heroes who so jar against our more fully conscious and respectable values that it is painful and threatening for us to acknowledge our attraction to them. Ironically, we can be ashamed of having these heroes, and ashamed of our shame for falling short of them, showing that our heroes are at war with other heroes within us. The underground heroes are likely to be heroes of vanity and violence who trade on our darker fantasies. If they are not there, why are Madonna, Sylvester Stallone, and Arnold Schwarzenegger multimillionaires?

Of course, a goal for most of us would be to become increasingly integrated people, not those who would obstruct and destroy themselves through internal friction and conflict. An integrated moral life involves being able to tell right from wrong, but not only that, it means actually doing the right. Even that is not all. Full integration of morality and heroism means that we love doing the right, we prize it, aspire to it, delight in it. It is heroic to us. C. S. Lewis expressed this in a down-to-earth way: "We do not wish to be, or live among, people who are clean or honest or kind as a matter of duty, we want to be, and to associate with, people who like being clean, honest and kind."[15]

Let me summarize. We have begun to develop the idea of what a hero is by distinguishing the hero from other exceptional people. We have reflected on the way he or she works in our lives and then considered the strength of the hero's influence. We have in heroism an immense force for good or evil, integration or disintegration within us individually and in society at large.

Pascal wrote, "The greatest baseness of man is the pursuit of glory. But it is also the greatest mark of his excellence."[16] He claimed that the pursuit of glory, or heroism, was responsible for the extremes of both human depravity and human greatness. How can this be? He saw the pursuit of glory as essential to human nature itself. People will pursue glory, glory of one sort or another. The all-important question then becomes, *What glory will we pursue?* We will grapple with these questions in the following chapters, but not until we take a careful look at the struggles of the heroic imagination in our own day.

HEROISM AND CYNICISM

The New Generation had matured to find all Gods dead,
all wars fought, all faith in man shaken.[1]
F. SCOTT FITZGERALD

Seventy percent of Americans now say that America has no
more heroes. Why are there no heroes today? There are no
heroes because we have ceased to believe in anything strongly
enough to be impressed by its attainment.[2]
PATTERSON AND KIM

Can a person be a hero if we know him better
than he knows himself?[3]
DAVID DAICHES

He who breaks a thing to find out what it is
has left the path of wisdom.[4]
RICHARD PURTIL

Premodern thought saw lust as confused love.
Modern thought sees love as rationalized lust.[5]
PETER KREEFT

We are living in a time when the very word *hero* has come to carry cynical connotations. What does the phrase "heroic medical measures" usually mean? Doesn't it mean extreme medical treatments given more for the vanity or protection of a physician than for the welfare of a dying patient? Heroism in this sense is at best self-serving and at worst sadistic—in any case, not admirable. As the ideas and structures of society change, earlier heroes get discredited and replaced by others more able to fire the imaginations of each new generation in its particular challenges. The heroes going into forced retirement have often been attacked ferociously—usually through satire. One thinks of the cowboy hero in Sam Shepard's play, "Fool for Love,"[6] born too late for cowboys to be heroes, and reduced to lassoing the bedposts in his hotel room. We have also seen heroic ideals in collision with one another, with all the conflict, recrimination, and ridicule that comes with it, as in the decade of the Vietnam War.

Yet in the late twentieth century we are seeing something different from what has gone before. Loud and learned voices are saying there is no such thing as heroism at all, and never was. This is not just an effort to hurry one outmoded heroic ideal into oblivion, it is a denial of the possibility of human greatness itself. Heroism has become a concept that is said to be "soft" in the light of sophisticated modern knowledge. In his study of heroism in American literature, Theodore Gross wrote, "For contemporary authors heroism is America's vestigial organ, buried somewhere in the body of the country—some lost useless organ whose nerve was never felt in the writers' own lifetime."[7]

Some say the absence of heroes is a hopeful sign. In Bertolt Brecht's play *Galileo*, when Galileo recants his views about the solar system in the face of the threats of the church, his student Andrea is crushed and disillusioned with his teacher. He says, "Unhappy is the land that breeds no heroes." Galileo's quick reply is, "No, Andrea, unhappy is the land that needs a hero."[8] Our willingness to discard heroes is seen as evidence of growing up; holding on to them as a sign of refusal to do so. Whether we see the loss of heroes as a cause for alarm or hope, most of us are affected in some way by the spirit of cynicism in modern society.

At the root of cynicism is the idea of "seeing through" deceptive appearances to the not-so-flattering reality that lies behind or beneath them. Take an example in the Bible, from the book of Ecclesiastes. The jaded preacher wrote, "Then I saw that all toil and all skill in work come from a man's envy of his neighbor" (4:4). Notice three things. First, he claimed to be able to see through appearances to the sources of motivation within a person, not to be fooled by surface impressions of competence and diligence. Second, he stated a universal motivation of human nature, including not just people he had personally observed but all people in all of their toil and skill. Third and finally, the motivation that is uncovered is clearly less heroic than what is visible on the surface. People are often admired for their hard work and skill, but how often are they admired for their envy?

Cynicism about heroes is a powerful voice spoken from both high culture and popular culture today. If heroes are to have any integrity for us in our lives, we must reckon with cynicism's claims.

HEROISM AND REALISM

Heroism can be defended in the late twentieth century, but not by supporting every so-called hero or heroic claim. In the last chapter we distinguished between heroes and pseudoheroes. This assumed that a realistic judgment can distinguish between the two. If we are to recognize true heroism, we must practice a realism that debunks some heroes but stops short of cynically debunking them all.

Realism approaches potential heroes in two ways. First, it unmasks virtues that have been treated as heroic and shows them to be vain, life-destroying vices. Second, realism sees through some individual heroes. That is, there are individual "heroes" who may have pursued valid goals but have blatantly insincere motivations or major flaws that discredit their heroic stature. We can criticize both ideas of heroism and individual heroes while still acknowledging that there is human greatness beyond the scope of that criticism.

Counterfeit Heroism

First, look at the unmasking of pseudoheroic virtues. Some of our society's debunking has been well directed. For example, one can only applaud the death of the heroic myths glorifying war. A common view of heroism has been that it finds its essential expression in war. War was formerly the stage where the ultimate human drama was worked out; it was considered the final test of masculinity. E. Merrill Root suggested that when the wholesome qualities of being a good soldier are suppressed (presumably by the regrettable absence of a war), they are driven into the subconscious only to explode in frustration at a later time. He wrote, "If you inhibit the soldier you incite the murderer."[9] Evidently war was psychologically necessary for the functioning of a good society and certainly necessary for the realization of manhood. This was not just the conviction that war is morally justified in certain cases, and that soldiers are sometimes heroes. It was the idea that war provides the only context for true human glory and honor to be realized—evidently only experienced by the lucky male half of the population.

Although this conception of honor and glory has centered on the soldier, it has never been restricted to the military. It has touched all walks of life and brought with it a macho exaltation of bravery, toughness, and competition; a love of violence and danger; a nonexpression of emotion; and a condescension to women (who have been superfluous except as mothers, admiring lovers, and victims). The myth of the glory of war in its purest form has been substantially exploded by the years of gloryless carnage of the First World War and the cynical cultural climate that followed. Since then, and particularly in the Vietnam era, the ever-improving media coverage of war has tended to keep its sordid reality well within view.

Counterfeit Heroes

The second side of realism about potential heroes is to accept only with caution the heroism of those individuals who appear heroic. For example, some human actions that appear to be admirable are done for all the wrong reasons. Many is the public figure whose heroic posture of crusading for justice for the poor is exploded by disclosures that he has amassed vast wealth for himself on his crusade. Centuries ago, Augustine observed that Romans, with great self-discipline, would put aside many vices such as lust or greed, all in order to indulge one vice—the love of praise.

Our celebrity culture mass produces a flow of "beautiful people" who are expected to function as heroes. When public exposure reaches their private lives they are revealed as not so beautiful. We have all seen examples of this.

Then there are heroes alive and dead who may have been inflated or whitewashed by their own efforts or by others who later found their heroism useful. If we look back in our own history it should not surprise us to find that some of our nation's heroes reveal signs of deflation, or of dirt showing through the whitewash. Washington, Jefferson, and Lincoln were great men, but we must not think that their heroic stature depends on their perfection—especially not according to late-twentieth-century doctrines of "political correctness." A shrewdness of moral vision that requires a certain amount of debunking is necessary to see others realistically. Without it we remain naive admirers of the con artist and the hypocrite. With it we can admire truly heroic things done by fallible people. Realism critically evaluates both heroic ideals and individuals' heroism.

But the vital question is, How far can debunking go and still remain realistic? At a certain point, the confidence that we can see through people to their inner, corrupt motivations could possibly blind us instead of sharpening our vision. Let us take a longer look at the full force of cynicism itself at the two levels we have identified—seeing through heroism and seeing through heroes.

SEEING THROUGH HEROISM—A CRISIS OF MEANING

There are many ways to understand the contemporary shortage of heroes. Some emphasize that technology and mass society have reorganized the world so that individuals are not noticed as much in the great strides of civilization. There is no Lindbergh-equivalent in NASA's space program. While this is true, the difficulties of heroism go beyond that. We are dealing not only with an absence of heroic people in national, "bigger than life" settings but with the inability to acknowledge heroism anywhere else.

Others suggest that we are living in a time of cynicism about all the major institutions of society—education, law, medicine, the arts, business, religion, the family, and government, to name a few. If one is cynical about an institution, one has difficulty seeing the heroism of a person whose main activity is within it. Although there is truth to this explanation also, it simply raises other questions: Why is there such cynicism about the institutions of society? Why do people today have such trouble identifying greatness anywhere?

G. K. Chesterton observed earlier in this century that "the eye that can perceive what are the wrong things increases in an uncanny and devouring clarity, the eye which sees what things are right is growing mistier and mistier every moment, till it goes almost blind with doubt."[10]

There seems to be a built-in disenchantment that neutralizes our appreciation of human greatness. Robert Nisbet wrote that heroes of the past "had audiences of greatness, that is, individuals in large numbers still capable of being enchanted," and that "the instinct to mock at the great, the good, and the wise is built into this age."[11] This observation is echoed by most observers of twentieth-century heroism. How can we explain it?

To understand this kind of perception we must not only think of the changes in society and technology, significant though they have been, but pay attention also to the role of *foundational ideas*. They can be so close to us that they are like our eyeglasses—*we do not see them, but we see the whole world through them.*

One of the most significant contributors to disenchantment with heroism is the widespread loss of confidence that human life holds any understandable meaning. You see, the very idea of heroism depends on having a comprehensible notion of life's meaning. This is obvious after a moment's thought. Heroes can be heroic only in terms of some worldview that provides a system of meaning and value. People do not just excel. They excel in terms of something that is valued. Without some criterion for human excellence, we cannot distinguish heroism from random behavior or villainy. Different worldviews with different meanings establish different heroic ideals that, in turn, are lived out by different kinds of heroes.

The extraordinary diversity of heroes in the world was brought home to me by the book *Peace Child* by Don Richardson.[12] It is a story of Christian missionaries among cannibalistic tribes in Papua New Guinea. After learning the native language, Richardson told the story of the life and death of Jesus to the tribespeople, and they applauded enthusiastically. But to Richardson's amazement, they were applauding, not Jesus, but Judas as the hero. Why? Because in their worldview, the highest value was treachery. For them, Judas added a new dimension in patient, shrewd deception and betrayal.

There has been a massive shift of ideas and attitudes in Western culture that has set the stage for the low status of heroes today. Anthropologist Ernest Becker has described this change as succinctly as anyone. He wrote that people have always believed in two worlds, one that you could see and one that you could not. The material world that you could see was where you lived your daily life. The invisible world was a greater and more powerful world upon which this visible world depended for its origin, power, and meaning. Becker pointed out that *the source of meaning, and therefore of heroism, has always been rooted in the unseen world.* Whether that world involved God, gods, spirits, dead ancestors, forces, or eternal principles, the final point of reference for what was heroic was never in the visible world itself.

Then in the last century, those who followed the developments in Western thought were informed that there was no invisible world, and never had been. What they could see was all that there ever was. Becker rightly attributed the beginnings of the modern crisis of heroism to that change. For those convinced by these new ideas, there was no longer a standard or voice *from beyond their own experience* to enable them to distinguish hero from villain. Meaning, such as it was, had to be manufactured from within the visible world without reference to anything beyond it.[13]

The visible world that surrounds us in our daily lives does not produce meanings all by itself. Even the spectacular achievements of science are only descriptions of facts and the relationships between them. Meanings, if they are not given from the unseen world, must be synthesized within human minds and attributed to the facts and activities of our daily world. But if there is no God or other reliable source of meanings, who gets to say whose meanings and values are true? The question about the meaning of human existence itself becomes an open question. What is it to be a human? Do we have special value or not? If so, why? Our society wants to hold these questions open in a special way. They must *stay* open, which is to say, they must remain unanswered. It is seen as both naive and as a betrayal of our advances in knowledge to believe that we could know the answers. Each of us as individuals can believe in whatever answers we like, just as we can have different private tastes and preferences. But we are told that we must never believe that one person's truth about ultimate meaning is truer than another's.

The Masters of Suspicion

The absence of answers to the questions of ultimate meaning has set the stage for the enormous influence exerted by thinkers who studied human nature and behavior under the prestigious new mantle of "science." Four giants are among those often called the "masters of suspicion"—Marx, Darwin, Freud, and Nietzche. Despite their many differences, their combined impact on Western culture had a certain coherence.

Karl Marx tried to show that a scientific understanding of human nature and history revealed that the vast array of human motivations were reducible to one root—economic self-interest. This motivation controlled individual attitudes and behavior in ways unknown to the individual. Economic forces also established the flow of history itself in a fixed, economically determined unfolding of events over which individuals had little control. *The significance of human choice was minimized, if not excluded, and the only human value was in a person's contribution to the state.*

Charles Darwin's theories raised suspicion about the uniqueness of human beings. No longer was the human race to be understood as the unique creation of God, made in the image of the Creator himself. Instead, humanity was the product of a mindless and impersonal biological process. *It became problematic to maintain human distinctiveness from the animal kingdom, which was simply different products of the same evolutionary process.*

Sigmund Freud, standing on the shoulders of Darwin, claimed that human motivations were reducible to biological drives, but that they were hidden from conscious view beneath the more respectable surface of the human personality. Freud claimed that, instead, *people are directed by unconscious drives shaped by early childhood experiences, especially those having to do with sexual development.* He attacked the common-sense idea that people rationally direct their knowing and doing.

These three men are among the "masters of suspicion" because they cast doubt on the high status of the human race, and also on the confidence that we know our own minds. Instead of "sticking out" from the rest of creation with a divinely appointed task, the human race became simply the accidental product of a mindless process that is going nowhere in particular. Our self-understanding is suspect since our rationally understood motivations are masks for deeper drives and needs more akin to the animal world than to anything transcendent.

Philosopher C. E. M. Joad described the implications of this revolution for human moral meaning.

> Although there was scientific basis for saying that man was the highest primate, there was none for placing him outside the animal kingdom in the matter of unique rights; he was only the star performer in the zoo. Suppose, then, some one put him in a cage or made a slave of him; was there any biological or sociological law which said this could not be done?[14]

Joad could see perfectly well that a man does different tricks than the other animals in the zoo, but these observations do not tell us anything about his value or why we should not treat him as an animal. Science is mute about all values and meanings of any kind. If, for example, a human being is only a biochemical phenomenon, differing merely in degree of complexity from the plant or animal, why should we consider his "heroic ideals" to be important? Are they not just mirages produced by the peculiar biochemistry of the human animal's overheated brain? Could it be that the attempt to create or retain powerful meanings or ideals on this foundation is an act of intellectual alchemy, believable only within the lingering after-shadow of belief in a Creator?

Perhaps it should not surprise us that 70 percent of Americans claim that the nation has no more heroes. Patterson and Kim, authors of the national survey *The Day America Told the Truth*, offer an explanation for this high figure: "we have ceased to believe in anything strongly enough to be impressed by its attainment."[15]

If larger meanings and ideals can be dismissed, then we have "seen through" heroism itself. If we believe that the very idea of moral excellence is bogus, what attainments would impress us enough to want to emulate them, especially if following heroes proves difficult?

Another master of suspicion was Frederick Nietzsche. He was known for his declaration that God was dead. God had only ever existed as a projection of the human imagination, but now humanity had outgrown its need for such a superstition. He saw with great clarity that losing belief in God meant the loss of all meaning, but he found that grimly exhilarating. Without meaning one was left with the will to power as the most basic human motivation. It was to be from the death of God that Superman would be born—a new heroic humanity—defining and creating itself, and reordering the meaningless world. Truth was not discovered, it was invented. Without the shackles of religion, the self-creating power of human will would bring a heroic affirmation of life.

The late twentieth century has seen enough self-creating murderous dictators to no longer be attracted to Nietzsche's Superman hero. However, Nietzsche's ideas of the loss of meaning and the centrality of power as the major human motivation have provided some of the foundation of post-modernism.

Post-modernists would tell us that to believe in ultimate meanings is naive, because these meanings are beyond our reach. We are so locked inside our own heads, with our own personal histories and private agendas, that we can never even understand one another, let alone the meaning of human life.

But post-modernism goes beyond this claim. It says, since no comprehensible universal meanings or heroes exist, that those who believe them do so in order to gain, advance, or preserve their *power* in society—especially along lines of race, gender, and class. The great ideals of Western culture are, when rightly understood, nothing of the sort. There is a hidden agenda, the post-modernist alleges, hidden even to many of the boosters of Western thought themselves. These "truths" are ideas built into the structures of Western society through language, literature, and education as well as political systems—to advance and maintain the power base of white European males who are economically advantaged. The popularity of these ideas of Western culture has been simply a smoke screen to hide the crude exertion of power over disempowered groups.

The heroes of Western culture, along with the historians who have packaged them for us, are all DWEMs—dead white European males. They play a key role in the transmitting of "ideals" for the preservation and profit of those in power. Calling attention to any hero is likely to be a power play designed to oppress the disempowered.

Post-modernism sees through human claims for truth or heroism with a cynicism informed by the biological interpretations of human behavior of Darwin and Freud, and the economic interpretation of Marx. But the thought of Nietzsche adds the distinctive idea of "the will to power" as the hidden explanation of human motivation.

The masters of suspicion had enormous significance for individual self-understanding. Marx, Freud, and Nietzsche all gave us tools that claimed the revolutionary power for the initiated to be able to see through people, so that nothing need be interpreted at face value. People's lives can be understood as controlled by a few very basic biological, economic, or power incentives—regardless of what they think they know about themselves at a conscious level.

Consider the impact of these ideas on heroism. Heroism, which by definition has to do with human choice and action measured by certain ideals of excellence, is leveled out. No one is more admirable than anyone else. One is left with heroism as a grand illusion, existing under a cloud of suspicion.

There is a great irony in this story. The giants who have so shaped our self-understanding and have withered heroism—Marx, Darwin, Nietzsche, and Freud—are themselves some of the few people acknowledged as heroic by society! They have had disciples who fought turf battles over apostolic succession, near-sacred texts, and vast cultural followings, perhaps more outside of their respective disciplines than within them.[16] In practice, the irrepressible human desire for heroes seems to have outweighed all the arguments that these men used against heroism—even in the minds of their followers.

SEEING THROUGH HEROES—CYNICISM UNCHECKED
If we treat people as heroes, we assume that they (like us) have some measure of conscious decision-making ability. To some degree at least,

they know their own minds. Their stature as heroes is undercut if their heroic actions or attitudes are fully explainable by nonconscious, self-serving, or sordid motivations. We are not usually drawn to admire those who are just hapless victims of forces unknown to them, or those whose motivation for good deeds was bad.

Take the classic example of heroism when a man or woman risks life or health to save another person from a burning car. One could take love and courage at face value and acknowledge it as heroic, or with the help of different psychological, social, or biological models see it in many different lights. Let us look at a representative sampling.

If the hero was a man, one expert might say that his risk taking was in fact a desperate attempt to win the approval of a long-dead father who had denied love to his son in his youth. His risk was a symbolic compensation for this lack, as well as for perceived failures in his adult life. If the hero was a woman, it could be said that she had lived all her life with the painful realization that her father had always wanted a son, not a daughter. This act of bravery was her unconscious compensation for being born female and an attempt, at last, to be noticed.

If we accept these interpretations, what has become of the hero? Someone who has done something heroic is transformed in our minds from a hero into a neurotic. By a slight turn of perception, admiration is changed to condescension.

Freud's Legacy
This direction of thought, usually loosely associated with Freud and his followers, sees through and discredits individual heroes. Freud's impact on our culture as a whole has been enormous, on the study of litera-ture, the arts, and history as well as on psychology and psychiatry. My concern at this point is not whether Freud's cultural impact was true to his original ideas. But by its emphasis on the unconscious and biologi-cal roots of human motivations, psychoanalysis has become a great lev-eler of heroes. Conscious motivations that were not biologically rooted were discounted. By its method, any heroic act can be seen to have unheroic roots just under the surface.

Erik Erikson, despite his deep involvement in the psychoanalytic movement, was frustrated with its inability to describe psychological health or well-being, let alone excellence. He wrote,

> We do our tortured best to express what we value in terms of
> double negatives; a person whom we would declare reasonably

well is relatively resistant to regression, or somewhat freer from repression, or less given to ambivalence than might be expected. And yet we know that in a state of health or of mental and affective clarity a process of order takes over which is not and cannot be subsumed under the most complete list of negatives.[17]

Although there have been many more recent variations of psychoanalytic thought, its debunking force has left a deep mark on our understanding of heroes. Modern biography bears this out. Michael Lesy, in his book *Rescuers, the Lives of Heroes*, evaluates nine heroes who are each rescuers in extreme, often life-threatening situations. He is able to admire very few of them at face value, and most he felt he understood better than they understood themselves. Of two winners of the Congressional Medal of Honor, he tells us "both men acted to atone."[18] A man called Mosher rescued a woman in the apartment above him from rape and murder and almost bled to death of a knife wound from the attacker. Lesy writes of him,

> Some might say that Mosher overcame his failure and frustration to do what he did. In fact, failure and frustration were the cause of his actions; they enabled him to act; they compelled him to act. If he hadn't been so unhappy, if he hadn't felt so trapped, he wouldn't have acted. Because he needed to be saved, he saved someone else.[19]

Lesy also said Curtis Sliwa, the founder of the Guardian Angels, a volunteer group that patrols the New York subways, was a person deeply divided between strength and weakness, security and vulnerability. "Sliwa was a kid with a fault line down his center. The tension between his halves and the need to resolve that tension impelled him to act."[20]

Of course, it is likely that guilt, frustration, and anxiety were involved in the complex choices made by these people in moments of extreme danger. But the biographer confidently sees through the appearances and "knows" that these emotions were really the cause of their heroism. When the "real truth" is told, the heroes sound more like neurotics, losers, or emotional cripples. Words like *impel* and *compel* eliminate their conscious choices. Their motivation for heroic action had to do only tangentially if not accidentally with the people that they saved. Their main motivation was self-serving, a compensation for their internal pain. Their shortcomings emerge as the causes of their heroic action.

THE MASTERS OF SUSPICION

Basic Ideas	Focus of Suspicion
Marx Economic motives are at the root of all social behavior. History is the unfolding of an inevitable process, moving toward a classless society.	Suspicion of any non-Marxist world-view or morality as a smoke screen to hide bourgeois oppression and exploitation.
Darwin The diversity of life forms and their apparent design (including human consciousness itself) are all the result of the mindless, purposeless process of natural selection.	Suspicion of all ideas that suggest that there is a qualitative distinction between human and animal.
Nietzsche God is dead, and with him all meanings. Truth is what you want it to be.	Suspicion of all human knowledge, especially knowledge about God and moral principles—except the Superman ideal.
Freud Freud applied Darwin's ideas to human psychology. Drives for sex and aggression are found beneath all decisions. Our conscious choices are shaped by unresolved childhood conflicts below the level of consciousness.	Suspicion of conscious motivation for all action.
Overall Impact Humanity has come of age and can understand itself without the superstitions of religion or the illusions of absolute knowledge. God is a projection of the human imagination. But people still struggle to distinguish themselves in some meaningful way from nature.	Human knowledge has come of age, but ironically, it is human knowledge *itself* that is now suspect as a result—especially knowledge beyond what is scientifically observable. What appears to be virtue in human affairs, when more fully understood, is likely to be either vice or a compensation for some inadequacy.

We should not think that this perspective on heroes is unusual. Joyce Carol Oates complained that biography has now become "pathography."[21] It seems to be expected that a biographer, in doing his or her "homework," will furnish the reader with an explanation of the "real" motivations for choices and actions. If these motivations are admirable, the biographer's job was not done with any thoroughness, courage, or honesty.

The Authority of the Human Sciences

Another important influence from the human sciences has been behavior in psychology. It offered little help in enabling us to understand heroes. In fact, its major contribution to this discussion is toward debunking human greatness and dignity altogether. For the behaviorist, all human responses are explainable by the anticipated payoffs or rewards that were their sole motivation. All behavior is thus conditioned by the stimuli that the surrounding environment provides. Freedom is an illusion. B. F. Skinner put it this way, "How one feels about behaving for the good of others depends upon the reinforcers used."[22] Such "decisions" are not so much the result of conscious choices as much as they are inevitable responses to the strongest environmental stimuli. He goes on:

> The amount of behavior generated by a reinforcer depends upon the contingencies in which it appears. In an extreme case a person may be reinforced by others on a schedule which costs him his life. Suppose, for example, that a group is threatened by a predator (the "monster" of mythology). Someone possessing special strength or skill attacks and kills the monster or drives him away. The group, released from threat, reinforces the hero with approval, praise, honor, affection, celebrations, statues, arches of triumph, and the hand of the princess. . . . The important fact about such contingencies is that the greater the threat, the greater the esteem accorded the hero who alleviates it. The hero therefore takes on more and more dangerous assignments until he is killed.[23]

Heroism is explained on the principles of conditioning found to describe the learning patterns of rats and pigeons. This description is a better one of the activity of a lemming than of a human being. It simply explains as insignificant the vast range of ideas, commitments, feelings, and choices that human beings make in the course of responding to danger in human life.

Biological determinism, as in the doctrines of sociobiology, provides "explanations" at a lower level still. The sociobiologist is concerned to show that human altruism is not what it appears to be—choices for the good of other people that involve self-sacrifice. Actually, we are told, altruistic behavior is not really chosen at all but is dictated by our genes, which are programmed through natural selection to perpetuate like genes. A person who seems to make an unselfish choice, such as rescuing a stranger trapped in a burning car, is actually only a pawn in the game played by his or her own genes, programmed through evolution to perpetuate their kind.

Other psychological theories offer still more varied interpretations of human motivations. The movement called humanistic psychology has chafed against both psychoanalysis and behaviorism because of what it saw as the imprisonment by those schools of human psychology within the categories of animal behavior. Humanistic psychology wanted to develop a view that did more justice to what is distinctively human, giving more room to the importance of conscious choice.

However, this movement's impact on our society has often trivialized the diversity and depth of different human motivations, and the role of values and ideals. The tendency, especially at the popular level, has been to see the person with only one overriding focal point of need—self-esteem. The insights of other schools of psychology are used, but the conscious self is the center with its need for self-love. Low self-esteem is seen as the basic psychological problem from which most others come.

Think again about our hero who saved the stranger's life at great risk. How would popular self-esteem psychology understand this? We might be told that we should not understand an act of courage as primarily an act of altruism rooted in care for the rescued person. The hero has anticipated benefits both from the approval of society and from an increased sense of self-esteem.

Once we see past the appearances, the heroic rescue was not actually altruistic but was ultimately self-referential. *Heroism has more to do with feeling good than with doing good.* We are told that people do heroic things ultimately so that they will feel good about themselves. Now what has become of the hero? The hero has become just one more self-centered person who expressed self-interest in a way that happened to benefit another.

Again, if we see through appearances with the eyes provided by such a psychological model, the result is a leveling process. The hero's moral excellence is "understood" out of existence. Since self-esteem is the foundational human drive, a heroic act is self-serving but appears to be something more.

From this perspective, some see the idea of having heroes as itself dangerous for psychological reasons. George Sheehan puts it this way:

> Where have all the heroes gone? They've gone with the sim-plicities and the pieties and the easy answers of another era.
> Our lack of heroes is an indication of the maturity of our age.
> A realization that every man has come into his own and has the capacity of making a success out of his life. Of being able to say,
> "I have found my hero, and he is me."[24]

This is a reversal of Pogo's substantial wisdom, "We have found the enemy, and he is us." The very idea of heroism assumes that one per-son can be better than another at something that is important. It implies that I could improve, and maybe even that I ought to. To self-esteem psychology, which builds psychological wholeness on self-esteem as the foundation for all other psychological growth, these ideas can be very threatening. They attack my self-esteem by suggesting that there might be things wrong with me and that I *might need to change.*

The danger of this view is that it sees psychological well-being as dependent on a fragile self-satisfaction, which is at risk if there is any-one that I have to look up to. I should have no heroes, not because oth-ers are not good, but because I must believe that I am so much better than they are.

The human sciences have taught us an enormous amount about ourselves, yet in much of that advance, heroism has been a casualty. Under the banner of advancing our knowledge of ourselves, vital aspects of human life, including moral categories, have been explained into nonexistence. It should not surprise us that the power of these ideas about human nature, meaning, and motivation have contributed to our society's cynicism about heroism. They did not stay in inacces-sible academic literature, but have found their way into novels, films, music, and with enough repetition, into the space between our ears.

HEROISM AFTER CYNICISM
Whatever else is said, it is not hard to see why people today might be suspicious about heroes. What sort of heroism could survive the kind of acid bath of cynicism that we have described?

In a society that claims no confidence in the ultimate meaningful-ness of human life, smaller meanings have to step in to support smaller heroes. But even with these smaller heroes, the sophisticated are lying in wait to reveal secret motivations and quirks. Our society tends therefore to focus on those whose heroism can remain undamaged even after passage through the filters of cynicism.

The Minimal Hero

First, the *minimal hero*. A minimal hero is one who inspires either a very low level of aspiration, or else aspiration for a restricted and banal set of achievements. Cynicism removes our will to emulate anybody. It takes too much effort. Jules Henry writes, "When cynicism, resignation, and passivity enter life the first makes all emulative choice of properties seem vain, and passivity and resignation sap the will necessary to the emulative decision."[25] One's highest ideal can be to lead a hassle-free life — to minimize frustration and maximize stimulation and comfort. John Travolta said his goal was "to enjoy myself and survive — that's a real challenge!"

Today one is respected who can work the system, not get too hung up on moral scruples, make enough money to fund an upwardly mobile lifestyle, and maybe be an expert in his or her field. There is no need for significant moral involvement. What can I do to end the world's suffering anyway?

Francis Schaeffer well described the values that have displaced the intense moral turmoil of the 1960s — the overwhelming goals of "personal peace and affluence."[26] Robert Bellah echoed the same message in *Habits of the Heart*, with his emphasis that today's main languages of meaning are those of the therapist (personal peace) and the manager (affluence).[27]

The strength of the minimal hero is in making no claim to possessing any of the heroic qualities that could be debunked by contemporary cynicism. There is usually no meaning system acknowledged beyond upward mobility and freedom from hassle. There is therefore no pedestal of moral stature to fall off or be pulled down from. If a cynic were to come as a subversive and charge that the minimal hero was "only in it for selfish reasons," that would be no challenge to the integrity of the hero. "Of course I am in it for selfish reasons. What's the matter with that?"

The Mock Hero

The *mock hero* is another who makes it safely through the net of cynicism. Let Russell Baker describe this hero:

If you want to do a swashbuckling hero like the fellow in "Raiders of the Lost Ark," you have to make a joke of the whole business. You want to make sure nobody in the audience thinks you're an outdated sap who really believes in swashbuckling. So you keep winking at the audience by making the whole thing so preposterous that they'll know you're only kidding. Then you justify it by saying it's the kind of baloney old dad and mom really took seriously back when they went to the Bijou on Saturday afternoon, and weren't they out of it, those poor old saps?[28]

The mock hero enables us to have our cynicism and our hero too. The James Bond films fit this pattern, as do many science fiction films, some of which have more moral heroes. We can get entertainment and a kind of emotional and imaginative "buzz" from films like these and still dismiss them as "kids' stuff," mumbling of the excesses of Hollywood. We are entirely safe, insulated from being personally challenged in the way we live our lives. We are able to have our secret longings stimulated but still retain a sophisticated self-image.

The Anti-Hero

The supreme achievement of modern cynicism is the third example, *the anti-hero*. The anti-hero is the protagonist who occupies center stage as did the hero in traditional drama, but who is a failure. He inspires not respect or even hatred, but pity. He is pathetic, showing himself unequal to the challenges of life. Most are found in very mundane roles, but they are not able to live them out successfully, being besieged with self-doubt, internal conflict, and incompetence.

Examples of the anti-hero are Arthur Miller's Willy Loman, the man who "never knew who he was"; T. S. Eliot's J. Alfred Prufrock, who struggled with whether to part his hair in the back; and James Thurber's Walter Mitty, whose heroic deeds in his private imaginative world were rivaled only by his klutziness in real life. Woody Allen has put himself in many anti-heroic roles—usually in order to deliver a satirical sting to contemporary superficiality. Logan Piersall Smith caught the spirit of the anti-hero when he wrote,

I am no thinker, no mere creature of dreams and imagination. I pay bills, post letters: I buy new bootlaces and put them in my boots. And when I set out to get my hair cut, it is with the iron face of those men of empire and unconquerable will, those Caesars and Napoleons, whose footsteps shake the earth.[29]

The anti-hero communicates, by the "heroism" of the person who is center stage, that the very idea of heroism is dead. We are invited to look on our hero and see how inadequate he is.

The minimal heroes, mock heroes, and anti-heroes pass through the filters of cynicism because they are stripped of moral stature. They present no moral challenge, having made their peace with moral mediocrity. The doctrines of modern cynicism are so far-reaching that if they are true, heroes are limited to this uninspiring cast. We turn now to evaluate the validity of some of these doctrines.

SEEING THROUGH CYNICISM

How can we know what the real motivations were of the man or woman who risked life and health to rescue a stranger from a burning car? Many powerful and useful insights from the human sciences give us extraordinary insight into human experience. But do they give us the x-ray vision that cynicism requires to eliminate heroism?

We have stressed cynicism's claim to see through both heroism and individual heroes. Cynicism stands above, looking down. It looks disparagingly on what it sees as naive, unscientific, and grandiose ideas about both human ideals and specific human beings. It is surrounded by an aura of sophistication, hardheadedness, and courage. Because of this aura, cynicism itself is seldom examined critically. When we challenge cynicism, it is hard not to appear unsophisticated and uninformed. But what if cynicism's claim to be able to see through all appearances is itself naive, unscientific, and grandiose?

There are two important questions to ask. First, What if cynicism itself can be "seen through"? That is, does cynicism make an overbite, in that its far-reaching claims are undermined by its own method of thinking? Second, Do the results of cynicism actually enlighten us, revealing deeper truths about human excellence, or not?

THE OVERBITE OF CYNICISM

The basic ability to "see through" that characterizes cynicism has always enabled the cynic to unmask postures of virtue and expose them as vice. But the masters of suspicion and their disciples have given modern cynicism new confidence that it can do far more than see through hypocrisy, deception, and con artistry. People today are invited to believe that they can decode surface appearances to see through to *un*conscious motivations, the "real," less than admirable motivations behind heroic action, motivations that are unknown even to the hero.

THE IMPACT OF THE HUMAN SCIENCES ON HEROISM

BASIC IDEAS	NATURE OF IMPACT
Psychoanalysis Non-conscious psychological drives of sex and aggression, shaped by early childhood experiences, are the main forces motivating human behavior.	Heroism can always be discredited because it can be explained by underlying motivations that are less than heroic. The only hero is the psychoanalyst, who fearlessly explores the terrifying depths of the human mind.
Behaviorism Human choices are controlled by the anticipated rewards provided by our social and physical environment. The stimuli in our environment dictate our responses. The human person is a psychological illusion.	There are no heroes because people are only helpless responders to external stimuli. The only hero is the social engineer equipped with an understanding of behavioral psychology.
Sociobiology Human behavior is directed at the genetic level, driven by the demands of the "selfish gene," for the survival of the gene.	There is no heroism because even altruism is not a conscious choice, but is controlled by the gene's demand for survival. The only hero is the genetic engineer who will be able to control our future.
Humanistic Psychology There is no meaning to human existence itself, but personal meanings are limitless. Self-esteem is the central psychological dynamic.	We are all heroes. The most important thing is to be a hero to yourself. Heroism is, as a result, diluted.

These motivations, which may be the alleged cause of heroism (as in the above interpretations by Michael Lesy), could be biological, social, psychological, economic, or political. The post-modern climate of suspicion lends plausibility to this kind of analysis. People are not what they seem to be, even to themselves.

But then we must look at the other side of the coin. To make these assertions about other human beings, the cynic must presume to have a near-omniscient viewpoint. It must at the very least be undistorted by his or her own conscious and nonconscious needs, fears, drives, and compensations. The cynic asks us to believe that he or she has an immaculate perception of the inner lives of other people, while at the same time telling us that the self-understanding of *those* people is irrelevant. We are asked to believe that the cynic alone is free from the corrupting motivations that skew the vision of the rest of the race.

The cynical people I know still persist in believing that they understand themselves, and usually give perfectly sensible reasons why they act as they do. Sometimes these reasons involve moral convictions. They expect to be treated as sincere, morally serious people who know their own minds. But if cynicism is right, the moral notions of the cynic must also be only a web of self-serving illusions, motivated by lower purposes or nonconscious drives.

This is the Achilles' heel of cynicism. The only way that these two claims can be held together is if the cynic is granted sole immunity from the critical debunking that cynicism uses on other people. There is a cynical elite, self-initiated into rules of critical analysis—whether they be the rules of psychoanalysis, sociology of knowledge, behaviorism, Marxism, feminism, deconstruction, or any number of other systems claiming explanations for the secrets of human motivation. The sophisticated tools of the cynic can equip him or her to see actions as masks for power plays of race, gender, or class, or else as sublimations, repressions, and denials of threatening psychological crises. But they need special pleading for immunity—that they in their cynicism not be subjected to the striking power of their own ideas. Why should we grant this special immunity to the cynic? Isn't cynicism a giant overbite? How do we know that there are no hypocritical motivations or nonconscious needs, fears, and anxieties fueling the cynic's cynicism, skewing the cynic's cynical perception of human nature and of individual people? We don't.

Could it be that the ideas and attitudes of cynicism, although not actually true, simply happen to be handsomely rewarded and therefore "reinforced" in certain parts of our society? Perhaps there are incentives for cynicism that are psychologically, politically, educationally, sexually, or economically self-serving and nearly irresistible—more powerful, for example, than the incentives for honest evaluation of the virtues of other people.

If cynicism about heroes is at least partially grounded in less than straightforward motivations, what could some of these motivations be?

What would be the realists' evaluation of the cynic? Two of the commonest incentives for cynicism are self-protection and self-elevation.

Self-Protection as a Motive for Cynicism

First of all, cynical ideas protect us from unsettling challenges to moral excellence. As Mark Twain said, "Few things are harder to put up with than the annoyance of a good example." In his essay "The Decline of Greatness," Arthur M. Schlesinger wrote, "An age without great men is one which acquiesces in the drift of history." He went on to say that great men remind us that the individual can make a difference, but "fatalism reassures us that they can't. It thereby blesses our weakness and extenuates our failure. Fatalism, in Berlin's phrase is, 'one of the great alibis of history.'"[30]

From the perspective of heroes in literature, the popular culture historian David Houston said,

> A person who sees no heroism in himself can generalize and decide that there is no such thing as a hero. There'd better be no such thing, because such people gave up trying to be heroic long ago; now they can't look up without being reminded how far down they are.[31]

These men saw that the desire to avoid personal challenge to excellence can color our ideas about human possibilities. With Schlesinger's analysis, it was that we want fatalism as an alibi to hide behind. Cynicism is a protection lest more be expected of us than weakness and failure. That protection is removed as soon as a hero appears who is not a victim of his or her "fate." David Houston stressed the comfort that comes from the absence of heroes—it is unsettling to be reminded of our mediocrity by looking up. If expectations are kept low, we reduce the risk of painful disappointment with ourselves and others. There is a certain relief in removing the top rungs from all ladders. It removes pressure from us.

If you are steeped in cynicism, it might be easier for you to walk past a car in flames and "interpret" any urges to intervene. Are you feeling compelled to rescue a trapped person only because of your own failures and self-doubt, or even because your "selfish genes" are pressing you to do it? If you believe that heroic action in dangerous situations is motivated mainly by low self-esteem or desire for power, then these ideas are likely to weaken your sense of obligation to respond to the moral reality in front of you.

Self-Elevation as a Motive for Cynicism

A second possible motivation for cynicism is self-elevation. To conclude that there is no such thing as heroism can be to decide that there is nothing in this world worthy of my commitment of myself. It can be part of a grandiose vision of my place in the cosmos. The act of putting other people down can also lift me up—at least in the eyes of a significant number of observers. We can see this everywhere from the school playground to the university faculty room to the corporate boardroom to the political arena. We all sometimes act as if there were a finite amount of admiration to go around, and as if what I took away from you might stick to me. More than that, my wit, humor, and insight in putting you down might in itself win me respect.

Modern interpretations of the old maxim "No man is a hero to his valet" point to the elevated social status gained by the cynic. The maxim has been attributed to Hegel, Goethe, Carlyle, and others. It probably originated earlier, in the reign of Louis XIV, and then was expounded, expanded, and claimed by others.[32] Its ambiguity has intrigued students of heroism ever since.

It is very likely that its original meaning reflected the elitist views that were widely accepted in the aristocracy of the eighteenth century. The idea was that a valet, because he was a valet, was unlikely to be able to appreciate the virtues of the great man who employed him. The valet's time and attention were so taken up with doing laundry, cleaning boots, and emptying chamber pots that his vision was too small to relate to the greatness of his hero-master. *The defect was not with the hero.* It was in the perception of the valet, who was so preoccupied with the ordinary that he could not recognize the extraordinary. This was the implication of the saying, especially as focused on by Hegel and Carlyle, in the nineteenth century.[33] In fact, Hegel expanded the saying to read: "No man is a hero to his valet; not, however, because the man is not a hero, but because the valet—is a valet."[34] It was a challenge to not be small-minded like the valet and fail to appreciate the greatness of the great. In fact, by failing to recognize the hero, you might be showing off your valet-sized, inferior spirit.

The interpretation favored in the climate of late-twentieth-century cynicism has reversed the challenge. Now people immediately expect to see the defects in all who might be considered heroes. They look first for the feet of clay and the evidence of spin control from the image consultants. Ironically, it is the valet who becomes the new hero. The valet is someone who sees the "great man" at close range and is able to see through the hollow veneer of virtue with sophisticated insight to the real, less admirable person beneath.

Today's versions of "No man is a hero to his valet" usually substitute modern translations for the valet. Now no man is a hero to his psychotherapist, his biographer, his *Time* magazine reporter, or to any literary critic. The challenge is that we all should aspire to the sophistication of the modern valet. The valet has now ascended, by acquaintance with the human sciences and critical theory, to the "knowledge class." If you still believe in the greatness of the great, that fact simply betrays your lack of sophistication.

In biography that proceeds in this style, there is an intriguing shift of roles. The subject of the biography is reduced to a fool or an object of pity or scorn, but the biographer emerges as the new hero of penetrating insight and refreshing, courageous honesty.[35] The biographer represents a heroism of sophisticated perception and fearless willingness to reveal the truth. As with the heroic stature of the masters of suspicion themselves, cynics become the only heroes in a heroless world.

The question that we are left with is whether we accept the message of the modern biographer-valet. We must start by admitting that the cynic, whether in the form of valet, biographer, reporter, or neighbor, is sometimes right. In fact, things with any one of us may be even worse than a cynical observer imagines.

Some of the cynic's true insight may also be due to specifically modern ways of understanding people. Because of hard work in the human sciences, philosophy, and literary criticism, we have learned a great deal about the way different biological, psychological, social, political, and economic forces affect human attitudes, motivations, and choices. People are not islands, making free choices as if in a vacuum, uninfluenced by parents, society, the unconscious, or biochemistry.

However, that is not to say that human choice is eclipsed, that every human decision could not have been otherwise. To admit that there are many nonconscious and ignoble factors at work in our decision making is very different from saying that the conscious process itself is illusory, and that all decisions were inevitable. Although they have offered many insights into our conscious and nonconscious motivations, the human sciences at their most reductionistic have gone far beyond this and offered an entirely different, miniaturized picture of what a human being is. In the words of Rollo May, they have been "making molehills out of mountains."[36]

Insofar as we believe that the cynic's critical methods of analysis can be valid, to that extent it should lead us to humility. This is because our use of that very analysis may well be controlled, directed, and skewed by our own not-so-noble motivations. Realism and humility will go hand in hand. Where there is humility, there will be plenty of room for us to recognize heroes. *This is because to eliminate all heroism, the cynic must be more than sometimes right. The cynic must be always right about heroism and heroes.* You can be *sometimes* right in negative judgments and still be a realist, well short of cynicism. *To remove the possibility of heroism, there must be no people who can slip through cynicism's net with heroic actions or choices intact.* Cynicism requires an extraordinary faith in the penetrating accuracy of our own perception, extended well beyond our experience. This would require a near-divine level of objectivity that few cynics would dare to claim.

We have seen that the doctrines of cynicism offer their own incentives of self-protection and self-elevation to the one who believes in them. However, we cannot dismiss these doctrines just because cynical people might have less than noble motivations for holding them. That would be to repeat the cynic's own mistake, and to try to destroy cynicism only by becoming a cynic—jumping from the frying pan into the fire. A person's motivations for believing something have no necessary relationship to the truth of whatever is believed. However, seeing the power of these motivations ought to give us reason not to be overawed by the cynic's claim to objectivity, sophistication, or scientific authority.

THE IMPOTENCE OF CYNICISM

Think of the contrast between Hamlet's evaluation of a human being, "How like God!" and that of Pavlov, "How like a dog!" We must judge which model better copes with the task of describing human existence in all its height, breadth, and richness as well as in its pettiness, degradation, and cruelty. We live in a climate that puts great confidence in simple explanations of complex things. As a result, there is the well-fed illusion that the burden of proof rests in the lap of one who claims that a human being is more than a biochemical phenomenon.

The question that we must grapple with is, Does cynicism actually deliver a description of great explanatory power, or not? A hero, by definition, is different from others in that he or she excels in some valued quality. Does cynicism account for the hero standing out from the rest of the nonheroic population, as any hero must do? Take the examples of heroic rescuers compiled by Michael Lesy. You will remember that he claimed that their heroic acts were caused by attempts to compensate for their own guilt, anxiety, frustration, and failure to cope with life. It was even claimed that their shortcomings "compelled" some of them to heroic action. They were portrayed as very normal people, except perhaps somewhat more dysfunctional than most.

The difficulty is that the vast majority of us, at least at certain times in our lives, also feel guilt, anxiety, and frustration over failure. This seems to be part of universal human experience, and so cannot be used as the factor that singles out exceptional people from the rest of us. If their psychological and social failures were what impelled them into heroism, what about the rest of us? Most of us, who also experience a wide range of failures, manage to avoid heroic action easily and consistently. There are countless other nonheroic ways that we are more likely to respond to our frustrations and inadequacies. Why did heroes respond heroically instead of with cowardice, denial, or heartlessness? Telling us that heroes experienced themselves as failures tells us nothing that would account for the *difference* between them and the rest of the population. Yet it is the very non-normality of the hero that demands explanation.

Joyce Carol Oates raised the same issue when she complained that many recent biographers of literary figures "so mercilessly expose their subjects, so relentlessly catalogue their most private, vulnerable and least illuminating moments, as to divest them of all mystery save the crucial and unexplained: How did a distinguished body of work emerge from so undistinguished a life?"[37] Her point is that the cynical "valet's perspective" will tell sordid facts that may be historically true, but it does not help us account for the main reason we are interested in the person in the first place—namely, that he or she has done something exceptional, even distinguished and admirable. Many people do sordid things. But how did these people rise above them? Cynicism levels out heroism itself and leaves it unexplained.

If cynicism cannot account for the single-act heroism of rescuing a trapped person from a fire or a murderer, how much less can it explain lives of heroic endurance? Remember the people of Le Chambon in Nazi-occupied France whose story began chapter 1? For four years they hid Jewish refugees or smuggled them to safety. Theirs is a story of sustained integrity of moral character, under threat of torture and death of self and family. It was tragically non-normal in France and in most of the other occupied countries.[38] Can we attribute their exceptional choices to low self-esteem, desire for power, or unresolved psychological conflicts—and still keep a straight face? Cynicism, for all its posture of enlightenment and sophistication, has little explanatory power to account for heroism.

In fact, one can go a step further. Cynicism about heroism is actually a source of darkness and confusion, making us less able to understand the people who have gone before us and who surround us. Psychiatrist and Harvard professor Robert Coles often tells the story of a profound change in his own thinking. It was occasioned by getting to know children like the six-year-old girl named Ruby Bridges, who was the first black child to attend a previously all-white school in New Orleans. We will let him tell his own story:

> In the late fall of 1960, my wife and I were told by a New Orleans schoolteacher: "I don't understand the child. She's only six years old, and she goes through so much, and her family goes through so much; yet, she comes into the classroom with a smile on her face, and ready to learn, and she forgives everybody!" The teacher went on to explain her observation: "The people in the mob—they shout at her every obscenity the human mind can imagine. They tell her they'll kill her. But when she comes into this school building, she tells me she feels sorry for them, and once she even said she prays for them, and she doesn't really blame them." As a proudly "aware" observer with prolonged training in the so-called helping professions, I listened, naturally, with skepticism. The poor girl, I thought, with self-satisfied sureness, trying to cover up the anger and resentment she felt by recourse to pieties. And the poor teacher, so naively puzzled, even admiring. If only she understood the subtleties and nuances of mental life. Incredulity would then yield to expectancy; the day would come when the child who demonstrated an abiding compassion for her own tormentors would become the child who openly protested her hatred for her enemies—and the sooner the better.

But Coles waited, and waited. Ruby did not behave as predicted. She just kept forgiving and praying for the angry crowd. Coles's wife began to argue with him about the way he was pressing Ruby into his own cynical categories of understanding. She finally handed him this typed note:

> For over six months we've been watching a little Negro girl face possible assault, if not death, every morning and every after-

noon. We've heard the obscenities the men and women shout at her, and we wonder how she can take it, day after day. She does though. She goes even further: she forgives her tormentors; she prays for them. She says, "God will understand them and teach them."

For speaking like that, she gets from us a smart-alecky condescension. We know what her problems are! We know what's really going on, deep inside her head. Anything she says isn't to be taken at face value — of course! Meanwhile, Ruby and the others we've met keep going through these daily hurdles, and we keep trying to find out what's wrong with them, or what will be wrong. And when we hear the children being considerate even to those who hate them, we're sure it won't be long before the psychological trouble we've been expecting unfolds before our eyes. I'm beginning to wonder whether there isn't some psychological trouble all right — with us, and with the way we think.[39]

Coles went on to speak of the impossibility of making sense of what he and his wife were seeing, within the categories of the psychiatry in which he had been trained, or for that matter, in the widely accepted contemporary theories of moral development.

Although many of the theories that we have discussed have been heralded as "breakthroughs" of our understanding of humankind, Coles found them to be proud intellectual barriers preventing him from seeing and hearing clearly and honestly. His views had to be deconstructed by the moral life of a six-year-old child. If adherence to a scientific theory blinds us to life itself, we lose our ability to do the very thing that science is meant to help us do — observe and describe our world with accuracy. Worse still, it is precisely the most important aspects of human life that are defined into irrelevance or out of existence. It is the human concern for justice, compassion, love, and beauty that must somehow be explained away by a host of lower-level motivations. The vast range of ideas, ideals, traditions, commitments, feelings, and choices that are involved in the course of responding to danger and moral challenge is simply considered insignificant.

Cynicism about heroes explains too little and claims too much. The loss of the possibility of heroes brings with it the loss of the possibility of villains as well. The cynical ideas that we have considered eliminate not just praise but blame, too. If heroes save lives for reasons beyond their awareness, the same kind of reasons can explain why cowards, murderers, racists, embezzlers, and rapists do not really understand what they are doing either, and can hardly be held responsible for their actions.

Without having witnessed twentieth-century cynicism, Ralph Waldo Emerson had seen enough to warn, "There is something in great actions which does not allow us to go behind them." It is just this "going behind" actions that is the "seeing through" of cynicism. He was suggesting that heroism is at some point opaque to the "seeing through" of cynical vision. Cynicism, by comparison, is confident to go behind great actions to the supposed self-serving and nonconscious motivations at their root. But as soon as we think we have explained greatness, we may have only miniaturized it down to the size of our own theories. We have turned a mountain into a molehill, but only in our own minds. The mountain remains a mountain. In that case we have not explained anything, we have just become confused.

Perhaps true honesty and courage demand a greater respect for heroes than heroes usually get. Thomas Keneally described the difficulty that an author faces who takes on the task of telling a story of heroic virtue. In the prologue to *Schindler's List*, he pointed out how much easier it is to write of vice than of virtue:

> It is easy to show the inevitability by which evil acquires all of what you could call the "real estate" of the story, even though good might finish up with a few imponderables like dignity and self-knowledge. Fatal human malice is the staple of narrators. . . . But it is a risky enterprise to have to write of virtue.[40]

Would that more storytellers would consider it a "risky enterprise" to write of virtue! Oskar Schindler's life would have offered a bonanza for a psychobiographer equipped with some knowledge of Freud. Yet in telling Schindler's story, Keneally resisted the temptation to go behind his heroism to explain it. The result is that Schindler's life is allowed to stand on its own and command respect and aspiration, despite a full catalogue of his vices.

Cynicism has not had the last word. We have seen some good reasons for not letting it intimidate us. However, it is a powerful force that cannot be ignored because it is so deeply rooted in the fabric of our thinking already, and in the academic disciplines that have been shaping the minds of future generations.

Many years before modern cynicism, Pascal wrote, "It is dangerous to make a man see too clearly his equality with the brutes without show-ing him his greatness."[41] We can become not only confused but actu-ally dangerous when robbed of powerful ideals and examples of good-ness that can grip our imaginations and personally challenge us. We turn next to a development in our society that applauds human great-ness, not from having thought through the questions raised by cynicism, but from having ignored them.

CHAPTER THREE

HEROISM AND TRIVIALITY

*No one can take the place of the superstars of
the last decade. I'll never forget what's his name!*[1]
MARSHALL FISHWICK

*Somehow we cannot make ourselves so uncritical
that we reverence or respect (however much we
may be interested in) the reflected images of
our own emptiness.*[2]
DANIEL BOORSTIN

*I want people to be able to recognize me by just
looking at a caricature of me that has no name on it. You see,
I want to be great and you can recognize great people like
Muhammed Ali and Bob Hope by just looking at a nameless
caricature. When everybody can look at my caricature and
say, "That's him, that's Richard Pryor!" then I'll be great.*[3]
RICHARD PRYOR

We look now to the bright lights, the big grins, and the white teeth—to the instant heroes that our culture specializes in. While in the last chapter we reflected on the changes in the ideas that surround us, in this chapter we will look more at the impact of new technologies in changing our lives. Despite their apparent differences, there is a strange, cooperative relationship between the sneering of cynicism and the beaming grins of triviality. Both do their part to discredit heroism. Simply put, the more cynical you are, the more life seems trivial to you. The more life seems trivial, the more cynicism is the only honest attitude.

The word *trivia* comes from two Latin words, *tri* and *vium*, a place where three ways or roads crossed. Evidently, this was where Roman gossips would congregate to make small talk. Since that time it has been used to describe things that are small and unimportant—that is, trivial.[4] There is nothing wrong with triviality—many things in the world are small and, relative to great issues, unimportant. Much of life is concerned with small things; it would be difficult to maintain sanity if we thought and spoke only of cosmic issues.

But trivialization makes things that are actually important trivial. It comes in two forms, both of which involve distortion and deception: first, when things or issues that are great are made to appear small and insignificant; and second, when things that are light and superficial become life-dominating, weighty matters. Both are forms of trivialization. Both make something trivial that is not. In the first case, the important thing or issue is trivialized. In the second, a person's life itself becomes trivial when it is dominated by the superficial.

Anthropologist Ernest Becker put his finger on one of the origins of the relationship between cynicism and triviality:

> Since the Enlightenment we have gradually drifted into a position of what amounts to calculated self-abasement, by actively forfeiting what the human animal needs most: a unitary, critical world view, infused by continuing moral awareness. Having lost this—and indeed having lost even the awareness that it is necessary—we should not wonder that we in the West are repeating too, almost exactly, the experience of the earlier time in which this was being lost: the fourteenth century experience of the decay of nature. . . . But, unlike this earlier time, our present disillusionment cannot be turned in the service of otherworldliness or religious morality. It is instead in the service of the new

cynicism, blind to both spiritual and human values, a headlong, consumer race to "enjoy" while there is still time.[5]

Having purged away the remains of a meaning system so thoroughly that we have forgotten our need for it, we are enveloped in a new self-abasing cynicism whose most powerful positive expression is a passionate commitment to buying things. Its heroic virtues include acquisition, display, competitive success, and fame. If we look at people who are heroic by this standard, it is easy to conclude that heroism is trivial. How did this come about?

THE BACKGROUND OF TRIVIALIZATION

It is impossible to account for the changes in heroism in the last 150 years without looking at the influence of communications technology. Social historian Daniel Boorstin refers to the "Graphic Revolution" that has taken place in this period.[6] In this relatively brief span of time, an extraordinary array of technologies have been invented and marketed, and are now necessities of modern life. We have seen telegraph, photograph, telephone, radio, film, television, video, and fax, along with all the techniques of high-speed printing, the multiplying of possibilities for all of these through the computer and satellite and the Internet telecommunications network. Our ability to send images and information to each other at the speed of light has increased by geometric leaps. This has changed the shape of our world more than we who have lived only in the latter stages of the revolution can imagine. As history has progressed, each new innovation of communication, from Renaissance portraiture to the printing press to television, has increased our ability to keep ourselves in the imaginations of our neighbors and their descendants. Each development has intensified the images that we send them, given them a greater impression of intimacy with us, and expanded the number of people that we can celebrate.

The first newspaper in North America was published in Boston in 1690. It was a monthly called "Publick Occurences Both Forreign and Domestick," but would be printed more often "if any Glut of Occurences happen." God (and the Devil) made the news; it was the newspaper's job merely to report it. If there was little news or if the report was unexciting, that was not the newspaper's fault.[7]

How different from today's news industry where large-city newspapers publish several editions each day! But there is more to this change than the growth of a particular industry. It represents a substantial shift in the way people see the world.

The Inflation of Fame

Arthur MacEwen, William Randolph Hearst's first editor of the *San Francisco Examiner*, said, "News is anything that makes the reader say, 'Gee Whiz!'"[8] The purpose of giving information is not so much to elicit action as to entertain and, of course, to inspire you to buy the next edition so that you don't miss anything. For our present discussion, the most important part of the Graphic Revolution is its attendant explosion of fame. Our ability to give many people high visibility, at least for a little while, has led to Warhol's (now famous) Law: that in the future "everyone shall be famous for fifteen minutes." Fame is dreamed about more but means far less in this climate. Our society is referred to as a "celebrity culture," where well knownness is the ticket to power of almost any kind.

The hunger for public recognition is not a new thing. In the early chapters of the Bible, the construction crew working on the Tower of Babel started work saying, "Let us make a name for ourselves" (Genesis 11:4). A reading of Homer reveals heroes like Achilles who were acutely concerned for their public image. Following in his footsteps with the ambition of surpassing him was Alexander the Great. He went to great lengths, employing his own historians, to ensure that he would be remembered by subsequent generations in ways that did him credit.

The same preoccupation was well developed among the leaders of Rome, many of whom advertised themselves as the Alexanders of their day. Julius Caesar was a master of self-dramatization by the use of theater, games, and triumphal marches. Cicero was even more shrewd in looking to the future with the publication of his orations, and in leaving a lengthy literary record of his views and accomplishments. Leo Braudy, in his extensive history of fame, *The Frenzy of Renown*, writes, "Cicero is the self-promoting entrepreneur whose lengthened shadow stands behind every media politician."[9] He remarks about this period of ancient history: "Fame for public action was so important to the Romans, as it was to the Homeric Greeks, because in a religion without a developed concept of the afterlife it was the only way to live beyond death."[10]

This is an important point for understanding today's celebrity culture. Without a clearly understood link to some invisible world, a bond reaching beyond death, your immediate contemporaries and those who follow you must fulfill your need for recognition, distinction, and significance.

Leo Braudy might also have pointed out that belief in life after death is not the only factor. Life after death is closely tied to a sense of the significance of life *before* death—that our actions, choices, victories, and failures here and now are part of some larger story that is not limited to our conscious experience—or to our individual span of life. If there is no such master story or higher system of meaning in which the stories of this life are a part, the admiration of our contemporaries can become a surrogate immortality, and a plausible goal of life. Who else is there to notice?

There has never been a golden age with a perfect correspondence between fame and virtue. Individuals in each age have wrestled with the ideas, technologies of communication, moral resources, and limitations they had available. Having said this, we must not underestimate today's unprecedented explosion of celebrity, especially since World War II. Braudy describes the concept of fame today as "grossly distended."[11] He writes, "In the last hundred years, the nature of fame changed more decisively and more quickly than it had for the previous two thousand."[12] *Fame is no longer just a perceived reward for some achievement, but is sought as the achievement itself, as if it was the ultimate vindication of our existence.*

Our society has produced the perfect soil for fame to grow in, with just the right nutrients and climate. Far more than in ancient Greece and Rome, there is now a confident disbelief in any invisible world that could have relevance to our affairs here and now. Moreover, we possess technologies of communication that the Romans and Greeks never dreamed of. You can make your name and face known around the entire planet in less than an hour! It would have left Alexander the Great dumbstruck. All you need to do is to shoot somebody who is already well known.

The Impact of the Graphic Revolution on Heroes

Let us look at several results of the Graphic Revolution as it touches the way we perceive exceptional people. First of all, we have an over-intimacy with public figures. Almost any public figure is treated to a merciless flood of information made public about himself or herself. Fueled by an insatiable desire to know and be intimate with the great, the public demands to know, and will pay well for it.

For example, if the President of the United States changes the part in his hair from the right to the left side of his head, it merits three columns of speculation in the weekly news magazines about how he might be trying to change his image—did he do it to appear younger and more vigorous or wiser and more authoritative, or was there some as yet unknown motive?

Or if another president bangs his head on a door frame or trips and falls down occasionally, it is given wide coverage as well, with dramatic photographs of the moments of impact. In our present political climate where so much of what we "know" has been processed, handled, and spun, when unscripted slips and gaffes take place, the media have a feeding frenzy. The assumption is that you for once get to see the real person behind the artifice. Image wizard David Gergen calls such a time "a naked moment in politics." Michael Kelly, a journalist critical of his profession, wrote,

> A single such event—Clinton and the haircut, Quayle and the potato(e), Carter and the killer rabbit, Bush at the checkout counter—its significance heightened with every retelling, can permanently scar a public figure, and several in a row can be fatal. Every year, a new species of misdemeanor is defined as a high crime. This year, inattention to the tax laws regarding baby sitters and house cleaners became the hanging offense.[13]

We are given famous people "up close and personal" in a way that tends to dissolve greatness—if there is any. It is not that human greatness can never stand close scrutiny. Rather, the scrutiny given to public figures must be of a quality to make the viewer say the modern equivalent of "Gee Whiz!" and thus tends to focus on unrelated fragments of a person's life, obscuring that life's overall story. It graphically displays life's failings—trivial and monumental—and its quirks, kinks, and eccentricities, all of which make good news. It is not hard to see how this process serves to trivialize public figures.

Perhaps it is like trying to appreciate the grandeur of the Grand Canyon with your face six inches from its floor. All you can see is sand and beer cans. It does not necessarily mean that the canyon is as trivial as the part of it that you have allowed yourself to see.

A second result of the Graphic Revolution is an overstimulation of the senses. In an age of greater and greater "spectaculars," one must keep raising the level of wonder, delight, or horror to even register on the Richter scale of our consciousness. Sex and violence are primary currencies of this escalation of sensual stimulation.

The effect on us is twofold. One more turn is made on the ratchet of what is needed to stimulate us. We become dependent on ever-more dramatic and unusual effects and events. The other side of the same process is that we become ever-more bored with daily life as we actually live it.

Modern Americans are without question the most entertained people in world history. To keep us entertained, our senses must be stimulated. The list of possibilities is endless, from museums to mud wrestling, with the ever-present option of around-the-clock radio and television.

Communications theorist Neil Postman argues that commercial television has had a profound impact on the way we think. He does not object to the trashiest of television wherein people get what they expect, nor to television's ability to provide superb entertainment. His warning is that when a medium that is intrinsically built for entertainment takes on a serious subject, that subject is trivialized.

Commercial television can only give you short bits and pieces of information, without context, shown from ever-changing visual angles. Notice that you almost never observe someone thinking. It is as if the most complex questions can always be resolved with a quip or wisecrack. Thinking takes too much priceless time, and the network must make sure that you do not get bored and change channels.

No matter what atrocity of war, mass murder, or disaster claiming the lives of thousands, the account is always followed by a reassuring word in a pleasant voice from a commentator chosen for attractiveness and easy listening. That, in turn, is followed by promises that the five products that brought you that exciting segment of the news will transform your life by causing you to fall in love with everything from denture glue to hemorrhoid treatment to chicken soup. The result of years of television viewing is a gradual Midas touch, not of gold, but of triviality about the whole human condition. After a steady diet of commercial television, one would be unlikely to conclude that the world was a serious place to live.[14]

A third result of the Graphic Revolution is the sheer power of the communications media to mediate reality for us. Think of the mystique that surrounds the media and those involved in it. It performs a priestly function, as mediator between us and the world, all the while possessing the power to give out that most sacred of all rewards—fame. Two examples will suffice.

In April 1953, in the midst of the Korean War, an American garrison on Pork Chop Hill, commanded by a second lieutenant, fought off the Communist Chinese for three days. The battle involved great bravery and endurance, but the press missed it, so it went unnoticed. However, it happened that a writer was present and wrote a book about it that was a commercial failure—until a film starring Gregory Peck was made out of two chapters. The film was a great success commercially, and now Pork Chop Hill is remembered as one of the great battles of United States military history along with the Alamo, Okinawa, and Iwo Jima.[15] Who is responsible for this battle being "history"? A good case can be made for Gregory Peck and the film company.

Neil Postman raises another example. He asks, why is it impossible to elect a president of the United States who weighs three hundred pounds? We once did (William Howard Taft), but it is no longer conceivable. Why not? The shape or bulk of a person's body would seem to have little relevance to the duties of the presidency. The Constitution does not forbid it. The laws of the land do not forbid it. But television forbids it. There might as well be a constitutional amendment with a presidential weight limit.[16]

So, we must say two things: The hunger for celebrity is not a modern development. At the same time, modern media have boosted our ability to celebrate ourselves and others in ways that open up new ways to self-deception and illusion.

IMAGE ORIENTATION IN MODERN SOCIETY

The place of image in modern society is a key part of trivializing heroism. It helps to explain the sheer power of illusion in the modern imagination in which some of the most passionately sought-for ideals are actually mirages.

People have always experienced some level of toil, boredom, and frustration in their everyday lives. Hopes and expectations have usually exceeded reality. However, there may never have been a society in which so many have believed that they can "have it all now." We are bombarded with visions of success, beauty, power, possessions, and prestige, and told to "go for it." It is all just beyond our fingertips. Expectations have even bounded ahead of the extraordinary advances in our affluent Western world's standard of living and freedom of opportunity. But when our personal experience falls short of our expectations, we feel frustration and disillusionment.

The Power of Expectations

One characteristic of our time is an extravagance of expectation—that we hope for more than is available to us in this world. Daniel Boorstin develops this theme:

> We expect anything and everything. We expect the contradic-
> tory and the impossible. We expect compact cars which are spa-
> cious; luxurious cars which are economical. We expect to be
> rich and charitable, powerful and merciful, active and reflective,
> kind and competitive. We expect to be inspired by mediocre
> appeals for excellence, to be made literate by illiterate appeals
> for literacy. We expect to eat and stay thin, to be constantly on
> the move and ever more neighborly, to go to the "church of our
> choice" and yet feel its guiding power over us, to revere God
> and to be God.[17]

The real world and our daily experience in it cannot measure up to our expectations—but the world of image can, at least for a little while. If we hold dearly to our expectations, the image world can become more real than reality itself. The real world becomes bland or gray in comparison. We *can* make images that *do* meet our expectations, or pay others to make them for us—and those images are far more vivid.

It is our expectations that fuel our image making. Only in the realm of images can you overeat and still remain thin, practice complete sexual freedom and also experience the intimacy and trust of a faithful life-long relationship. Images in this sense are not direct lies but are deliberately confusing ways of stating a truth.

For example, one familiar image has been the Marlboro Man. He does not make rash promises that Marlboros cause less cancer, have less tar, or even taste better than other cigarettes. In fact, if you look closely at the advertisements you will see that he is often not even smoking a cigarette. (It could even be that he has read the surgeon general's health warning and given them up.) But there he is, usually on his horse, in the midst of vast mountain scenery, striking an image in our minds of masculine strength, freedom, and the heroic history of the American West.

There are no lies, no overt attempts to persuade, no silly promises that you, too, can leave your office and become a cowboy if you will only smoke a pack of Marlboros a day. The image leaves you with nothing to reject, refute, or argue against on a rational level. If there are any lies told, it is you who tell them to yourself. It is only a picture, after all.

There is just the association between this cigarette and rugged individual freedom in beautiful scenery. The advertiser realizes that the image itself works so powerfully that a cigarette is superfluous. The picture is so laden with cultural meaning that it suggests a seductive kind of participation in the ethos of freedom and individual self-reliance, away from the urban sprawl. It suggests to you that this cowboy is the real you underneath the mundane life made up of petty obligations, commuter traffic, air-conditioned offices, and bills to pay. Its message has an ambiguous relationship to truth. One can judge its effectiveness only by its extraordinary longevity.

Think of how much political discussion concerns the images of electoral candidates. One of the main requirements to gain office seems to be the ability to project a certain image, whether it be to get the California vote, the black vote, or the women's vote. A candidate must appear to be what the voters want to see, whatever that is.

Linked closely to this phenomenon is what Daniel Boorstin calls a "pseudo-event" (now more sympathetically called a "media event"); that is, an event that happens primarily to be reported. If the press were not there to report it, it probably would not happen. The question is not whether it is true or important, but whether it is fascinating and, therefore, newsworthy. Of course, much of what goes on in the modern political world falls into this category—the press conferences, news leaks, interviews, innuendoes, public relations banquets, riots, protests, and even battles. The believability of images can become the most important determining factor of political decision making.

Individual Self-Image

One of the most important areas of image orientation is in our individual lives—the images we project of ourselves to one another. Here again, we can do wonders at the level of image that would be impossible for a person in reality. How much easier it is to develop and project a certain image of yourself than it is to actually be that sort of person. One can wear the clothes and adopt the mannerisms and vocabulary of Tom Cruise more readily than one can live out the kind of lives he does on film. Likewise, one can affect the image of an intellectual, with a certain wardrobe, glasses, demeanor, and vocabulary, more easily than one can actually become a learned person. It is easier to dress for success than to actually be competent in the corporate world.

We cannot expect to communicate very much about who we really are to most of the people we meet, especially if we live in an urban setting. This means that we will communicate far more image than sub-stance to most people, whether we like it or not. Also, there is always a performance aspect to our lives. We cannot help letting others' obser-vation of us influence our actions. We vary enormously from one another in what image we try to project and in how much we care about what others think about us. Erving Goffman, in *The Presentation of Self in Everyday Life*, calls this whole process "impression management."[18]

A distinctive aspect of our society is that impression management is taught and encouraged. Vast amounts of time, energy, and money are devoted to consciously staging our appearance. We can buy books by the top "image consultants" that will tell how to "radiate success," "upgrade your image," "achieve total confidence in your appearance," and "transform you into an executive headhunter's dream."

But the problem is, if we are concerned only about managing our own image and not about who we really are behind that image, we are likely to live only for the mask. *The more time we spend fashioning that mask, the less likely that there will be anything behind it.* Christopher Lasch complains that many people seem to pay more attention to how they appear than to who they are, and are "unable to express emotion with-out calculating its effects on others."[19] Andy Warhol dwelt masochisti-cally on this theme. He wrote about standing in front of a mirror:

> Nothing is missing. It's all there. The affectless gaze . . . The bored languor, the wasted pallor . . . The graying lips. The shaggy silver-white hair, soft and metallic . . . Nothing is missing. I'm everything my scrapbook says I am.[20]

As one who devoted much time and energy to his self-image, Warhol said he was obsessed with the idea of looking in the mirror and "seeing no one, nothing."[21]

While Daniel Boorstin could warn in 1961 of this preoccupation with artificiality as a danger, the post-modern thought of today wants to celebrate it. It would say there is no real self beneath the roles we play. Our projected images are not contrived expressions of the self; they *are* the self. There *is* no coherent self that is genuine in contrast to images that are artifice or manipulation, it is all artifice. Does not life have more freedom and richness without the burden of a coherent self? MTV is one of the strongest expressions of this selflessness, where there is no coherence, no story, no objectivity to reality—just vivid images.[22] In order to sustain themselves, our unrealistic expectations grasp onto gratifying images, but the shortfall in the real world brings frustration and disillusionment. In an image-oriented and therefore increasingly artificial society, there is still an unceasing hunger to believe in, and have contact with, human greatness. If we have turned away from a meaning system that could provide soil for moral greatness to grow in, artificial, instant heroes seem the only ones available. They are as close to us as our television set. However, they are apt to be trivial heroes of the surface, of style and not of character. It is not clear that even in the post-modern generation they can provide anything beyond narcissism.

THE DYNAMICS OF CELEBRITY

In the first chapter we distinguished between different types of exceptional people—the talent, the celebrity, and the hero. The talent was someone who had a skill, who could do something—just about anything—well. The celebrity was someone who was famous. Both the talent and the celebrity were distinct from the hero, who was defined by moral character. The three can coexist in the same person or be independent of each other.

Hero as Celebrity

Here we look in greater depth at celebrity because of its relationship to trivialization. Boorstin claimed that the celebrity is "neither good nor bad, great nor petty. He is the human pseudo-event."[23] Where the hero is respected for some achievement, the celebrity is envied for being famous. While one can substantially agree with Boorstin's analysis, it is important to remember that the celebrity's fame does not usually occur by sheer accident, but because of some attention-getting talent.

The majority of our celebrities are seen as partial people in the sense that they are known for one thing, which has attracted attention. They are rather like the female body in many magazine advertisements—all you see is a hand, a foot, a bust, a waist, a neck, or a shoulder, not the whole person. So with celebrities, we see their talent or gimmick, but that's all we see. We have tried to show that celebrity and heroism must be separable, that simply being well publicized for a talent is not all there is to human greatness. However, some would disagree with this view. Roger Rollin, an observer of popular culture, wants to make heroism entirely dependent on publicity: "All heroes . . . are celebrities; no hero is not a celebrity." He makes his reasons clear:

> The sine qua non of heroism is publicity. Without publicity an
> act of heroism is like the sound made by the tree that falls in the

empty forest. A hypothetical case in point: the farm woman who risks her life to save her two-year-old from a rampaging bull and mentions the incident to no one. Even she may not think of herself as a hero, only as a negligent mother or as someone who just did what had to be done. But most of us would impute high values to her act—courage, selflessness, and so on—or, more precisely, to her. Values, however, can *only* be imputed: they *inhere* in nothing and no one, for they are created by human consciousness. Such a woman might impute value to her act and to herself. But if no one becomes aware of what she did other than her two-year-old, who might not understand the event and would at any rate soon forget it—if she were never, in other words, to receive publicity for it she would only be a hero to the gods. And the gods have long been silent, even about heroes.[24]

Here again we can see the working together of cynicism and triviality. Rollin articulates the doctrines we discussed in chapter 2: that the only meanings in the world are ones that we ourselves attribute to events and actions. The idea that there are ultimate values that give value *to* us, and to which we are then answerable, is therefore a fantasy, since there are no gods to care or to reveal themselves to us. Values are therefore tacked onto acts and events by admirers, according to the way things look to them at the time. But who then gets to tell hero from villain?

Rollin is very clear about his answer. The gods are silent. The heroes themselves cannot decide because then their heroism would only be self-proclaimed. He writes, "All that is left is 'the people,' the non-heroes who witness and communicate the heroism and those who accept and validate that communication."[25] The only standard of human greatness is fame.

Rollin presses home the significance of God's abdication by stressing that the media have taken over where God left off—"the mass media giveth and the mass media taketh away."[26] If the essence of heroism is fame, it does not guarantee that all heroes will be trivial, but it certainly encourages it. There will be more heroes, and they will have a shorter shelf life because a winning image is very difficult to maintain over time.

Heroes of the Surface

Heroes are heroes of surfaces. As Marshall Fishwick, another student of popular culture, wrote, "Only by responding to the public's insatiable passion for poetic stimulation can the hero remain 'on top.'"[27] Celebrities are seen as public property, to be discarded when they are worn out. Public attention span is not long, especially when there is so much competition for it. If I had tried to include the most up-to-date celebrities as examples in this book, they would still be people long forgotten by the time you are holding the book in your hands.

When you look at what makes the difference between a celebrity and an "unknown," it seems somewhat haphazard. Of great importance might be dimples in the right places and the correct distribution of fatty and muscle tissue on the body. In some fields extraordinary talent is not enough. There are too many people around with extraordinary talent. You need a gimmick, any gimmick, something to distinguish you from the masses of other aspirants to fame.

Taking a strong moral stand on anything except what happens to be in vogue at the moment can be a liability—fatal to one's long-term celebrity standing. Think of the media attention given to Aleksandr Solzhenitsyn during the 1970s, as he was exposing the inhumanity and hypocrisy of the Soviet Union, and getting exiled from his own country for it. He had immense popularity in Europe and North America. But then came a marked turning point in his public fortunes: in a 1978 commencement address at Harvard, he turned his seering, prophetic, moral vision from his own country (as we had become accustomed to hearing it) to the United States in its spiritual decadence.

Although he received a standing ovation at the time, the measured response of the academic and media worlds was one of icy, sputtering indignation. "How dare he? What does *he* know about us?" He was substantially dropped from public view (until the time of his return to Russia). His shelf life was over. He could no longer be counted on to give us what we wanted to hear.

THE TRIUMPH OF TRIVIALITY

We can see two great waves of the trivialization of heroism: that the truly heroic are trivialized, and that the trivial are inflated to heroism. In the first wave it is the heroic individual who is reduced in stature; in the second, the status of heroism itself, the very idea of human greatness. Together they turn heroism upside down.

Trivializing the Heroic

Let us look at two examples of the first wave. Test pilot Chuck Yeager, the man with the "Right Stuff," has been seen as a hero, and rightly so.

His courage and service to the nation have been extraordinary. Yet in some news magazines in the late 1980s we could read the following copy beside his smiling face:

> He went on to become the first man to break the sound barrier, the first to travel at more than twice that speed (over 1600 mph) and one of the first pilots to reach the edge of space, taking a plane above 100,000 feet. If there's ever been anyone who had "the right stuff," it's Chuck Yeager. Especially when it comes to the Scotch that he drinks: Cutty Sark.[28]

What happens when we see the zenith of a test pilot's career as being able to lift a glass of Scotch to his lips and drink it? When we put courage, service to one's nation, and drinking whisky together in a list of achievements, courage and service are trivialized by the absurdity of the association. Perhaps few take it seriously, and he is still better known as a test pilot than a drinker of whisky, but it is too familiar a story. Virtue becomes reduced to its commercial value. We quickly tire of the commercial grins of the last Olympics' most photogenic gold medalists, and we know that even talents can be trivialized down to their commercial value.

Take the experience of Lenny Skutnik. He was a government employee who, in January 1982, jumped into the icy Potomac River after an Air Florida plane crashed into the Fourteenth Street bridge. He did it to save a woman who was drowning. He was hailed as a national hero and also became a celebrity because the rescue was captured on a video and shown on television. He was applauded and decorated by people from all over the world, and was asked to stand beside Nancy Reagan during President Reagan's State of the Union address. He had some very astute things to say about this experience:

> What I think I'm getting now is publicity on top of publicity—like that State of the Union thing. That made 'em forget. It put what I actually did on a lower level and put that (the appearance with Nancy Reagan) on top. A few people said to me afterward, "Hey, aren't you the guy who was on the State of the Union?" That kind of thing. Not, "Hey aren't you the guy who jumped in the river and saved that lady?"[29]

Although what he did remains, his heroism is obscured by his media appearance, dissolved in part by the sheer quantity of publicity.

What is remembered is as much the achievement of the media as it is his heroism. In the minds of many, the indelible impression of him will be the television appearance and the Reagans' handshake. In a society where fame is sacred, any hero who becomes a public hero is suddenly plunged into a halo of imaginative confusion in which there may remain little of the original deed or virtue.

Inflating the Trivial

In the second wave of triviality, true heroism is not brought down but rather, talents are inflated. This second wave is the more powerful of the two, and it leaves us with a new cast of "fascinating" people each week.

Heroes' stories in the past have often undergone modification to increase their dramatic effect. There have been many in the pattern of the legendary Mike Fink of the Mississippi, who could dive deeper, swim farther, and come up drier than any other person alive. But today's heroes do not, for the most part, come to us in this way. In 1985, *U.S. News and World Report* published an article entitled "Heroes Are Back,"[30] pointing to a greater willingness to talk of heroes in the mid-eighties than a decade earlier. After taking a national poll, they named the top ten American heroes at that point in time. Seven of the ten were from show business, most of them esteemed not for anything they had done in their real lives but for their fictional roles played out on the stage of rock concerts or in celluloid. The heroism that has captured the imaginations of millions was the heroism of their images. The style of American heroism has not changed significantly in the time since then.

We are not dealing only with the mindless screaming of early adolescents who see their first rock star. Jane Fonda, Jessica Lange, and Sissy Spacek were called to testify before a congressional committee on the economic problems of farmers. Were they called because of their particular expertise in agricultural economics? Not quite. They were called because they had all played farm women in recent films. One legislator defended their testimony by pointing out that "at least people will listen." He was probably right.

The intriguing question remains: what relationship does the imaginative power of these celebrity-heroes have to reality? It is not a simple question, but millions of people are preoccupied with fantasies of people who are not actually there at all. The celebrity whose image I might try to project to others (as if it were the real me) is not only not me, but he or she does not exist anywhere on this planet. We become like the desert wanderer who navigates by mirages.

We can see this most clearly in commercial advertising. One editorial put it this way:

> With lots of blusher but no shame, the peacock profession of modeling gives face and body to our covetous dreams, then mocks us as we press our noses against the window glass. What unimaginable delight made the pretty lady swirl and smile as the photographer snapped her picture? What season of debauchery brought the sulky thrust to this beauty's lower lip? At what groveling serf does the fine young lord in the Ferrari scowl with such contempt? Nothing; none; at no one; these glossy apparitions are moments that never were—yet they tease us because their reality is beyond question, while our own stored moments, caught in snapshots and thrown into a drawer, are obvious and pallid fakes. Fascination sidesteps good sense, and we wonder; How was this lovely bunkum done?[31]

At a conscious level, we may debunk this bunkum, yet modern marketers are not so stupid as to pay the billions they do if advertisements had no measurable leverage on what we buy. But they do not only affect the way we spend our money. They also help form images and ideas about what is important in the world, what brings satisfaction, and what real greatness is in our whole society. It is done not by direct lies but by images, mirages, and vapors, all of which have fascinating but ambiguous relationships to truth.

The political world is no stranger to the mirage either. There is now a whole new generation of political image consultants, hired to promote and manage the images of political candidates. Although they keep a relatively low profile, they wield enormous power from behind the scenes. They conduct polls, raise funds, and produce advertisements; put the best "spin" on all events; but also decide on issues and policies to be followed and emphasized. Ron Suskind of the *New York Times* described the efforts of Malcolm Wallop, a Republican from Wyoming, to win election to the Senate:

> In 1976, Wallop, then a 43-year-old State Senator from Big Horn, hired Bob Goodman to run his campaign for the United States Senate. From Goodman's point of view, Wallop had certain disadvantages as a candidate in Wyoming. He was born in New York (although he was raised in Wyoming), educated at

Yale and descended from British nobility. Goodman's television commercial sought to compensate for all that. It showed Malcolm Wallop riding at the head of a troop of 75 galloping cowboys. "Ride with us, Wyoming," the narrator intoned at the end of the spot as the music swelled. By most accounts, the ad—which is shown in university communications classes as the epitome of political salesmanship—was a crucial factor in Wallop's eventual victory.[32]

After the election, Bob Goodman went so far as to claim, "I invented Mal Wallop."[33] There was a parting of the ways due to questions about who was leading whom, and Wallop hired a different consultant for the next election.

My point here is not to dwell on the very real dangers to representative government that are foreshadowed, but to reflect on the way people in political life are perceived by the public. Elected officials have always been some of the most respected people in the land, and are a natural focus for the public's ideals and aspirations. Whether politicians are or ever have been worthy of that respect has to be evaluated in each individual case. However, the style of political life in a media age tends to remove the politician as he really is farther from our view in each successive election.

The political world in the United States has created a vicious cycle of cynicism and trivialization. The more candidates and their handlers try to fine-tune the candidates' images, the more the media "retaliate" by exposing the theatrical dimension of the campaign and hunt for the gaffes, slips, and "naked moments," hoping to get a view of what is real. Of course, this encourages handlers to even greater vigilance to let no unprocessed information out to the public. It is a spiral of illusion in which candidates' competence is increasingly measured by their ability to master their own illusions.[34]

The second wave of trivialization, then, is energized by the most visible of public figures, whether political or not. They are mirages created by media images reflecting off the heat of our expectations. What is envied is superficial and trivial, but it is also artificial. What is imitated is not character but style—how we look holding a cigarette or making a pronouncement; how we stand as we lean against a wall; how we buy clothes, car, house. And the people who model those styles, who carry them into our living rooms, are make-believe. Their clothes fit so beautifully only because they are held by rows of pins up and down the torso, arms, and legs (on the side that is away from the camera), so that no wrinkle is visible to us.

As long ago as 1959, Earl Blackwell and Cleveland Amory compiled the voluminous *Celebrity Register*, including in it over two thousand biographies. They assert that "it is impossible to list a man's social standing—even if anyone cared; and it's impossible to list accurately the success or value of men; but you can judge a man as a celebrity—all you need to do is weigh his press clippings."[35]

If, as Roger Rollin claimed, after the death of all gods the only standard of evaluation of human greatness that matters is fame, then human value *will* be measured by the weight of press clippings. In the *Celebrity Register*, the television comedienne Dagmar is listed beside the Dalai Lama, Dwight Eisenhower beside Anita Ekberg, and Bertrand Russell beside Jane Russell.[36] Why not? They are linked by their common status as celebrities. As long as we hold fame to be the overarching value, it seems pedantic to make more meaningful distinctions between them. In a context where well knownness is exalted, moral distinctions tend to melt down or disappear.

We are not dealing here with just an appreciation or interest in celebrity. We are dealing with celebrity as society's great blue ribbon or first prize—for many, the conception of greatness itself. Not only does this tend to trivialize persons, but it trivializes the very idea of human greatness.

We are left with lite heroes who can stimulate the imagination without challenging us to change. There is little danger that the lite hero will unsettle us very much, because he or she is usually perceived only as a partial person, or has a very short shelf life, or both. Glory is in the brightness of the lights, the frequency of the press clippings. It becomes a vapor—here now, and then gone in a moment as if lighter than air. A lot of it is needed to fill the emptiness of the human heart and its need for aspiration.

The celebrity world takes a sinister turn as terrorists and murderers find it the perfect stage on which to play out their particular objectives. Any terrorist can be sure that the media will oblige him with millions of dollars of free publicity for his cause—just for the price of the bullets or explosives. One murderer complained bitterly in a letter to the Wichita police, "How many times do I have to kill before I get a name in the paper or some national attention?" It was only after his sixth killing that he began to get the coverage he felt he deserved.[37]

The two waves of trivialization have come together in a triumph of triviality. It has meant pulling heroes down into celebrities, and inflating public figures to pseudo greatness. We can go on to summarize the contrast between celebrity and heroism with three points. First is the question of depth. The celebrity is usually perceived as a partial person, known for some skill that might have nothing to do with his or her character. Second is the question of time. The celebrity is likely to stay on the shelf only a short time, often not even long enough for aspiration to take aim at the moving target. And third, the question of reality. The celebrity can be a human mirage, or as Daniel Boorstin has claimed, a "human pseudo-event." What you aspire to might not exist anywhere, let alone be realistically accessible to you.

When Combined Forces Meet

When we combine the forces of trivialization with those of cynicism, we can see something of the impasse of heroism today, and the difficulties that it poses to the development of an imaginative vision of excellence. Cynicism, with its appearance of sophistication and courage, tears down human greatness and gives us a landscape with no heroes left standing. Trivialization, in trying hard to produce the human greatness that people crave but are unable to find, inflates and deflates celebrities before our eyes like soap bubbles in the wind.

These two forces, cynicism and trivialization, start off in opposite directions but ironically circle around and meet behind our backs. They meet at the point of herolessness, where there are no believable public heroes and the search for private ones seems a waste of time. Cynicism and trivialization have a symbiotic relationship, each feeding the other. The more we give in to cynicism, the more that life can only be seen as trivial. On the other hand, the more triviality we see around us, the more cynicism seems to be the only honest Conclusion. The world of professional sports has encouraged this cycle as so many athletes have become known less for heroism or even talent, as for greed, strikes, and cocaine.

Our culture teaches us to identify with the stars and to quietly despise the anonymity of the "herd." Much of the psychology of celebrity involves projecting ourselves in our fantasies into the glamorous shoes of the well known. From that vantage point we can feel lifted out of the faceless mass of humanity and recognized as great. However, it does not take very much insight to realize that we all *are* the herd (except for a very select few). One psychologist wrote with unassailable wisdom, "most of us are average." If we maintain unrealistic expectations of the world through building our lives around images that sustain those expectations, the relentless erosion of the real world will always win out in the end. Even the images, dreams, and mirages of post-modernism are no match for the pitiless efficiency of frustration, disappointment, disease, and ultimately our own personal death. Boorstin wrote, "Never have people been more the masters of their environment. Yet never has a people felt more deceived and disappointed. For never has a people expected so much more than the world could offer."[38]

We ended the last chapter with the insight of Pascal, and shall continue his thought here:

> It is dangerous to make man see too clearly his equality with the brutes without showing him his greatness. It is also dangerous to make him see his greatness too clearly, apart from his vileness.[39]

The danger is that through cynicism we might lose the vision of our true potential for greatness. We are left without a positive force to jar us out of comfortable mediocrity and banality. There is also danger in protecting us from an understanding of the evil that we do now and are capable of in the future—what Pascal called our "vileness." Trivialization has done this effectively by dazzling us with what is young, rich, and beautiful. It helps us to ignore our brokenness, our finitude, and our mortality.

Our culture has flirted with Pascal's worst fears in that it has delivered neither a clear vision of our greatness nor of our vileness, but has insulated us from both. Evaluating the impact of this situation for the person in the street is the next step in our journey.

CHAPTER FOUR

HEROISM AND THE PERSON IN THE STREET

≈

Let us not be complacent about our supposed capacity to get along without great men. If our society has lost its wish for heroes and its ability to produce them, it may well turn out to have lost everything else as well.[1]

A. M. SCHLESINGER, JR.

≈

The chance of becoming famous might be called the great American jackpot. To be a celebrity, to appear on television, to be applauded, to have necks crane when you enter a room—that is the warm and not-so-secret dream of countless Americans in a society that is becoming more and more an audience directed by mass communication.[2]

ORRIN KLAPP

wo themes have emerged from our discussion thus far that make it hard to take heroes seriously. Contemporary cynicism tells us there is no such thing as human greatness, so don't get your hopes up that you will meet people you would want to be like. What looks like strength in another person is very likely weakness in disguise. Also, the forces of trivialization have degraded public heroes into celebrities and catapulted trivial people into places of high visibility to be admired and envied. These people substitute so poorly for heroes that heroism itself has a bad name. On the positive side, there are plenty of people around who do heroic things, most of whom are unsung, local heroes. A few public heroes have been able to retain their integrity. There is still true heroism to be seen in film and on television—if you look for it. Every liberation, protest, or politically active movement will have its heroes.

Most important of all, there still exists a deep hunger in our society for true heroism, a desire to believe that there is such a thing as human greatness, despite the condescension of cynicism and the erosion of triviality. The hope is that we might find heroism in others in order to share in it ourselves. A time when old models are falling to pieces is also a time when good questions are asked with renewed seriousness. If there is a growing concern over the crisis in heroism, it can only be a positive development.

Having said all this, one cannot disguise the crisis of heroism in our society today. This crisis is not only a matter of concern among pundits and cultural critics. It has a profound impact on the day-to-day life of the person in the street. It is to that impact that we now turn.

HEROISM OUT OF REACH
The heroism that survives the acid bath of cynicism and the inflation and deflation cycles of trivialization is apt to be a heroism that either offers no imaginative challenge to life or else is inaccessible to the vast majority of people. This is because modern heroism has substantially separated itself from moral reality. But this should not surprise us. There is probably an educated consensus in our society that believes there are no final standards of right and wrong and that all human values are just "imputed" to actions by individuals or groups (as was suggested by Rollin). There is therefore no reason to expect any specific moral values to have enough widespread cultural authority to build a concensus on heroism.

In the second chapter we discussed various heroes who pass through the net of cynicism simply because the "heroic" qualities are themselves imbedded in cynicism. They cannot be toppled by the cynic because they are already on the bottom and have nowhere to fall. The minimal heroism of the hassle-free life does not challenge your aspirations, it simply legitimizes your apathy. We discussed the mock hero who is always winking at you to be sure that your cynicism is alive and well. He doesn't take himself seriously, why should you? Likewise, the anti-hero leads only to a deeper conviction that you are a victim of overwhelming forces that are larger than you are.

Then there are those heroes who do challenge us imaginatively, but whose challenge is outside the context of morality, at least as it has been perceived in the Judeo-Christian tradition and most of Western culture. We can make only loose distinctions, but let us divide these heroes between those who are heroic for immoral reasons (immorality appearing heroic) and those who are heroic for nonmoral reasons (a morally neutral "virtue" appearing heroic).

Immoral Heroism

Let's take up immoral heroism first. Here, true heroism is sought in freedom from moral restraints. Lives of those who have broken free from the dead and constricting expectations and judgments of others to violate society's moral norms can be portrayed as highly attractive. They are contrasted to the majority who do not possess the courage or stature to seize their freedom. Nietzsche is their patron saint.

The three most common examples of immoral heroism today are in the areas of unrestricted freedom in sex, money, and violence—all variations on the theme of abuse of power presented as highly attractive. At the level of our pseudosophisticated pop culture, sexual promiscuity is healthy and liberated, shows an acceptance of one's body, and only occasionally has unhappy consequences. The power of seduction—to be so magnetically alluring that one can pry a member of the opposite sex away from any and all other loyalties—is a high and fascinating prize of self-affirmation. In the modern media it holds an *imaginative power* of attractiveness far beyond that of sexual faithfulness within marriage, which by comparison can easily be made to seem rigid, fearful, uptight, and unhappy.

Likewise, there is only thinly veiled admiration for those who exploit others financially, as long as they have a spectacular lifestyle to show for it. Money "talks," after all. Think of the various and sundry personal shortcomings that are "forgiven" if the person is rich enough.

Thousands will line the streets for the Rolls-Royce funeral of a flamboy-ant drug baron knifed to death in prison.

Violence also has a powerful imaginative attraction. Some critics have maintained that the secret to Clint Eastwood's rise to success was his distinctive style in shooting people. No one could rival his image of transcendent indifference to his dead and dying victims. Why is vio-lence evidently so fascinating and attractive? It represents the primal thrill of power. But it offers also an illusion of transcendence over our own death when we can identify with the killer.[3]

All of these heroics of power have a strong appeal to the imagina-tion of a society uncertain about ultimate meaning and anxious about its own helplessness in a threatening and unpredictable world. If these are the hero systems presented by our culture, what is their significance to us as potential aspirants? As we try to follow the lead of our imagi-native attraction to these heroes, we immediately sense a curious difficulty—what if we should succeed and actually become like one of these immoral heroes? Is that what we really want?

Most of us have seen enough of the world to realize that if we did succeed, we would make a shambles out of the relationships that we care most about. In fact, in the real, off-the-screen world, it might bring only loneliness and addictions, if not the emergency room, the morgue, or a career making license plates in jail. And we know this. Do we really want to "live fast, die young and leave a beautiful memory"?[4]

What does this mean? Apart from any matters of conscience or moral principle, sheer self-interest forces us to be ambivalent about these dreams. We are attracted to them but we need, for the sake of sheer survival, to simultaneously hold them at arm's length. Admira-tion may be present, but aspiration becomes very cautious. The result is usually that the dream stays a dream, "safely" embedded in our imag-ination and pursued only in the faltering ambivalence of our daydreams.

Morally Neutral Heroism

Most of what passes for heroism today is morally neutral. That is, the admired qualities are not in themselves morally significant one way or the other. Take, for example, the celebrity hero. Being well known is itself not morally good or bad. Yet the pulse of many people will quicken if they catch a glimpse of a television "personality" on the street, in an airport or restaurant. A celebrity may have a talent, even if it is only that of self-dramatization, but the actual ingredient that is admired does not come from the person. It has been created by the media. It is only because of the media that his or her face is recognized in most of the households in the country.

The heroism of most people with talent is equally independent of moral truth. Most of the rock stars and professional athletes and experts from all different fields do not seem to need moral stature to maintain competence in their fields.

Heroes have not always been removed from moral life. Take, for example, the heroes of Shakespeare. None of them is perfect, but each is heroic for basically moral reasons. The villains also are, for the most part, not as bad as they could be, but they are villainous for immoral reasons. The difference between hero and villain was significant because the heroic virtues were also seen in that culture as the highest moral values. Both *Macbeth* and *Hamlet* are dominated by a violation of the moral structure of the universe and are bound up in the resolution of that moral conflict. Such an agreed moral framework for heroic virtue is the very thing that is in doubt in the modern imagination.

How do we respond to morally neutral heroes? Here too we find difficulties. The gnawing question is, how many of us will really be able to reach heroic status within the context of fame, sports, music, wealth, physical beauty? If the "great American Jackpot" is "to be applauded, to have necks crane when you enter a room,"[5] it does not take long to realize that people won't do that for everybody who enters the room. If they did, it would lose its meaning for us, since this heroism is intended to distinguish us favorably *from* the others in the room. In fact, very few people command that level of attention, and most who do, do not do so for very long. It is only for the multimillionaires, the superb athletes, the brilliant musicians, the stunningly beautiful people, and only for as long as they can maintain their fortunes, gifts, and appearance. For the rest of us, our noses are pressed against the glass on the outside. Even Warhol's plan for fifteen minutes of fame for each of us is not much to live for.

While our pursuit of immoral heroism is clouded by our awareness of the dangers of success, our pursuit of nonmoral heroism is discouraged by the remoteness of the possibility of success. There are simply too few spots available up there—not enough room at the top of the charts. Having many multimillionaires could only be the result of catastrophic inflation. And how many of us are, or are likely to become, stunningly beautiful people, superb professional athletes, or brilliant musicians? To become heroic in these fields we need extraordinary gifts and levels of proficiency well beyond the capabilities of all but a very few. Aspiration is apt to be short-lived. As our adolescence wanes, the glorious possibilities before us begin to appear more unrealistic and are usually replaced by a more vicariously experienced heroism.

For example, watching a ninety-yard touchdown run is inspiring. But for most people it inspires only a trip to the kitchen for another can of beer during the commercial break that follows. In the same way, the adoring fans of a rock guitarist are inspired to invest fortunes in CDs, tapes, posters, and clothing, but comparatively few get beyond "air guitar" to actually learn to play the instrument.

Think of the idea behind chamber music, which was written to be played by members of a family or small group of friends in their own homes. Now we hear it in impeccable better-than-life recordings made in studios, with every imperfection electronically removed. The modern attitude is predictable—why bother with your own scraping and squeaking when you can hear better than the best on your CD player? What we can get vicariously in all these areas is at a much higher level than what we could ever realistically aspire to, so why bother aspiring?

Some welcome the rise of the celebrity hero as a proper expression of democratic principles. Leo Braudy describes fame as the "democratic descendent of honor."[6] By this he means that when the criterion of honor is simply well knownness, you are not barred from it by a class system in which you lacked an aristocratic pedigree. It is perfectly true that class barriers to public recognition have dropped, but they have been replaced by new ones—the new elite is made up of the beautiful people of the celebrity culture. They have a shorter shelf life than the aristocrats of old, but for most people, their world is just as unattainable. In fact, the celebrity culture fosters the illusion of a more democratic heroism and holds the false promises before our faces. But for all but a few, the reality is as far away as it was for a serf under feudalism.

If heroism is separated from moral truth, whether by being immoral or morally neutral, it moves out of reach for the majority of people. Of course, some of the nonmoral hero styles are easier to pursue than others. Sex is cheap and the heroism of money, fame, and expertise are ever-present carrots in front of our noses, so they at least seem potentially available. But those who get enough of them to experience heroic status through them are few. For the majority, heroism begins to work in a different way.

A DYSFUNCTIONAL RELATIONSHIP TO HEROES
The role of the hero in the traditional sense has been to stretch us into larger people because of the hero's example. Heroes showed us our

ideals in flesh-and-blood stories, and so provided us motivation to engage in our own stories more fully. If people are left with heroes who are out of reach, their imaginations may still be engaged in admiration, but it is admiration without aspiration. There is veneration of a person without the intention to emulate him or her.

Admiration Without Aspiration

Admiration without aspiration ends in frustration. It centers not on constructive growth or change but on daydreaming and self-hatred. We develop a dysfunctional relationship to our heroes.

A typical victim of inaccessible heroism is Walter Mitty, who becomes the anti-hero of James Thurber's short story "The Secret Life of Walter Mitty."[7] Walter Mitty lives a very ordinary life, doing very ordinary things, but he has a secret life in his fertile imagination. While doing some unheroic task such as driving his wife to get her hair done, his imagination starts to work and he is suddenly single-handedly averting disaster, taking over the controls from a panicked pilot of a plane that is about to crash. But his glory is interrupted by the harsh and scornful voice of his wife, who tells him that he is driving too fast, and that it is not the first time she has had to tell him about it. Minutes later, as he waits at a stoplight outside of a hospital, he is suddenly a doctor, brought in at the last minute to save the life of a friend of the president. But this dream too is broken by the blast of a horn from behind him as he has been sitting immobile at a green light. In an amusing but merciless way, Thurber explores in several episodes the agonizing chasm between the ecstacy of the secret, imagined glory of his fantasy world, and the shame and humiliation as his daydreams are exploded into the real world. The heroism of his fantasy world is unlimited, but it is so self-engrossing that it makes him into a real-world incompetent. His daydreams do not stimulate him to grow; they just make it hard for him to concentrate enough on his own life to notice a green light.

Our imaginations often work in the same way—we produce daydreams by the hundreds that feed our sense of vanity by projecting us into all kinds of heroic roles. They are binges of self-esteem at the fantasy level. But if we spend much of our time daydreaming about heroes that are out of reach, and if we do not also have heroes that are within reach, we too will be less effective in the real world. On top of that, we will also despise ourselves. These out-of-reach heroes become tyrants making us ashamed and disgusted with ourselves because of the contours of our bodies, our lack of physical coordination, our inability to think quickly on our feet, our anonymity, our poverty, or what seems to us a dull life by comparison to Hollywood norms. What pathetic creatures we are when put beside the glory of the stars!

This is not at all to say that fantasy itself is destructive. On the contrary, fantasy is a wonderful, important, and much-neglected gift. In fact, some of the best fantasy literature embodies a heroism that is entirely accessible, although the story may be set in the midst of elves and unicorns. Even if we are dealing with a science fiction story with bizarre technology and extraterrestrial life, the moral issues raised in the story can be recognizable and translated into our lives. In fact, one of the characteristics of moral heroism in any setting is that it puts heroism too close to us for comfort. The problem comes when the heroism of our fantasies is disconnected from moral reality, becoming inaccessible, and our involvement in it becomes addictive and escapist. If we are very involved with these fantasies, they tend to displace accessible heroes.

Compensatory Heroes

This raises the issue of what has been called "*compensatory heroism*."[8] A compensatory hero is not a certain kind of hero but a certain kind of relationship to any hero. We build compensatory heroes when our attitude is not that of emulating the hero but of letting the hero compensate for what we cannot or will not do ourselves. The hero is used for a vicarious voyage of the identity, an aid to creative daydreaming.

To illustrate the point, let us look at a hero who is clearly heroic for moral reasons. Just as immoral and nonmoral heroism is usually out of reach, so moral heroism is within reach in the sense that it deals with thoughts, words, and actions that are realistically possible for each one of us. Take Mother Teresa as an example of someone who is heroic for moral reasons. She spoke to auditoriums in the West that were packed with admirers. They gave her standing ovations, honorary degrees, and a Nobel prize. She has been listed as one of the "top ten" American heroes in many polls for years. But what is the nature of this admiration? Many admirers' knees would turn to water if it was suggested that they should go to Calcutta and care for the poor and dying. Hearts would melt if allegiance to her should call even for a minor change of lifestyle in her direction.

As she spoke, she made it clear that emigrating to Calcutta is not the point, but that there are staggering needs all around us in the affluent West that cry out for love and care of a costly, sacrificial kind. In other words, opportunities to live out her heroic virtues are eminently available to us—as close to us as our neighbors. To be sure, she has inspired genuine aspiration in many lives, not only in those who have joined her order, but in people throughout the world who have caught from her a glimpse of the true heroism and joy of caring for other people. But one fears that the subversive force of her message was lost on many others in the audiences, as she told of a poverty in America and Europe that is even deeper than that in Calcutta, and that there is joy and freedom in giving a costly love in response to God's prior love for us.

For some, then, she does function as a wonderful model for their aspirations. She fires their imaginations and redirects the course of their lives by her extraordinary example. They are stretched toward God and greater humanness. For others, through no fault of hers, she functions as a compensatory hero. Dreaming about her can make us feel better about ourselves in the midst of a self-centered way of life. It is comforting to know that *someone* is out there doing something about these awful problems of poverty and disease in the Third World! Her heroism can compensate for our lives of relative self-indulgence, enabling us to stay as we are with a clearer conscience.

A compensatory hero is one who, in the words of Orrin Klapp, is a "vehicle for psychic mobility to those who see themselves as nobodies."[9] That is to say that this kind of heroism functions as a fuel for imaginative dreams and projections, but not for mobility of character or real personal change.

If we can use moral heroes (whose greatness is accessible to us) as compensatory heroes, how much more likely that we will use intrinsically inaccessible heroes in this way. In the various stars of the celebrity world we can always find the fulfillment of what we lack, and be satisfied to admire it, envy it, and identify with it in our imagination.

If fame eludes us we can become a fan, basking in the reflected glory of the star by following his or her every move and statistic from an involved distance. Being a fan helps to bridge the gap between the oversized expectations encouraged by our society and the comparatively meager allotments of public status dispensed by that society.[10] The compensatory hero offers the possibility of "psychic hitchhiking" if we attach ourselves as fans to one who is "making" it in a big way.[11]

If I am a fearful person, identifying with the most recent incarnation of James Bond can make me feel better—I can picture myself in his shoes and try to experience something of his omnicompetence and coolness under pressure. If I feel ignored, insignificant, and unnoticed, I can be a fan of the top celebrity of the popular-music world, and I may derive a sense of importance by being in touch with the action. Perhaps this is one of the reasons the American televangelists received so much financial support—even after moral disgrace should have driven them into humiliated oblivion. If I contribute to such obviously "successful" people, a bond is formed between us (the charitable contribution makes the bond stronger than just being a fan). This is psychic hitchhiking on the illusion of being a winner myself.

Of course, all this imaginative involvement is vicarious. I am not a participant or even an aspirant, just an admirer. This heroism helps me to be more comfortable with an unheroic life without changing it. It helps me to make my peace with my mediocrity or anonymity.

It can be even more difficult if we have tasted acclaim at some point in our lives. Take the classic example of the star high school athlete. Within his social world, he received a high level of recognition. But then what? Most do not go on to excel to the same extent in college sports, and still fewer find professional careers within their reach. What else in their lives is likely to give them the level of audience attention that they once had when they were eighteen? They can take the nostalgia route by reliving past "glory days," but this gets old quickly as our listeners lose interest. One of the roads most taken is to a religious commitment to televised sports, which takes more hours of our Sundays than Puritan sermons ever did.

Compensatory heroism does not let heroes provide an ideal to be striven for, but it is a way of using heroes to substitute for lack of ideals. It compensates both for our lack of ideals and lack of the motivation to pursue them. It disguises alienation to look like integration. If enough people do it together, it gives a sense of togetherness in adherence to shared images, stars, and statistics, even though those images are part of an imaginative compensation for the absence of vital meaning in life.

THE HERO AS THE OPIATE OF THE MASSES

Few visions of life today seem to have the power to motivate people to widen their circle of caring beyond their own private interests. Our society has destroyed many of its myths and symbols, and it has not replaced them with anything that can help us toward meaning or dignity of life. In the midst of this symbolic poverty, we need powerful stories and heroic ideals if we are to be stretched beyond the insatiable, one-dimensional demands of self-gratification.

The *New York Times* reported a Yankelovich poll indicating that . . .

63% of the American public is ambivalent about embracing a totally self-centered, self-fulfilled style of life, asserting that the old standards are still important. However, 80% admitted that they have been affected by the new mentality and feel that their own need for sensation, novelty and ego-fulfillment takes precedence over the needs of all other people.[12]

The analysis of polls is notoriously difficult, but even if the 80 percent were cut in half, it is deeply threatening to the fabric of a democratic society, let alone a just one.

In the West we experience a level of economic prosperity unknown in most of the world, and a freedom that has been experienced only by very few. Is it not strange that two very prevalent attitudes of young people are boredom and escapism? Why boredom, when so many opportunities exist for so many? What is so terrible that we need to escape from it?

Michael Novak answers the question this way:

In a pluralistic culture, in which many stories are simultaneously and powerfully presented to the young, a certain confusion, malaise, and loss of confidence often result. No one story commands allegiance. Action, therefore, lacking a story to give it significance, seems pointless. Why bother with anything at all? What is worth trying to become? The young often begin to sleep alot.[13]

Whether the heroes are too far out of reach to bother with, or whether they change so fast that it is impossible to take aim at them before they disappear from view, there is a disengagement of the moral imagination. There seems to be no believable story of which we are a part.

Heroes and the Status Quo

Is there anything powerful enough to lure us beyond self-gratification and conformity to our consumer culture? Many of today's heroes act as opiates to the masses. (Ironically, this was just as true in Marxist countries, which used to have ubiquitous, ten-times-life-size portraits and statues of Lenin.) Far from inspiring growth of character and motivated positive engagement in life, heroes can acclimate us to the status quo. This is true of the compensatory heroes whose function is such by definition—to help us sink more deeply into the overstuffed couch of the fan without losing too much self-respect. The so-called psychic hitchhiking that they offer is vital dreamworld compensation for all that we lack in this world. Leo Braudy described the way cynicism about heroes can be fed by the fear of nonconformity—lest we be challenged by heroes to be different from the herd.

> No one considered Alexander Pope's twisted spine or Napoleon's short stature or Caesar's baldness or Alexander's mother or Byron's club foot reason for their aspirations until the compara-tively recent present. But we invoke them as "explanations" because they reassure us not only that such out-of-scale aspira-tion is essentially freakish (and not like our own), but also that it is a freakishness that affirms our own grander aspirations—if we would choose to indulge them. For who in a democratic society wants to be excessively different without a good excuse?[14]

He has pointed us again to the cynicism of our supposed psycho-logical sophistication—we know the heroes of the past better than they knew themselves, and we can explain their aspirations as neurotic com-pensations for their deficiencies. However, this may not be just the pure, brave advance of scientific understanding. It could also be evidence of our own psychological and moral deficiencies. Could it be that we *must* see these heroes as freaks—in order to legitimize our own fear of being as different from the herd as they were?

Domesticated Heroes

Then we are offered the *domesticated heroes* produced by the needs of the materialistic consumer society itself, inspiring us to reaffirm our commitment to its heroic priorities. Domesticated heroes will be made up of combinations of immoral heroes and morally neutral heroes. There are two sides to this domesticated hero. The first side has to do with life in the public, working world. There he or she fits in and never goes to extremes, makes trouble, or lets it be known that there might be values beyond the efficiency of the workplace. If too much individ-uality or eccentricity is shown, the hero might get low marks for no longer being an exchangeable unit in the system. It is important to not have fanatics and individualists, but "steady, efficient, little men."[15]

The second side of the domesticated hero has to do with the pri-vate world of leisure time. There he or she is the heroic consumer, liv-ing up to and beyond his or her means, each year faithfully making the proper translation of luxuries into necessities. It is the ecstatic payoffs in this heroic arena that make the domesticated hero endure the frustrations and sacrifices of the working world.

The public and private worlds come together where work and consumption meet—for example, in the clothes one wears to work. Here we can see the force of conformity leveling out individuality. John Molloy, of *Dress for Success* fame, earnestly entreats us to tune in to the corporate style favored by our company, and by all means find out where its top executives buy their clothes even before we go to an interview. "The style of dress and behavior that works for one company may be all wrong for another, and nothing can trip you up faster than marching to the wrong drumbeat."[16]

Observe how the little word *behavior* is slipped in. It is one thing to have to buy a "uniform" for a job in the form of the correct suit, tie, or trench coat, but how much of our behavior needs to conform to the corporate drumbeat? It all depends on how badly we want the prize. We need a very good reason to be different if that difference may cost us the next rung on the ladder.

This domesticated hero can be made to seem very dashing and bold, but the risks are all within carefully prescribed boundaries. Our society is skilled at glamorizing those traits that it wants to find in us. But actually, domesticated heroism is "roaming on a short tether . . . leading the horse from a romp in the pasture back into the barn."[17]

It is not as if the life of the modern imagination is dead. The imagination of millions has been captured and is hard at work. The advertising industry is the major broker of imaginative images in modern Western society. Even if no one else appreciates the power of the imagination, the advertising industry certainly does. It defines for us the symbols of success and status with artistic and technical brilliance. It constantly verifies its own effectiveness through marketing surveys. One of its greatest successes has been marketing the illusion of freedom—in enslavement to the priorities of the commercial world. This heroic freedom finds its fullest expression at the shopping mall with a credit card. Needless to say, the advertising world is not dedicated to the enrichment of your life or to social good, but to maximizing the market share of its products with your cooperation.

Without an active moral imagination modern men and women are defenseless against the seductions of conformity in our materialistic society, resulting in what Erving Goffman calls the "bureaucratization of the spirit."[18] If success in an organization dictates that everyone must buy their clothes at the same store, how likely is it that anyone has the strength to stand against practices that are morally dubious but profitable? Remember that Adolph Eichmann's main mistake was that he did as he was told. He "only" followed Hitler's orders to murder Jews.

To break free from this conformity, we must have something more to follow than the domesticated success story offered us by our consumer society. We need a powerful story, and a strong imaginative involvement in it, to be able to evaluate society's claims on us, not to mention to stand against the tide if we think those claims are going in the wrong direction. Psychologist William Kirk Kilpatrick described the shock to the citizens of Argentina when they lost the war in the Falkland Islands. They had thought they were winning the war because they had only heard the government-controlled news and had no other story to make them question it. He wrote,

> What can happen with news stories can happen also with life stories. You can be left with only one version of reality. It is important, therefore, for a storied people to keep their story fresh in mind for, despite their claims to the contrary, modern societies do usually have a story line they are anxious to push on us—either Marxism, or humanism or consumer hedonism.

He pointed out that in Poland, resistance to the communist state had been possible only "because the people have not forgotten to which story they belong."[19]

Think of Mother Teresa again. Her story did not come out of her own head or thin air. She has lived by the story of one whose compassion for the poor and helpless has been a standard of love and caring for two thousand years. There is a hero behind her heroism. It was in the name of that hero that she stood against resignation toward suffering and death that was the status quo in Calcutta.

One could say the same thing about the life and death of the Reverend Martin Luther King, Jr. His most famous sermon was built around the phrase "I have a dream." The phrase was used as a rhetorical device, but it was also true. He did have a dream. Yet his dream did not die as a daydream. It was a powerful outworking of moral imagination—a vision of justice for all people, without violent revolution or bloodshed. One need not agree with all that he said and did to see that, through his courage and conviction, his vision grew out into the world and broke the status quo for the good. We can easily produce a generation too sophisticated or too overstimulated to have positive dreams that find their way into real life. In that case the heroes that are left are no longer an unsettling boiling force, they simply make inertia more interesting through psychic hitchhiking projects, vicarious escapes, and distractions of the imagination. Insofar as this is so, there is a reversal of the work of the hero—from a source of aspiration and change to a means of making banality and boredom more bearable.

MODERN SOCIETY AGAINST ITSELF

Heroes have been destroyed by the corrosive power of cynicism and the inflation/deflation cycles of triviality. The most common direction taken by the hungry imagination is to feed itself on minimal or compensatory heroes. But this is a starvation diet. We still want to feel heroic ourselves, to know that the project of our life is a good story. We still seem to feel the need to relate to glory, honor, some form of human greatness or excellence. There is the wistful longing for a heroic act to do, so heroic that it permanently justifies our existence and settles our anxieties about our own worth once and for all.

A Double-Bind

This puts us into a dilemma. On the one hand we do not believe in heroes, and on the other, we want to be heroic. We are sophisticated enough to feel the need to despise heroes as adolescent folly. Yet at the same time we are unable to get along without them in our own imaginative life. There is the widespread belief that the old-fashioned virtues of courage and honor cannot float in this century. Theodore Gross wrote that those in the world of the arts today find heroism professionally "embarrassing," but at the same time cannot help but respect it in their private lives and despise its opposite.[20] There is a mind/heart division in which the mind remains cynical and the heart keeps a closet heroism alive. Heroism is therefore publicly ridiculed by those who privately, secretly, seek it. It is the modern cynic shooting himself or herself in the foot but still demanding to run the race.

Several of the thinkers of the last century who were concerned with heroism saw the hero as a great man who was so powerful that he could boldly break all the rules and transcend the normal boundaries set by society. Nietzsche wrote of a hero who, by sheer power of personality, would bring a "transvaluation of values" and enable everyone to see the world with new eyes through him. The heroes of Thomas Carlyle were similar, as were those of Emerson later in his life.

Within their schemes, the hero was meant to be adored and revered but not seriously emulated. There was room for only one or two on earth at a time. The rest of us were called to be followers, to be docile—to respect and obey. According to Carlyle, to be able to recognize the "great man" among one's contemporaries was itself a high calling.[21]

These men wrote at a time of large-scale revolt by educated people against belief in the God of the Bible. However, more than in our time, they were trying to face up to what the world was like without belief in God. Nietzsche wrote of there being a loss of all points of reference, that there was no longer any up and down or any horizon to guide us. For Nietzsche and Carlyle, the hero was a God-substitute, a compensator for lost faith in God. The only people in his century who qualified as heroes for Carlyle were Goethe, Napoleon, and Frederick the Great.

As a God-substitute, the role of hero is obviously inaccessible to all but a few people in each century. When such a larger-than-life hero hits the political world, his heroic style itself can create a spirit of docile reverence on the part of the populace—the very thing such a hero needs to fulfill his dream. But as a human God-substitute, the hero is likely to be a scourge to the planet. Think of the twentieth-century contenders and the trail of blood and barbed wire that they left behind them.

Much of what I have written so far is the sad story of the confusion about heroism in our day. The problem is not that there are no longer any heroes. It is that we have learned to not recognize them, or if we do, to confuse their heroism with their talents or publicity. This loss has left its mark on our imaginations.

The Christian faith has lost the role it once had in influencing the imagination of Western culture. It is a long way from being able to offer substantial leadership in this area again. Ernest Becker complained that the church does not offer "its ideal of heroic sainthood as an immediate personal one to be lived by all believers." Instead it "openly subscribes to a commercial-industrial hero system . . . to this empty heroics of possession, display and manipulation."[22] Insofar as he was right, the church has domesticated heroism and shaped itself around the consumer culture. Rather than challenging banality and evil in our time, the church has at its worst moments given banality a spiritual dimension and outright evil a theological justification.

However, in reflecting on the history of the Christian faith, G. K. Chesterton observed, "At least five times the Faith has to all appearances gone to the dogs. In each of these five cases, it was the dog that died."[23] He was pointing to the extraordinary resilience of the Christian faith to recover from times of defeat, compromise, and cultural containment through self-criticism, repentance, and reform.

Implicit in much of what I have said so far is that there is another possibility, another framework within which heroism can make sense and be powerful enough to fire even modern and post-modern imaginations. Heroism is not an illusion produced by human cultures that leaves us in disillusionment or perpetual adolescence. Rather, it is a pointer to glory and honor that actually exists in the character the Creator. In the light of the Christian faith, the deepest human aspirations are not absurdities but are longings that make sense if a personal Creator actually does exist and cares about us. It is to find a fulfillment for that longing that we turn to the second part of this book.

PART TWO

A NEW LOOK
AT HEROISM

A FOUNDATION FOR HEROISM IN THE TWENTIETH CENTURY

If the greatness of man has come to seem an illusion,
how can there be great men?[1]
JOY GOULD

We continue surreptitiously to wonder whether greatness is
not a naturally scarce commodity, whether it can ever really
be synthesized. Perhaps our ancestors were right in
connecting the very idea of human greatness with belief
in a God. Perhaps man cannot make himself.[2]
DANIEL BOORSTIN

When I look at your heavens, the work of your fingers,
the moon and the stars that you have established;
what are human beings that you are mindful of them,
mortals that you care for them?
Yet you have made them a little lower than God,
and crowned them with glory and honor.
PSALM 8:3-5, NRSV

I t is no small thing to have real heroes in the late twentieth century. So many ideas and practices cast doubt on any human greatness that is beyond publicity, personality, and talent that it seems naive to believe in it at all. Unless these doubts have some satisfactory answers, all we can do is to call out wistfully for something desperately needed but that does not exist on this planet. Is there a way to understand human nature and experience that makes sense of heroism? It is to that investigation we now turn.

POSSIBLE SOLUTIONS

Although there have been many attempts to affirm human greatness, very few of them take real measure of the problems raised by cynicism and trivialization. Let me give three examples.

Orrin Klapp

Orrin Klapp, in his book *Heroes, Villains and Fools*, warned that the impact of relativism produced the idea that "every opinion is as good as every other" and that "is not an adequate basis for a good society."[3] He saw the crippling impact of cynicism about ultimate moral truth. But he went on to say, "If the American character has been deteriorating—and I must regretfully admit that I think it has—the very first thing to arrest the drift is to check the compass, refer to the chart, and set the course."[4]

One can hardly quibble with this advice—who would be against checking one's direction? Yet as a solution, it begs all the serious questions. What is a compass in the world of today's relativism, postmodernism, and multiculturalism? Where is the chart? Whose chart? Even if we had a compass and a chart, who says there is a "north" or that the human mind can even comprehend what "north" means? We are living in an intellectual climate that has dismissed the forms of moral navigation that might have helped us. How can we derive hope from "checking the compass" unless we know that there is a "north," what a compass is, and where to find a chart?

Norman Corwin

Then there is Norman Corwin, whose *Trivializing America* took almost three hundred pages to chronicle the woes of trivialization in sports, entertainment, music, publishing, law, politics, sex, religion, education, death, and many other areas as well. There is much that is valuable in his analysis. However, only in the last six pages did he turn to his solu-

100

tion. He admitted that any solution would be difficult because "Rescue by fiat is impossible, and the trouble with heroic measures is that they require heroes."[5] Nonetheless, the answer was that we need a "conspiracy of good people" to set an example against the forces of trivialization and function as a "saving minority," heroic models for society.[6]

But this is no more helpful than being told to "reset the course" without knowing where to find a compass or chart. Where is a view of human nature that will stand against the forces of cynicism that surround us? What are the values that will challenge the immense, economically driven forces of trivialization in our society, and how can they become imaginatively powerful? How can we appeal to "good people" when doubts about goodness itself are part of the problem?

Joseph Campbell

One modern prophet who has certainly not avoided the large questions about heroism is Joseph Campbell. He was a student of mythology, heavily influenced by Freud's ex-disciple Carl Gustav Jung. He was a prolific author and popular television presenter. He wrote and spoke powerfully about the need for heroes in today's world, where they are either very shallow or nonexistent.

Campbell's interest was in the "monomyth"[7], a universal, three-stage pattern of heroic life that he found in ancient mythology—separation, initiation and return. The theme was that the hero would leave the common, ordinary world, and go to a faraway place where he won great victories and received new powers. He would then return to the ordinary world and save his own people from some crisis.[8] But Campbell saw that there has been such a loss of the sacred in the modern world, that we cannot hope to reinvent such mythic heroes. Don Quixote found no dragons to slay, only a mechanical windmill to battle against—without much success.[9] In the present world, the "timeless universe of symbols has collapsed."[10] Campbell was careful not to prescribe new heroes for us, but did an enormous amount to stimulate hope in our contact with a nostalgic mythic era when people were more in touch with the basic realities of life.

Joseph Campbell was the source of fascinating insights from vast varieties of cultures and time periods and has been an inspiration to many in the arts. However, does his view of the hero deal with the problems that we have raised? Can it provide direction for the present loss of heroism? I will mention two difficulties.

First, although the study of mythology can be intriguing and enriching, Campbell himself did not believe in the myths *in the same sense* that those who originally lived by them did. Historian, Christopher Lasch wrote of the false hope that is often encouraged by followers of Jung. It is that love for the beauty and power of myths can compensate for the loss of belief in the living religions that supported those myths. He puts it this way: "But aesthetic appreciation, alas, cannot take the place of an authoritative spiritual discipline. Nor can mythology mean for us what it meant to those who took it as literal truth. The critical elucidation that makes it accessible to us simultaneously destroys its value as a guide to conduct."[11]

For people who lived by the ancient myths, their myths were an integral part of their religions or worldviews. Their myths were, in Lasch's words, "anchored in the eternal order of things"[12] in a way that they cannot be for us. The heroes of those myths can never have moral authority over our conduct. Theirs is a heroism radically removed from us and therefore inaccessible to us not only by elapsed time, but by their whole conception of the world. Joseph Campbell's heroes were also removed from us in that they were limited to his public heroes who lived out the life pattern of his monomyth. His scheme seems to have no room for the heroism of men, women, and children who never left home to slay dragons, let alone returned to save the common world, but who lived honorable lives of faith and courage against appalling odds.

Second, the worldview of Campbell himself is pantheistic in the traditions of Hinduism and Buddhism. He wrote, "You are God, not in your ego, but in your deepest being, where you are at one with the nondual transcendent."[13] All opposites are illusory, including the opposition of good and evil. In this light he taught his students to, "Follow your bliss," and the heroes of mythology will grab you deep inside.[14] It is hard to see how heroism in this framework, stripped of confidence in moral distinctions, can have the moral backbone to stand against the forces of commercialism and materialism which are also telling us, "follow your bliss."

Dismissing the ultimate distinction between good and evil results in a cynical devaluation of heroic moral virtues. On the other hand, "follow your bliss" seems to cooperate quite nicely with modern trivialization.

Before turning to another way to understand heroism, we will first look at another side to the problem. We will then be able to see the full force of its difficulties.

HEROISM AND THE PROBLEM OF DEATH:
We have already looked at the forces of cynicism and trivialization that have come together in powerful ways in relatively recent history. However, Ernest Becker, one of the most significant twentieth-century students of heroism, focused on a more longstanding problem for heroism that has been in the background of our discussion all along—the reality of personal death.[15] Any affirmation of heroism must face it.

Death Mocks Heroism

The reality of death has always stood against heroic claims. It is not that there is no heroism in one's manner of death (actually, giving one's life for others has been considered by many to be the ultimate heroic act). It is rather that the state of being dead is a negation of what heroism usually stands for. We return to the dust from which we came—"dust to dust, ashes to ashes." What is less heroic than ashes? What becomes of our magnificent dreams and aspirations, our hopes, plans, achievements, possessions, and treasured relationships? In this light, how foolish, arrogant, and pretentious it seems for us to speak of human greatness at all—even the greatness of a sacrificial death. Ernest Becker focused on this dilemma with painful sharpness:

> Man is literally split in two: he has an awareness of his own splendid uniqueness in that he sticks out of nature with a towering majesty, and yet he goes back into the ground a few feet in order blindly and dumbly to rot and disappear forever.[16]

These ideas are not the inventions of twentieth-century cynicism. They are not new at all. They have been present in some form as far back as we can trace human thoughts, and were well developed by biblical writers thousands of years ago:

> Even the wise die,
>> the fool and the stupid alike must perish
>> and leave their wealth to others.
> Their graves are their homes for ever,
>> their dwelling places to all generations,
>> though they named lands their own.
> Man cannot abide in his pomp,
>> he is like the beasts that perish. (Psalm 49:10-12)

The outrage of death has not changed in the roughly three thousand years since this psalm was written. Death ends all of our hopes on earth and equalizes all the differences between people, between people and the animal kingdom, and finally even between people and the ground they walk on. Dust and ashes level the difference between wisdom and folly, wealth and poverty, power and weakness, courage and cowardice.

On the surface, human beings seem only to be animals programed for self-deception. There is nothing to sustain our illusions of grandeur— we are only "like the beasts that perish." Yet our awareness of our uniqueness and dignity, that we "stick out of nature with a towering majesty," is not silenced or crushed either by the awareness of death's negations or by its inevitability. Human history shows the irrepressible desire of men and women to leave their mark on earth in the form of something lasting or "immortal" to show for their lives. Heroic ambitions often seem designed to defy the leveling powers of death. So the quest for heroism has sometimes been a theater in which people tilt against the windmill of death and the eventual anonymity that it forces on us.

Heroism, by definition, deals with human differences, with those who "stand out" for showing glory and honor by the way they live. Yet if death is the eraser of differences, it leaves glory and honor in this life as a fleeting mirage. Perhaps this is why Paul compared the human body at death to a seed falling to and decomposing in the ground, being sown in weakness and dishonor (1 Corinthians 15:42-43). Death represents an end to our dreams of honor. Any twentieth-century belief in heroism must either be able to answer these difficulties or put them in some wider framework in which they do not negate heroism. Otherwise, our personal death puts the finishing touches on cynicism and makes all our aspirations trivial.

How to Proceed?

There is no neutral, objective, or obvious position from which all people can address these questions. There is no self-evident set of "default" beliefs to fall back on. Everyone has some sort of a worldview, however undeveloped it might be. It is held by faith, however unconscious or intuitive that act of faith might be. Their view about what— if anything—is heroic will be rooted in the values explicit or implicit in that worldview. A worldview provides a program from which to be able to tell the hero from the villain—if there is a difference. Suppose one believes that there is no God and that that means there is no such thing as heroism or villainy. Even these ideas rest on certain convictions about the world and our place in it. And even these convictions are held ultimately by faith.

A possibility that has been only in the background up to now in this discussion is that there is a personal Creator who made all that we know and have experienced. If there is such a God, and we can know him, it will make a great difference to our understanding of heroism. It is perfectly legitimate to ask for a justification of that belief, although it is beyond the scope of this book to offer it. I have found that the God of the Christian Scriptures gives the only adequate accounting of human nature and experience, of its heights and depths and its grappling with good and evil. What follows will be only a small piece of that justification. We will attempt to see what heroism looks like in the light of his existence.

You may believe, along with the masters of suspicion, that turning to God at this point is grasping in anxious arrogance for some way to believe in our own greatness. Fair enough. But the God who exists only as a means to the end of establishing human dignity, sustaining society, or justifying our need for heroes, is not the God of the Bible. The God of the Bible is not the means to any end. He is the Alpha and the Omega, the beginning and the end. You will have to make up your own mind about him.

THE CHRISTIAN FAITH AS A FOUNDATION FOR HEROISM

God the Creator is personal. Human personhood is only a reflection of God's Person. He is like us, only it is actually the other way around. It is we who are like him. He is not an impersonal force or ultimate energy source but a self-conscious and self-determining Being. He thinks, acts, feels, and uses human language. He is also the Absolute in that there is nothing in this universe that he did not make in its original form. He is unchanging. Final control over what takes place in the world is in his hands, not in a void of cosmic randomness.

Many human efforts to think about God try to make him either personal and limited (as in the gods of ancient Greece), or else absolute and impersonal (as in the God of many philosophers since then). The God who reveals himself in the Bible will not be forced into any such polarization. He is both a Person and the Creator of all that exists. In the light of his revelation in words and action in history, Christians have been able to cope, albeit with enormous struggles, with the evil and apparent irrationality of many of the events in the world. They know that there exists a larger framework of understanding than their own, within which higher purposes than theirs are worked out.

Theologians use another pair of terms to describe these related truths about God—*immanent* and *transcendent*. He is immanent in that he is near to us. He is concerned for us. He numbers the hairs on our heads and knows that it is a different number today than yesterday. He knows of every sparrow that falls, and his steady love does not leave us. But he is also transcendent, the creator of everything. His being is unaffected by our opinions about him. There is no fate behind him to which he must bow, and no greater mind to which he must turn for advice. Before him, the greatest of all human governments, with all their economic power and megatons of destructive capability, are like dust on a set of scales (Isaiah 40:15). He introduced himself to Moses with the words "I AM who I AM," revealing his entirely self-sufficient and self-determining identity.

God as the Source of All Glory

We can know many of the attributes of God because he has described his character to us. They include such things as being all-powerful, all-knowing, and existing forever, and also things that correspond more directly to human experience such as loving, forgiving, grieving, and being faithful. In many Christian descriptions of God, glory is the attribute of God discussed last. This is not because it is least important but because it summarizes the excellence of God in every area of his existence.

The word for glory often means radiance or splendor, and is associated with brilliant light. We often use it in this way today to describe our most recent celebrities and their "moments of glory" in front of the cameras, microphones, and amplifiers. Glory in today's context indicates high visibility, recognition, and praise, but is a quality lighter than air, ephemeral, famous for fifteen minutes. When glory is used of God in the Bible it does carry the sense of radiance, but the force of the word could not be more different from the momentary glow experienced by the celebrity.

Actually, the root meaning of the word is to weigh heavily, to be solid and hard to lift from sheer weight. It is used to indicate honor, greatness, excellence, and being worthy of praise. True glory is splendor, yes, but it is also something of great gravity. It is solid, substantial, and is not going to blow away in the wind or grow dim in time. The glory of God draws on these two ideas, radiance and weight. God is associated with glory many times in the Bible—he is the King of glory, the Father of glory, and the Lord of glory (Psalm 24, Ephesians 1:17, 1 Corinthians 2:8).

God's glory is his alone. Glory is rooted in his character. His glory is not to be confused with what is attributed to counterfeit gods or to overinflated men and women. He says through Isaiah, the prophet,

> "I am the LORD, that is my name;
>> my glory I give to no other,
>> nor my praise to graven images." (Isaiah 42:8)

But because he is Creator, his glory is reflected in the things that he has made. The psalmist writes that the natural world bears the mark of its Maker's creativity:

> The heavens are telling the glory of God;
>> and the firmament proclaims his handiwork. (Psalm 19:1)

In a vision that the Old Testament prophet Isaiah experienced, he heard these words:

> Holy, holy, holy is the LORD of hosts;
>> the whole earth is full of his glory. (Isaiah 6:3)

God's glory is his own, but it is seen mirrored in the world that he has made that is full of reflected glory—in the excellence of the beauty, power, wonder, and goodness of creation. In the words of Gerard Manley Hopkins, the whole world is "charged with the grandeur of God."[17]

God's Glory Shared with Humanity

If the God of the Christian faith is true, it means that there is not some mindless, random process behind an accidental order and beauty in the world. It means that at the ultimate level in the universe, there is not blank indifference to the human condition. There is rather the intelligent mind of a personal Creator who cares for those he has made and who is the source and standard of all glory. It also means that each human being has a special place of value, made in the image of the Creator himself.

In a unique way, the glory of God can be reflected in and through the lives of those made in his image. But there is a particular problem in giving this reflection because people are alienated from God in a profound way, and their lives are twisted away from the image that God had intended. The world is a fallen world. Theologian Francis Schaeffer spoke of humankind as a "glorious ruin." This captures the core of a Christian vision of humanity. We are glorious creatures of God, but through trying to live independently, in self-sufficiency and rebellion against him, we are twisted out of shape. The Christian worldview sees the human race as fallen from God's intended pattern of life, no longer perfectly imaging him, but morally estranged from him.

Nevertheless, because God is a God of mercy, he has opened a door to reconciliation, forgiveness, and new life through the life and death of Christ, the Messiah. We will develop this more fully in subsequent chapters, but we will point out here that it is possible, with his help, for us to live out something of the glory of God. This means that we can, in spite of the highly flawed way we live, still reflect something of God's character. This is true human greatness, or heroism.

THE POSSIBILITY OF A HEROIC LIFE

It is all fine and good to declare that a human being can be heroic in reflecting the glory and honor of God, but how does it actually work out concretely? A good place to begin is with a poem written by David, the second king of Israel, which was a prayer addressed to God himself:

> When I look at your heavens, the work of your fingers,
>> the moon and the stars which you have established;
> what are human beings that you are mindful of them,
>> mortals that you care for them?
> Yet you have made them a little lower than God,
>> and crowned them with glory and honor.
> You have given them dominion over the works of your hands;
>> you have put all things under their feet. (Psalm 8:3-6, NRSV)

There are two themes important to heroism here: God is mindful of us, and he gives men and women dominion over the earth. We will look at each in turn.

The Care of the Creator

King David was frankly mystified about why the God who made the whole universe should pay attention to creatures so tiny, seemingly insignificant, and rebellious as we are. David did not need to know what we now know about the sheer size of the universe to feel the problem of human puniness before the vastness of space and time. Despite his greatness and our smallness, amazingly, God knows us and cares for us. This is important to the way we view ourselves.

Each one of us has a deeply felt desire to understand and evaluate our own uniqueness. We live inside our heads in a way that prevents us from ever sharing our experience completely with another person— even if we wanted to and had a thousand years to do it. We know ourselves in a way others cannot, and this creates a certain isolation between us and other people. How do we evaluate that self in its uniqueness? Are we good or bad? Healthy or sick? Successful or failures? Generous or greedy? Kind or cruel? Useful or superfluous? Heroic or shameful?

We seldom dare to trust ourselves alone to answer these questions, so we turn to others. We try to evaluate ourselves by watching others' faces as they respond to our words and actions. In our society, it is very easy to feel "I am noticed and admired, therefore I matter." Leo Braudy in his book about the history of fame points to a widely felt "lust for recognition."[18] This lust usually demands that we distinguish ourselves from others by being more successful than they are in terms of some valued currency of achievement or status. We feel the need to stand out, not to be lost without distinction in the faceless crowd and therefore cease to exist. Nietzsche voiced the fear of this fate as he lectured to aspiring heroes, or Higher Men: "And let us not be equal before the mob."[19] It is by the admiration of our contemporaries that many of us have learned to measure ourselves. None of us is untouched by the power of their approval or censure.

If the God to whom David prayed exists, and we acknowledge him, that changes our picture of the world and of us in it. There is suddenly another personal response to take into account in our evaluation of ourselves. In fact, the stature of God and the importance of his response dwarf our opinion and that of our contemporaries.

If the maker of the farthest galaxies is mindful of me, knowing the most intimate details of my life, and I am aware of that—then that relationship must become central to my life. Everything else must turn around that axle. No longer can I say that I matter in my uniqueness only if I am admired by myself or by other people. I will still care what others think of me, probably far more than I ought to. But there will be a different relationship, which repeatedly pulls me toward being independent and free from the tyrannies of others' opinions and expectations. The overarching motivation becomes not just public recognition but acceptance, approval, and affirmation by the Creator.

We are dealing here with far more than adding a "spiritual dimension" to one's life, but rather a relationship with one so great that it can counterbalance all others. One can see this clearly in the life of Dietrich Bonhoeffer. He was imprisoned in Germany during the Second World War for his resistance to Hitler, and was finally hung just as the war was ending. While he was in prison, he was left without the normal resources of human security and comfort. He wrote a poem entitled "Who am I?" that reflects on the struggle of how to understand himself.

> Who am I? They often tell me
> I would step from my cell's confinement
> Calmly, cheerfully, firmly
> Like a squire from his country house.
> Who am I? They often tell me
> I used to speak to my warders
> Freely and friendly and clearly,
> As though it were mine to command.
> Who am I? They also tell me
> I bore the day's misfortune
> Equably, smilingly, proudly,
> Like one accustomed to win.
>
> Am I then really all that which other men tell of?
> Or am I only what I myself know of myself,
> Restless and longing and sick, like a bird in a cage,
> Struggling for breath, as though hands were compressing
>   my throat,
> Yearning for colors, for flowers, for the voices of birds,
> Thirsting for words of kindness, for neighborliness,
> Tossing in expectation of great events,
> Powerlessly trembling for friends at infinite distance,
> Weary and empty at praying, at thinking, at making,
> Faint, and ready to say farewell to it all?
> Who am I? This or the other?
> Am I one person today and tomorrow another?
> Am I both at once? A hypocrite before others,
> And before myself a contemptibly woe-begone weakling?

Or is something within me still like a beaten army,
Fleeing in disorder from victory already achieved?

Who am I? They mock me, these lonely thoughts of mine,
Whoever I am, thou knowest, O God, I am thine![20]

He wrote as one who had experienced the truth that God was mindful of him. He was forced back past the confusion of self-canceling opinions, and even past the exhausted reserves of his own knowledge of God, to the conviction that God knew *him* and that he belonged to God.

Even if we are in a state of confusion or despair, God is greater than our state of mind. God is the most important person in our audience. We live "before" him, within the theater of his observation and care. This affects our view of ourselves even in the most extreme situations.

Heroism and the Presence of God

When the desire for the affirmation of our uniqueness is fulfilled through others, it can become insatiable. Leo Braudy wrote, "When all distinction comes from public action, the stakes of fame get higher, the actions more grandiose, and the players look for theatres larger than the normal round of public office."[21]

Yet if God is in our primary audience, that brings two changes. We can be assured of being accepted and loved by him—apart from public admiration—as we come to him in humility and faith. Also, he unmasks our attemps at impression management. He sees through anything and everything—even our thoughts. Every moment is a "naked moment" before him. Therefore, he can bring us both deep confidence in his love and also powerful incentive for our own integrity.

Ernest Becker, although a secular prophet, realized the impact that belief in a personal God had on our desires for heroism. He looked back wistfully to a more "primitive" time when Christianity could be believed more widely in our culture. He saw that if a person was confident in his or her relationship to God, they "could achieve even in the smallest daily tasks, that sense of cosmic heroism that is the highest ambition of man."[22]

Becker realized the scope of the Christian solution to the problems of heroism in a remarkably clear way: "If one is a servant of divine powers everything one does is heroic, if it is done as part of the consecration of one's life to those powers. In this way meaning can be extended up to the highest level, to the cosmic, eternal level, and the problem of highest heroism is solved."[23]

He has put his finger on a key point. If human greatness, or hero-ism, is determined more by the evaluation of God than by the opinion of men and women, then one need not go to outlandish exploits or accumulation of gadgets to establish heroic status. The opinions of oth-ers will finally be of little consequence compared to God's.

One need not be a Napoleon, a Madonna, an Elvis Presley, or a mythic figure from the pantheon of Joseph Campbell. Heroism is com-patible with "ordinary life" lived well. Thus Becker praised a prayer of Pascal as laying the foundation for both humility and a high level of moti-vation for activity in the world: "Lord, help me do great things as though they were little, since I do them with Your powers; and help me to do little things as though they were great, because I do them in Your Name."[24]

Becker saw this in stark contrast to the inaccessible, fragile, and trivial heroism of the modern world. If the Creator himself is mindful of us, our goal can be that he would ultimately say of our life, "Well done." You can see how this strikes at the core of both cynicism and trivialization. Meaning in life is found in relationship to this mindful God who gives us criteria for greatness that are anything but trivial.

GOD GIVES DOMINION OVER HIS CREATION TO HUMANITY

The second theme raised in the eighth psalm echoes God's words at Creation. Men and women are to have dominion or stewardship over the rest of God's creation as his guests in that creation.

> Yet you have made them a little lower than God,
>   and crowned them with glory and honor.
> You have given them dominion over the works of your hands;
>   you have put all things under their feet. (Psalm 8:5-6, NRSV)

The idea is that we were created to have mastery in the world that God made. We are guests who are called to be stewards or caretakers, not exploiters. Our limited mastery in this world must mirror God's final mastery over it. We are called to be creative in the world over which God is creator. Even after the catastrophic changes brought about by rebellion against God, God speaks of crowning us with "glory and honor" (verse 5).

Dominion Versus Determinism

The idea of dominion assumes a certain level of free agency on the part of those made in God's image. That is to say, we are actors, not just receptors or automatic responders to nonconscious forces. It is clear that there are many organic, psychological, and social forces at work in and around us that affect our feelings, attitudes, and behavior. But what is not at all clear is the contention that human choice is thereby obliterated or that we can understand the human race accurately by any one of the deterministic models. On the contrary, our freedom over conditioning forces is increased the more we understand those very forces. Complete determinism makes human life and choice unintelligible, including the theories of determinism themselves.

Reductionistic and deterministic views of humanity march under the banners of scientific respectability. Yet they owe more to a faith commitment to certain methods of investigation than to faithfulness to the observation and description of human life in all its richness and diversity. In his book *The Hero in History*, Sidney Hook makes a wry observation about determinists:

> For all their talk of the inevitable, the determinists never resign themselves to the inevitable when it is not to their liking. Their words, however, confuse their actions both to themselves and to others. In the end we understand them truly by watching their hands, not their lips.[25]

The discussion of determinism is not an ivory-tower matter. Deterministic ideas are responsible for much of the cynicism about heroism that we encountered in chapter 2. These theories have washed over us like waves, claiming that all human choices are conditioned by internal self-seeking motives, unknown to the human choice-maker. Human responses were determined, inevitable; they could not have been otherwise, so the very idea of human greatness becomes a hollow posture.

From the perspective of the eighth psalm alone we have the beginning of a worldview that offers an alternative to both the cynicism and the trivialization of the modern world. The mindfulness of a personal and absolute God and the task of dominion form a foundation for the possibility of heroism. We turn now to preview the substance of what that heroic vision could be.

DOMINION IN THE IMAGE OF THE CREATOR

As we begin to explore the shape of dominion or mastery more fully, we are brought back to its core, which is that it is found in imaging the character of God. We reflect the glory and honor that can crown us, having been made "a little lower than God" (Psalm 8:5). This leads us beyond the eighth psalm to the New Testament. Jesus Christ was the image of God in perfect focus and clarity, so that in looking at him we learn what glory and honor can mean in flesh and blood. We are told that God has given us "the light of the knowledge of the glory of God in the face of Christ" (2 Corinthians 4:6). In the life of Christ we can see God's glory as much as it can be seen in human form. He becomes the standard of heroism.

Dominion and Glory

This means that true glory is ours insofar as we are Christlike. We will devote several chapters to this theme. We will look at some of the most important of the virtues of Christlikeness: humility, love, willingness to suffer unjustly, forgiveness, courage, and service. These are not just good things to do. They are good to do because they reflect the character of the God who created us to do them. Therefore if we want to be the persons that we were created to be, and to realize our true selves, we will reflect these virtues.

The extremes of obedience and disobedience to God are described in the Bible in the vocabulary of heroism—of glory and honor as over against folly and shame. Our ordinary lives are made up of daily choices between them.

Sin is not only violating moral rules. It is described by the apostle Paul as falling "short of the glory of God" (Romans 3:23). Note that he does not say falling short of the "law" of God, but of the "glory" of God—that is, short of the excellence of God in every area of his existence. It is certainly moral failure, but God's moral excellence does not exhaust his nature. The seriousness of our sin is that we use our God-imaging capabilities to think, say, and do things that oppose, defy, and misrepresent God himself. As we misrespresent God's image, we also misrepresent the selves we were created to be.

For example, Ahab was a king in Israel in the ninth century BC. To satisfy his pride and greed, and his wife, he murdered one of his subjects in order to annex his land. The prophet Elijah met him at that very piece of land when Ahab arrived to take possession of it, and told him, "You have sold yourself to do what is evil in the sight of the LORD" (1 Kings 21:20).

He had clearly broken God's command. But in so doing he had also violated the character and glory of God, living out a catastrophically misshaped image of his Creator. Therefore he had "sold himself." What had he sold? He had sold the glory of what it could have been to reflect God's likeness in his life. Instead he imaged greed and murder. Being made in the image of God, he was made for something better, more heroic, than to be bought off by his own greed and cruelty to kill an innocent person to satisfy those vices. He had degraded and shamed himself by selling out on the glory of what it was to be a human being.

Our Lives Are Subplots in a Larger Story

So far we have looked at life before God in terms of individual acts that can be right or wrong, heroic or dishonorable in God's sight. But life is not made up of single acts and events. It adds up—we hope—to a story. As philosopher William Barrett wrote, "Life is many days, day after day. But it is not, we hope, a mere succession of days. We long that these days shall somehow add up to a meaning or a drama that we can call a life."[26]

Each person has a worldview, an overarching picture of the way the world is, as he or she sees it. When this worldview is expressed in narrative form it is called a "master story."[27] We live out the story of our own lives, with more or less success, against the backdrop of our master story. It is in terms of our master story that our own life story is measured—to be a story that is good or bad, meaningful or pointless, in character or phony.

The Bible itself is largely a story of the dealings of God with the human race. The story takes us from Creation and Fall through the risings and fallings of the Jewish nation, to the incarnation of God himself in human form—the coming of Christ. It tells of his death at the hands of those whom he had come to save, his resurrection, ascension, and sending of God's Spirit to build the church and spread the message of his gospel. This gospel is the good news of pardon for the guilt of sin and the promise of new life that will last forever. The story then tells of the present era leading to a future time when God will bring history as we know it to a culmination with the return of Christ, coming this time not as a servant but as a king to bring a renewed earth and heaven. That is the Christian master story.

We are part of the overarching story that is the ongoing work of God in the world. It is as if the master story of God were a cable running from past to future. Our own life stories are strands in that cable. By the way we live, we can strengthen or weaken the cable. We can either be an integral part of bearing the weight, or on the other hand, be a frayed end that carries nothing and only sticks out ineffectively.

One who follows Christ is not first loyal to a set of ideas or to the institution of the church, but to God and the story that God is working in the world. God holds out the promise to us that our lives can be good stories as they are part of his work on earth. It is not that heroism is merely possible. Actually, heroism is expected. We are living in a world where the power of evil is enormous and ever-present. We are called to join a heroic battle against it, in God's name and with his help. Life cannot be lived in some morally neutral space. There is no such space. The battle is fought against untruth, suffering, injustice, and hatred in the outside world, and against self-deception, pride, hypocrisy, and selfishness within our own lives.

The Christian story is not a drama that is enclosed within our space-time continuum. It reaches beyond the world that we can see or touch, because we are interacting with a living, personal God. It also reaches temporally beyond our physical death and into the future. Christ's promise was eternal life with him.

Death Itself Is Mocked

We mentioned the unheroism that the apostle Paul associated with human death by saying our bodies are perishable and "sown in dishonor." He said this because of the glory of life that is lost in death. In death, God's purpose in creation is reversed, and the earth takes dominion over men and women. But the apostle goes on in the same sentence to say that as a result of Christ, "it is raised in glory" (1 Corinthians 15:43). He spoke of a resurrection of the body to eternal life, for which the resurrection of Christ was the precursor. He even dares to mock death itself: "Where, O death, is your victory? Where, O death, is your sting?" (1 Corinthians 15:55, NRSV).

We are dealing here not just with our lives lasting an infinite extension of time. Aldous Huxley once said, in mockery of the Christian idea of afterlife, that he could not imagine anything worse than living with Aldous Huxley forever. One can see his point. Perhaps we would say the same thing of ourselves. But that is not the hope that Christ left us with. We are to be transformed and made new — the Bible even uses the term *glorified*. C. S. Lewis captures the idea well at the end of his children's book *The Last Battle*, when he writes of eternal life being a story that never ends, and in which each chapter is better than the one before.

Such a future hope casts its light back into the present, because it gives a heightened sense of who we are and of the importance of what we are doing with our lives now.

Again, C. S. Lewis expressed well the extraordinary significance of human choices about what kind of glory we will pursue:

> In the end that Face which is the delight or the terror of the universe must be turned upon each of us either with one expression or with the other, either conferring glory inexpressible or inflicting shame that can never be cured or disguised. I read in a periodical the other day that the fundamental thing is how we think of God. By God Himself, it is not! How God thinks of us is not only more important, but infinitely more important. Indeed, how we think of Him is of no importance except in so far as it is related to how He thinks of us. It is written that we shall "stand before" Him, shall appear, shall be inspected. The promise of glory is the promise, almost incredible and only possible by the work of Christ, that some of us, that any of us who really chooses, shall actually survive that examination, shall find approval, shall please God. To please God . . . to be a real ingredient in the divine happiness . . . to be loved by God, not merely pitied, but delighted in as an artist delights in his work or a father in a son—it seems impossible, a weight or burden of glory which our thoughts can hardly sustain. But so it is.[28]

A FOUNDATION FOR HEROISM

One need scarcely point out that this is an extraordinary claim to make in a world confident in its cynicism and sated in trivialization. The approved master story of secular orthodoxy is that life is a tale told without intelligent author, full of sound and fury and signifying nothing. It sees the human race as having emerged by accident in the past, and ending by some accident in the future. Against this backdrop of nihilism, secular orthodoxy welcomes us, with a smile, to manufacture our own personal meanings, stories, and heroes.

The Christian approach to heroism is very different. The Bible speaks of an integration of the individual's story with the master story of all of life. The small portrait of our personal lives gets its meaning from being part of a vast canvas. Our personal meanings are not just our own personal inventions, projections, or comfort zones.

In the Christian faith there is no desperate strategy to manufacture much-needed synthetic heroes. We start with a God who stands above the whole creation, yet is intimately involved in it. He is the source and standard of true excellence or glory. We were made to know him, be known by him, and to reflect his character by the way we live. Ernest Becker saw the enormous psychological significance of this. He marveled that the Christian "links his secret inner self, his authentic talent, his deepest feelings of uniqueness, his inner yearning for absolute significance, to the very ground of creation."[29]

Heroic living is held before us at all times, no matter who we are—whether a leader of state, a celebrity, unemployed, or permanently confined to a hospital bed. Heroism is not built on surpassing our contemporaries in some currency of competitive success, but by living out the imitation of Christ in relationship with God. Each person has the opportunity to play an irreplaceable part in the cosmic drama, even though many strands in that drama will be understood only in eternity.

Thomas Merton queried,

> How did it happen that, when the dregs of the world had collected in Western Europe, when Goth and Frank and Norman and Lombard had mingled with the rot of old Rome to form a patchwork of hybrid races, all of them notable for ferocity, hatred, stupidity, craftiness, lust and brutality—how did it happen that, from all this, there should come the Gregorian chant, monasteries and cathedrals, the poems of Prudentius, the commentaries and histories of Bede . . . St. Augustine's *City of God?*[30]

Merton's words raise the question of what intervened between the barbarity of decaying Rome and the flowerings of culture to which he referred? The crucial event was the coming of Christ and the impact of those who followed him. The truth of God reached out through what was said and lived, despite the many failures of God's people. It affected the cultural imagination of the Western world in a positive way. Into this world of cynicism and triviality, his truth can reach out again.

In the next chapters we will explore the positive shape of heroism in the light of the weight of God's glory. But before we get to positive heroes, let us consider what to do with the pseudoheroes who demand that we march to the beat of their different drums.

FOOLS AND FOOLWORSHIP: KNOWING THE PSEUDOHERO

*The most ignominious defeats of all are held in store
for those . . . who fail at something that was not worth doing
in the first place.*[1]
WILLIAM GADDIS

*To deal adequately with folly it is essential to recognize it
for what it is. This much is certain, it is a moral
rather than an intellectual defect.*[2]
DIETRICH BONHOEFFER

*There is . . . a love by which we love
what should not be loved.*[3]
AUGUSTINE

*Turn my eyes from looking at vanities;
and give me life in thy ways.*
PSALM 119:37

t takes little wisdom or experience to know that before we paint a house we need to scrape off the loose, flaking paint from the last paint job and make the surface clean. If we are going to renew our imaginations with true heroes, we are likely to need to do some paint scraping first. True heroes will have no imaginative grip on our lives if they are just spray-painted over the top of the flaky pseudoheroes of our culture. Unless the pseudoheroes are identified, dethroned, and stripped away, they will simply keep us in confusion, conflict, and needless shame. If we are to give ourselves wholeheartedly to what is excellent, they must go.

Breaking the grip that false heroes have on us and chasing them out of their place of authority in our imaginations is a formidable task. We cannot expect much to come of it if we politely ask them to leave, try to argue them out, or wag a disapproving finger at them. Their authority is usually deeply imbedded in us in the form of ideals, dreams, and habits from childhood years. Pseudoheroic values in our culture resonate with our own unique styles of insecurity, pride, and vanity. They are old friends, although I hope to show that their friendship is overvalued.

If we want to speak of heroism and the Christian faith together, some heroes must go. This is because certain heroes obstruct us from even beginning to take Christ seriously. In the minds of many, the Christian faith itself carries a stereotype of negative heroism—it is only for wimps, depressives, and fanatics.

The "big-time sinner," renowned for fearless scorn of God and his authority, is a powerful hero from the local bar to the university faculty room and in too many pulpits in between. The imaginative power of this hero is so strong that it blocks rational, critical judgment on the most important issues of life and death.

There is a term for pseudoheroism used by many of the writers of the Bible. It is meant to help us identify the pseudohero and escape his or her authority. It is the "fool." The intention of many of the biblical writers was to help us unmask the pseudoheroes around us. They wanted us to experience fools as negative heroes, blind guides, and losers, so that our aspiration for being like them would evaporate and leave aversion in its place.

WHO IS THE FOOL?

There are many meanings of the word *fool*, several of which are found in the Bible itself. There is the fool who is really the person of wisdom but is considered foolish by the world in its hostility to God's truth and moral vision. In this case what is called "foolishness" is actually wisdom, seen through darkened eyes. Then there is the wise person who allows himself or herself to be seen as a fool in order to subvert the self-assurance of those who are wise in their own eyes (but are actually blind). The goal of this subversive fool is to help the foolish see themselves truly, to help them abandon their folly. This was the fooling used by the court jester who, because of his role as humorist, was able to get away with saying outrageous things that went beneath the psychological defenses of the proud, pompous, and powerful. The fool of Shakespeare's *King Lear* and of Erasmus's *In Praise of Folly*[4] follows this pattern. But the main "fool" in the Bible is the person who might appear heroic in the public eye, but who is a sham hero and is heading for self-inflicted disillusionment and ruin.

The Fool as a Negative Hero

The fool as a negative hero is not to be confused with the modern anti-hero discussed in the second chapter. The anti-hero is the product of modern cynicism. He occupies the space in a story where the hero used to be—center stage—but appears unheroic, not so much for reasons of moral evil but for just being a failure at the project of life. He might be the kind of person who wishes he had the courage to do something really good or bad, but never manages it. No one is in danger of mistaking him for a hero or of ever admiring him. He is pathetic, so we are torn between pity and scorn. Anti-heroes can be destructive in that they seem to communicate to us the cynic's message that there is no such thing as heroism. On the other hand, at least they do not tempt us to follow them. They exert no imaginative attraction on us at all, so they do not need to be dethroned or debunked. They are already on the bottom with nowhere to fall. Who could be seduced into wanting to be like Willy Loman?

The fool, on the other hand, *is* often mistaken for a hero, and is emulated with passion and determination, with a vicelike grip on the imaginations of admirers. For example, powerlessness is a common experience felt by people living in a mass society where many of the decisions that affect their lives are made far away, by people of high importance. It is seductive to adopt compensatory heroes who are powerful and confident.

Some of the most common heroes today are heroic for exploiting other people—sexually, psychologically, economically. We must make no mistake, it is not that some are perceived as heroic despite lapses into exploitation; it is that power through exploitation is itself seen as attractive. Heroes who point the way to self-gratification at the expense of others possess vast imaginative authority. But they are pseudoheroes, if not heroes of evil, who must be exposed for what they are and avoided. The writers of the Bible give us the "fool" to help us break their power. The teaching on the fool becomes a paint scraper to our imagination.

The overarching attribute of the fool is not low intelligence or lack of education but a lack of humility before God and other people. This is the root cause of all the other attributes we will explore.

The Fool Is Without Glory

In the perspective of the last chapter, the fool reflects nothing of the glory of God in the way he or she lives. The potential of glory possible to each of us as images of God is forfeited by the fool's quality of life. This is an important theme in the wisdom literature of the Bible.

> Like snow in summer or rain in harvest,
>   so honor is not fitting to a fool. (Proverbs 26:1)

In fact, the fool cannot show honor at all. We discover more about why this is so a few verses later:

> Like one who binds the stone in the sling
>   is he who gives honor to a fool. (Proverbs 26:8)

This image sharpens the point. The fool is as effective at showing honor as the stone bound in its sling is in killing its prey. (Perhaps we should compare it today with going hunting with a steel plug welded into the barrel of our rifle.) If we try to give honor and glory to a fool, it is no longer honor and glory, and our attempt to honor him or her comes back to destroy us. The sling becomes a weapon that is only effective against us. The stone swings back to hit us in the head as we "release" it, as the rifle would explode in our face if we pulled the trigger. It seems that the fool and honor cannot go together, by definition. One destroys the other. The fool represents negative heroism, dishonor, and shame, and there is no greater fool than the one who sees himself or herself as a hero.

THE WAY THE FOOL IS EXPOSED

Remember that in dealing with heroism, we are dealing with the domain of the imagination. The vocabulary of the imagination is not made up of fine-tuned arguments in carefully reasoned essays but of sights, sounds, smells, stories, models, and myths. We are motivated to live as we do, not only by abstract ideas of right and wrong, but by vivid images and narratives. These are created, adopted, stored, developed, expanded, and treasured by our imaginations.

The Battle for the Imagination

It would seem that God has understood the nature of our struggle in helping to scrape off the old heroes from our lives. In the Bible we are not given long, linear arguments or moral essays against having the wrong heroes. Instead, its writers meet our imagination on its own turf, using the imagination's vocabulary and exposing our false heroes with literally hundreds of visual images, parables, narratives, satires, and street theater—so that the fool might be seen and felt to be the fool. There is much in it that is not nice or polite. One often feels that the words are used in a raging, full-scale battle to win over our imaginations.

Take, for example, the image we just considered, of the mighty hunter who binds a stone in his sling. It is not an argument. It is not a lecture. It is a very short but suggestive slice of a story. But think of how it works. With no conscious effort at all you may find yourself stretching it into several short stories. You watch the hunter carefully wind the string around and around and then tie the stone firmly to the leather sling with a double knot for fear it might come loose. Then you imagine him setting out on the hunt, perhaps spinning the sling menacingly in his hand as David might have done as he approached Goliath. In a few seconds you have imagined several different outcomes, perhaps even seen it enacted by Charlie Chaplin, Woody Allen, or Chevy Chase. It is an invitation to your imagination to participate in an open-ended, interactive story and follow it through to some sudden, humiliating breakthrough of the truth.

But of course this image is not in the Bible just to give us a laugh. It is a simile where the comedy is fastened to the futility and self-destructiveness of giving honor to a fool. This is the serious issue that seems carried along on the coattails of the story, but which is actually the whole point. As we find the mighty hunter to be ridiculous, and find ourselves laughing at him, we are pressed to ask ourselves some questions.

We like the idea of honor. We do not like being a fool. We dread being laughed at or ridiculed the way we find ourselves laughing at the mighty hunter in his moment of illumination. We go to extreme lengths to avoid that sort of shame and dishonor ourselves. What could "giving honor to a fool" mean? I wonder if it could refer to anyone who tries to honor himself or herself? Is that person automatically a fool? Do I know people who do that? Do I do that myself?

Right away we find ourselves asking very searching questions, and also feeling a sense of aversion to the predictable endings to the story. It could be that an image like this can help jar us out of our vanity to recognize a fool as the dishonorable person he or she is.

Most of the satire in the Bible—and there is quite a lot of it—is aimed at the pseudohero. The Bible has plenty of argument and moral exhortation, but it also makes use of a vast variety of highly imaginative literary forms. Some of the most persuasive writing about moral values in all of literature is in the form of stories.

Think of Hans Christian Andersen's children's story "The Emperor's Clothes." He could have written an essay against arrogance and another against conformity. But what he did rivets the mind not on abstract ideas but on a very concrete, pompous man whose vanity made him easily duped and then humiliated. We focus on a crowd of conformists whose fear of being seen as a little bit different made them tell lies, deceive themselves, and become fools. The child-hero, whose freedom from the pretenses of the adult world enabled him to see and tell the truth, exploded the illusion and plunged everybody into well-deserved shame.

As we hear and reflect on "The Emperor's Clothes," it tends to create within us a fear of the blinding consequences of arrogance and conformity. The satirical tone insures that they have no glamor in our eyes. We would not want to be like the emperor or the crowd, and we want to believe that we would have had the child's vision, courage, and integrity. Notice that we are dealing here not primarily with a story helping us to discern right from wrong, but with a story making us desire to do the right and dread doing the wrong.

The Imagination and Evil

It is intriguing to see how God presents radical evil to us in the Bible. It is not the way one might expect. Scholars of heroism such as Orrin Klapp put before us three imaginative categories of human evaluation: heroes, villains, and fools.[5] The hero is worthy of emulation, the villain is wicked, and the fool is incompetent—a buffoon who is bumbling but usually harmless. The writers of the Bible draw the lines differently. If we expect the fool to be an innocent incompetent, we are in for a surprise. A typical example is Jeremiah's prophecy:

"For my people are foolish,
        they know me not;
they are stupid children,
        they have no understanding.
They are skilled in doing evil,
        but how to do good they know not." (Jeremiah 4:22)

If we were to think in the categories of Orrin Klapp, Jeremiah put the villain as a subheading under the larger category of fool.

Remember that the fool is without honor and glory and therefore, rightly understood, inspires aversion. If the villain is a fool, we are discouraged from linking the villain to the glamor of heroism. This pushes against a deep and mysterious tendency within us, coming from the effect of sin on our imaginations. It is that we tend to find evil attractive in an ambivalent and perverse way. Evil is fascinating, intriguing, and we are drawn to it sometimes even against our will. It seems to have a special appeal to us. Think of the fascination with Al Capone, Billy the Kid, Jesse James, and Hitler, or the preoccupation with horror, accident, and disaster. Exposing the badness of evil may not necessarily be a deterrent to doing it. That may just make it more interesting and strangely glamorous, giving it a bigger place in our daydreams.

Compare the way Milton treated the figure of Satan in *Paradise Lost* to the way Satan is treated in the Bible. Milton gives Satan a great deal of attention, and in so doing makes him more interesting than God, although that was probably not Milton's intention. One scholar called Milton's Satan "splendidly wicked." Satan is presented as evil, to be sure, but we are allowed to find a certain glamor and dignity in his rebellion, and marvel at his fiendish challenge to God. By contrast, the Bible gives Satan almost no footage at all—especially considering his cosmic importance.

The biblical story gives our imaginations no encouragement to wonder about him, his story, or his motivations. We are told just barely enough to know that he is the archfool and loser, who through suicidal vanity, naiveté, and treason spoils God's creation, bringing death to billions, and who finally will destroy himself. In no sense do we get the impression of glamor or glory. He is a liar, a murderer, and the fool of fools.

The biblical authors condemn evil as clearly as can be done, but never in such a way as to offer it as food for our aspirations. Our imaginations are vulnerable, so easily enticed to find attractiveness in evil. Evil itself gets little attention in the Bible. Its disastrous results, incarnated in the life patterns of people who are shown to be fools, receive biblical attention.

In much literature goodness appears preachy, excruciatingly earnest, or sentimental. Moral goodness and imaginative power are too seldom on the same side of the battle lines. The challenge is to learn to use the language of the imagination to tell what the world is really like, to communicate the beauty of goodness and the dreariness, banality, and folly of evil.

As we turn to explore the characteristics of the fool in the Bible more closely, notice the way the fool is brought to us. The writers of the Bible aim at the redemption of our imaginations. This means helping us aspire to the hero's height of glory and honor, and also to dread falling to the fool's depth of shame. Their goal is that we would jump back from folly as from a rattlesnake on the path in front of us.

THE GENERAL CHARACTERISTICS OF THE FOOL

The fool is not someone who is either uneducated or lacking in mental equipment. At the most basic level, the fool lacks humility. Sooner or later this lack of humility makes him or her a loser. In biblical terms, "fools despise wisdom and instruction," and so "they set an ambush for their own lives" (Proverbs 1:7,18). Although this is the overarching pattern of folly, there are many variations on it. Just as the fear of the Lord is the beginning of wisdom, so folly begins with a denial of God and his authority. King David put it this way, "The fool says in his heart, 'There is no God'" (Psalm 14:1). What matters is not so much what is said out loud but what is said in the heart. Perhaps their folly is greatest whose mouths are full of God-talk but who, in their heart of hearts, believe none of it.

The psalmist confronted rulers who crushed God's people, killed the widow and the sojourner, murdered the fatherless, and then said with confidence, "The LORD does not see; the God of Jacob does not perceive" (Psalm 94:7). In other words, we can do as we please because there is no personal God who can see or hear us, and who has the power or authority to do anything about it if he cared. The psalmist's response is in the form of several questions: .

Understand, O dullest of people!
Fools, when will you be wise?

He who planted the ear, does he not hear?
He who formed the eye, does he not see?
He who chastens the nations, does he not chastise?
He who teaches men knowledge,
>the Lord, knows the thoughts of man,
>that they are but a breath. (Psalm 94:8-11)

God knows our thoughts, not only our words said out loud or our actions done in public. It is not God who is just a mist, a vapor, or an abstraction. It is the self-important plans of proud people that are "but a breath." But even if only a breath, they do not escape the eyes and ears of God, who sees and hears everything. Only a fool would think that the one who created these organs with their intricate functioning would be deaf, dumb, and blind. Only a greater fool would think that God would not care. The charge of "fool" is used also by the prophet Jeremiah, speaking the words of the Lord, as he takes the argument another step:

"Hear this, O foolish and senseless people,
>who have eyes, but see not,
>who have ears, but hear not." (Jeremiah 5:21)

The Fool's Strategy

The fool is *one who thinks he or she has beaten the system, outwitted an absent, impersonal, feeble, or uncaring God in order to have a more fulfilling life than God would have allowed.* Jeremiah's rejoinder here is both a warning and a protest that the fool has gotten the truth exactly backwards. They who count on God's blindness and deafness for their freedom are themselves without either the sense or the senses they were born with.

The writings of the prophets are filled with protests against the self-destroying folly of those who reject God and are satisfied with gods of their own making. Isaiah complained about the enchantment of self-deception that comes with idolatry, making it impossible to recognize folly for what it is. He told of a man who cuts down a tree, uses half of it for firewood to cook his supper, makes a god out of the other half, and worships it: "He feeds on ashes; a deluded mind has led him astray, and he cannot deliver himself or say, 'Is there not a lie in my right hand?'" (Isaiah 44:20).

Later Isaiah asked,

"Why do you spend your money for that which is not bread,
  and your labor for that which does not satisfy?"
    (Isaiah 55:2).

This makes even less sense when he goes on to point out that the only thing that does finally satisfy is both priceless and free—the mercy and love of God.

Our view of God does not stand in a vacuum but is ultimately connected with our view of ourselves. The fool's view of himself or herself is therefore predictable. The book of Proverbs puts it this way:

The way of the fool is right in his own eyes,
  but a wise man listens to advice. (12:15)

Why listen to advice if I know it all already? The fool consequently tends to be gullible:

The [fool] believes everything,
  but the prudent looks where he is going. (14:15)

If I can have a lofty sense of the importance of my own decision to believe something, it overshadows the need to carefully investigate its truth. The main thing is that I have come to believe it. Closely akin to the fool's self-confidence is his stubbornness:

Crush a fool in a mortar with a pestle
  along with crushed grain,
  yet his folly will not depart from him. (27:22)

The picture here is of the fool whose foolishness has brought about his own destruction, but even this does not dim self-assurance.

It is usually with the tongue that the fool blows his or her cover and comes out into the open. We are assured that

Even a fool who keeps silent is considered wise;
  when he closes his lips, he is deemed intelligent. (17:28)

But this silence is uncharacteristic because "the babbling of a fool brings ruin near" (10:14), reminding one of the babbling of a brook that runs tirelessly, year-round, without stopping. Also,

> A fool takes no pleasure in understanding,
>> but only in expressing his opinion. (18:2)

In case we have difficulty seeing the contemporary relevance of these warnings, the French sociologist Jacques Ellul has pointed out that it is the educated population who are most vulnerable to the influence of propaganda. Three reasons are summarized by Konrad Kellen in his introduction to Ellul's *Propaganda*: first, educated people absorb more secondhand and unverifiable information than anyone else; second, they feel the need to have an opinion about every important subject; and third, they consider themselves capable of judging for themselves, therefore they need propaganda in the worst way to maintain their self-images.[6] This is not a denial of the value of education, but a warning of the occupational hazards of education without the requisite humility for wisdom.

Self-confidence is a powerfully seductive heroic virtue, displacing painful self-doubt and uncertainty. We therefore want heroes that are always sure of themselves—people of action, not indecisive, anxious, or hesitant. The writers of the wisdom literature of the Bible offer a necessary debunking of overconfidence in today's world. Seen in the light of their realism, the powerful attraction of the confident fool is less alluring, less heroic.

The pseudohero who is admired for "looking out for number one" also falls within the domain of the fool who knows what he wants and goes to get it, but in the process lets the hungry starve, slanders his neighbor, and gets rich unjustly. It is good to stay away from this person because "the companion of fools will suffer harm" (Proverbs 13:20). We are warned also,

> Let a man meet a she-bear robbed of her cubs;
>> rather than a fool in his folly. (17:12)

The society of fools is not a good place to live.

Proud, self-confident, and stubborn, the fool denies God and his authority and deems himself capable of true judgment apart from any other advice or accountability. He loudly assumes the role of pseudohero.

SPECIFIC FOOLS

Having looked at some of the general characteristics of the generic fool or pseudohero, let us look at more specific kinds of fools. Although popular heroes change with extraordinary rapidity with the twists and turns of popular culture, some hero systems have shown staying power since biblical times. One is the heroism of money and property.

The Pseudohero of Wealth

A classic attack on the heroism of wealth is in a parable told by Jesus (Luke 12:13-21). He tells the story to an anxious man who tried to enlist Jesus' help in getting his share of his family's nest egg. It went like this. There was a rich farmer whose land had produced such bumper crops that he could not store them all. He decided to make a major investment in new, larger barns. He was a hero in the world of investment capital. The difficulty came as he planned his new investments. He said to his soul,

> "'Soul, you have ample goods laid up for many years; take
> your ease, eat, drink, be merry.' But God said to him, 'Fool! This
> night your soul is required of you; and the things you have pre-
> pared, whose will they be?' So is he who lays up treasure for
> himself, and is not rich toward God." (verses 19-21)

It is important to note here that Jesus did not even hint that the investor's money had been gained through dishonesty, or that wealth itself was immoral. His folly had two sides to it. First, money had been his whole life. His fortune seemed to be the farthest horizon of his caring. Secondly, since money has always translated into power, he had an inflated sense of his ability to control his own life (and health). He had lost the realization that every breath and heartbeat was sustained by God.

This man's counterparts are still the heroes for many today. Our hero has done well. He might have started with almost nothing and lived through hard times, but now he has made it according to the most widely acknowledged criterion of success. If he happens to be a church-goer, there is a better than even chance that he has been asked to take some sort of leadership in the church. ("He has managed his own investments so well, we need him to help us run the church.") He might be the picture of self-satisfaction and security.

Yet think of the way this investor is rebuked by God. It is not a typical moral rebuke. He is not told that he should have given more of his money away, or that he was greedy, although those things might have been true. He was simply told that he was a fool, a loser even according to his own practical standards. He may have been everybody's hero, but he was bankrupt where it mattered most.

If one faces God at death with only money or material possessions to show for life, one might as well face the cashier at a supermarket with a full shopping cart but a wallet full of oak leaves—it is the wrong currency, not legal tender. Jesus exposes him as a fool by looking at the end of his life and showing him to be a loser. By a catastrophic miscalculation, he has forfeited the glory of God that was his by creation and could have been his by redemption.

The Drinker as Pseudohero

Another pseudohero who has lasted for thousands of years is the heroic drinker. Isaiah's searing scorn is perhaps the sharpest. He warns,

> Woe to those who are heroes at drinking wine,
>   and valiant men in mixing strong drink. (Isaiah 5:22)

He exposes the heroism of the connoisseur of fine wines whose life revolves around the dates on his wine bottles and his ability to identify by taste the valley in France from which each one came. But he also satirizes the hero who basks in his reputation of being able to drink all competitors under the table at the fraternity house or local bar.

Isaiah deliberately used the language of military valor to satirize the heroism of drinking. He invites you to visualize crowds gasping in admiration as the hero mixes a martini, raises it to his lips, and then drinks it—standing in awe as he is awarded medals for such valiant achievement above and beyond the call of duty. Although utterly absurd, the picture is not that far removed from the average beer commercial in which a can of beer with the boys is the great reward for a heroic day's work.

The Pseudohero of Sexual Conquest

The sexual conqueror has also retained powerful imaginative attractiveness through the ages. This is the heroic stud. There is great admiration for the man who can have sex with many women—but the same honor has never been extended to his wife or girlfriend. The writer of Proverbs sees this drama in a fresh light. As the man goes after the woman to sleep with her, he goes not in triumphant conquest but "as an ox goes to the slaughter" (7:22), an animal stupidly falling into a trap that leads only to death.

Can you think of an image less heroic and less suggestive of conquest than that of an ox going to a slaughterhouse from which it will emerge packaged in hamburger, steaks, and roasts? An ox is not known for its brilliance, but is so strong that it could escape straight through the walls of most slaughterhouses—if it only knew what was happening. But the ox hasn't the faintest idea of what is going on, and so is quite docile. We are given images like this not that we would skip quickly over them, but for our long, thoughtful meditation.

Female Pseudoheroes

Women pseudoheroes do not escape the exposure of biblical writers— especially those of high society, the rich and the proud. They were respected and envied by much of the population, but the words of the prophet cut through the admiration:

> "Because the daughters of Zion are haughty
>> and walk with outstretched necks,
>> glancing wantonly with their eyes,
> mincing along as they go,
>> tinkling with their feet;
> the Lord will smite with a scab
>> the heads of the daughters of Zion,
>> and the LORD will lay bare their secret parts."
>> (Isaiah 3:16-17)

This is not a very nice image, but it was not meant to be. It captures God's attitude toward their superiority and finery. Look through the fashion supplement to your Sunday newspaper and notice the haughty eyes of so many of the models. This is for only one reason, because of the heroic attraction of being able to look down on others from a pinnacle of beauty, power, wealth, and sophistication. Isaiah wanted us to go home with a different image in our minds—the image of scabs and humiliating naked exposure. Likewise, the writer of Proverbs tells us that

> Like a gold ring in a swine's snout
>> is a beautiful woman without discretion. (Proverbs 11:22)

Think about this for a moment, try to make a picture of it in your mind. It is a visual image, and that is what it is there for.

THE FOOL'S COUSINS

In the wisdom literature of the Bible, the fool has two close cousins. They are the scoffer and the sluggard, and they are presented as pseudoheroes who work together in any society. The scoffer is the cynic who sees through everyone. There is nothing in the world that is worthy of his or her commitment or hope. The scoffer does not just withhold commitment but scorns and tears others down who are trying to do something positive with their lives. The sluggard is the natural byproduct of a society that has a lot of scoffers around. In an atmosphere of cynicism nothing seems to be worth the effort. It all seems phony, corrupt, or useless, so there is no point in any exertion. The sluggard, then, is self-justified in doing as little as possible, and so will aspire to a hassle-free life.

The Cynic as Pseudohero
Take *the scoffer* first. He or she is not just cynical in inward attitude but outwardly scornful in criticizing the naive and unsophisticated, which includes most of the human race. The idea of heroism or human excellence itself is particularly held up for mockery.[7]

The cynic is usually conscious of taking a "realistic" view of things in contrast to the naive and hopeful who cannot see the flawed character of people, society, and the world. To be fair, there is plenty to encourage cynicism if we look around us with our eyes open, and many avoid it only by putting their heads in the sand. However, in the Bible the scoffer is not praised as a person with courageous clarity of vision. To the contrary:

> "Scoffer" is the name of the proud, haughty man
>   who acts with arrogant pride. (Proverbs 21:24)

Why such a negative judgment when the biblical writers themselves have plenty of uncomplimentary things to say about human nature and behavior? It is because cynicism, and its outward expression in scoffing, takes important steps beyond the realism of the Bible.

The cynic goes beyond the diagnosis of the Bible, and so undercuts its solution. We are told that "A worthless witness mocks at justice" (Proverbs 19:28). This describes a person who has probably seen a good deal of injustice—injustice from ignorance, malice, and greed. He or she then concludes that there is no such thing as justice at all. This is a giant step—from the fallibility of human legal systems to the amorality of the universe. Not only is this arrogant, but *this scoffer then becomes a worthless witness*. Justice is not even worth striving for. The scoffer fails to contribute to justice *in that particular part of the world where he or she could have made a difference.*

The writer of the first psalm has to warn us against sitting "in the seat of scoffers" (verse 1), a seat that is high and lifted up in the public eye, a seat of pseudoheroism. Ironically the scoffer, while disapproving of heroism, enjoys heroic status in others' eyes because of the transcendent superiority implied in scoffing itself. It is the same phenomenon that we observed about the "masters of suspicion," Darwin, Marx, Nietzsche, and Freud. People look up to the cynics because cynics spend so much time looking down that they must know what is going on.

The heroic status of the scoffer is dangerous both because it is contagious and because it is so easily confused with courage and honesty. It can destroy vision, hope, and courage by the atmosphere that it exudes, without even giving an argument. The German philosopher Sloterdijk has noticed the growth of cynicism and written that it is "the main feature of the post-modern world." He observed the change that "modern cynics . . . are no longer outsiders."[8]

The final word about scoffers is said by God himself. He puts them with fools.

> Toward the scorners he is scornful,
>> but to the humble he shows favor.
> The wise will inherit honor,
>> but fools get disgrace. (Proverbs 3:34-35)

Here is the ultimate sting to the scoffer. There is a God who sees through and scorns the cynic's cynicism. This is something that the cynic in all his or her sophistication had never imagined—that there could be a God who laughs at cynicism, a laughter not of glee but of pity and sadness. The cynic must face the very disgrace that he or she inflicted on others.

The Sluggard as the Pseudohero

The second cousin of the fool is *the sluggard* or *the slothful*. Sluggards flourish best in the environment of the scoffers, where all sources of motivation have been debunked. The sluggard does not just want more than he thinks God allows, but wants it for less, without effort or risk. Sloth is not a vice that has only to do with the body. It embraces all of life. The sluggard is one of today's "minimal heroes." People can be considered heroic for how much they can get away with and for their mastery of the hassle-free life. The sluggard is seen as heroic for beating the system, getting most for least, and being free from a passionate involvement with anything.

Again, the book of Proverbs has some of the sharpest things to say:

> The sluggard says, "There is a lion in the road!
> There is a lion in the streets!"
> As a door turns on its hinges,
> so does a sluggard on his bed.
> The sluggard buries his hand in the dish;
> it wears him out to bring it back to his mouth.
> The sluggard is wiser in his own eyes
> than seven men who can answer discreetly. (26:13-16)

The humor of these proverbs is not just to entertain you, it is to jar you free from behind your defenses so that you see laziness from a different, less heroic angle. In another place we are told,

> Go to the ant, O sluggard;
> consider her ways, and be wise. . . .
> A little sleep, a little slumber,
> a little folding of the hands to rest,
> and poverty will come upon you like a vagabond,
> and want like an armed man. (6:6,10-11)

These are powerful visual images that we need to hold in our mind's eye to displace the opposing images of the glamor of the hassle-free life. They must also counter the extravagant images of compensatory heroism, which by their sheer vicarious grandeur enable us to sink a bit more deeply into our sofas. The sluggard's life pattern begins with avoidance of hardship but leads to the collapse of its many enticements in a collision with harsh reality.

Dorothy Sayers describes sloth as one of the seven deadly sins and manages to strip it of its accustomed glamor:

> In the world it calls itself Tolerance; but in hell it is called
> Despair. It is the accomplice of the other sins and their worst
> punishment. It is the sin which believes in nothing, cares for
> nothing, seeks to know nothing, interferes with nothing, enjoys
> nothing, loves nothing, hates nothing, finds purpose in nothing,
> lives for nothing, and only remains alive because there is nothing it would die for.[9]

We have looked at the biblical project of unmasking, demythologizing, and dethroning the fool in the human imagination. We've also exposed the pseudoheroes of wealth, sexual conquest, alcoholic consumption, and high society, as well as the fool's close cousins, the scoffer and the sluggard. It turns out that these "minimal heroes" aren't heroes at all when seen through the lens of Scripture. It is only as we experience the fool as a fool that we can get free from the power of his or her heroic leverage on our imaginations. We turn finally to the positive side of the biblical hope.

GOD'S GRACE TO THE FOOL

The fool is not a fixed category in the Bible as is your height or skin color. It is not as if some people were fools consistently and forever, and others not at all. It is not so much a question of fate as it is of choice. Foolishness is only as permanent as the duration of the fool's stubbornness. Despite all the satire and ridicule of the fool in the Bible, he or she is not put on God's trash heap and discarded. Violent language is used to dethrone the pseudohero, that we might learn to associate sin with folly and shame. It is not to make us think that anyone is a lost cause, but to lead us all beyond folly to truth and repentance.

The fool is not beyond God's grace, and that is a very good thing, because *we all* walk in the shoes of the fool some of the time. We dare not look condescendingly or self-righteously at the fool. If we do, we have already solidly joined ranks with him—by definition! This is because the very essence of folly is that lack of humility that would allow us to put ourselves over others in an attitude of superiority.

The apostle Paul puts it to Titus this way:

> For we ourselves were once foolish, disobedient, led astray, slaves to various passions and pleasures . . . but when the goodness and loving kindness of God our Savior appeared, he saved us, not because of deeds done by us in righteousness, but in virtue of his own mercy. (Titus 3:3-5)

Paul makes it very clear that he had numbered himself among the foolish, and that the gospel of Jesus Christ applied supremely to the fool. The fool's hope begins with awareness of the need for the mercy of God.

We see the same message in a psalm of thankfulness:

Some were [fools] through their sinful ways,
>   and because of their iniquities suffered affliction;
they loathed any kind of food,
>   and they drew near to the gates of death.
Then they cried to the LORD in their trouble,
>   and he delivered them from their distress;
he sent forth his word, and healed them,
>   and delivered them from destruction.
Let them thank the LORD for his steadfast love,
>   for his wonderful works to the sons of men!
And let them offer sacrifices of thanksgiving,
>   and tell of his deeds in songs of joy! (Psalm 107:17-22)

In this case their foolishness had resulted in all sorts of suffering, even sickness to the point of death. Their cry to God was itself a turning from folly, an acknowledgment of their dependence on God, and God heard it. The extraordinary thing in this psalm is that only when their folly had brought them to ruin did they turn to God. But like the returned prodigal son and the repentant thief crucified beside Jesus, they were still received by God joyfully. This is the humility of God, that he is willing to receive us even when we turn to him as a last resort.

The challenge from God is that no one should lie down and accept being a fool, or mistake a fool for a hero. *You can resign from the ranks of fools.*

If you have been foolish, exalting yourself,
>   or if you have been devising evil,
>   put your hand on your mouth. (Proverbs 30:32)

Or again,

O simple ones, learn prudence;
>   O foolish men, pay attention. (8:5)

If we think we have been playing the fool, the place to begin is to stop talking and start listening, to learn the wisdom that only God can teach us.

If we are instructed by his wisdom, we will be able to see the world for what it is. William Gaddis wrote what could well be an epitaph for the fool: "the most ignominious defeats of all are held in store for those . . . who fail at something that was not worth doing in the first place."[10] Folly cannot succeed, nor is it worth doing in the first place. If we understand this, it becomes harder to be dazzled by its heroic attractiveness.

The biblical teaching on the fool is designed to help us avoid self-deception. Its purpose is not to "put down" anyone but to point the way to humility and therefore to wisdom and life. The prophet Isaiah wrote of a time when there will be a king who rules in righteousness, and princes who rule in justice. At that time,

> The fool will no more be called noble,
>   nor the knave said to be honorable. (Isaiah 32:5)

The aim of this chapter is to hasten this time, when fools will be recognized as fools and no longer praised as heroes. The focus has therefore been largely negative, putting off images, stories, and tyrannies that would destroy us. The reverse side of the coin is positive, that we need to "approve what is excellent" (Philippians 1:10). The two together constitute a transformation of our imaginations which in turn reaches out into our entire lives.

If we know the fool and the hero for who they really are, we have a foundation for motivation in the twin forces of aversion and aspiration. It will stretch us toward God and human excellence. If you see the fool truly you will want to do all you can to be free from folly. If you see the hero truly you will likewise want to do all that you can to be heroic. We turn, then, to the main focal point for heroism.

TRUE HEROISM: WHY THE IMITATION OF CHRIST?

Storytelling is not a luxury to humanity;
it's almost as necessary as bread.[1]
ROBERT STONE

The imitation of Christ cannot . . . be a prerogative
of a special category of people: monks, martyrs, ascetics,
or itinerant preachers. It is the privilege of every
recipient of grace.[2]
G. C. BERKOUWER

The glory of God is humanity fully alive.[3]
IRENAEUS

Our ability to act well "when the time comes"
depends partly, perhaps largely, upon the quality of our
habitual objects of attention.[4]
IRIS MURDOCH

f anything is clear from what we have already said, it is that heroism today is in difficulty—whether that be a vacuum where the hero once was, the wrong person in his or her place, or the right heroes with dysfunctional attitudes toward them. These difficulties are not automatically overcome when we introduce the idea that Jesus Christ is the hero or ultimate standard of human excellence. In fact, because of Jesus' unique identity and place in human history, it is not surprising that a number of perversions of heroism have emerged from the idea of imitating Christ.

I knew a young woman who was told that in order to be accepted by God, she would have to be like Jesus. She took this more seriously than her advisor had intended and used to get up often in the middle of the night, steal out of the house, and go to a church to pray for her life to be Christlike. The more she prayed, the more aware she became that she was not like Jesus at all, and even seemed to be getting less like him the more she tried. For her, the imitation of Christ had become a road to despair.

The imitation of Christ has at one time or another led to everything from a grim and joyless moralism to self-styled spiritual elitism to bizarre behavior bordering on the psychotic or suicidal. As with any of Jesus' important teachings, when it is distorted it creates havoc on a grand scale. Before turning to the specific heroic virtues involved, we will look more generally at the idea of the imitation of Christ.

THE IDEA OF THE IMITATION OF CHRIST

Thomas á Kempis wrote a spiritual classic called *The Imitation of Christ* in the late medieval period. It was titled by the first line of the text, according to contemporary custom, and not because its subject was actually the imitation of Christ. Although it has been helpful to generations of Christians, it does not actually develop what Jesus and the apostles had meant by imitating Christ. For that we will have to go to the New Testament itself.

The writer of the book of Hebrews described Jesus as the "[hero] and perfecter of our faith" (12:2). The word translated "hero" (*archegos*) has the connotation of founder, of a pioneer as well as an ideal. The goddess Athena was the "archegos" of the city of Athens. She was the founder of the city and also represented all the virtues that the city stood for. So Jesus is the "archegos" of the Christian faith, being in a unique sense its originator as well as its ideal or model.

The idea of the imitation of Christ goes back to the beginning of the Christian story and is woven deeply into it. The twelve men closest to Jesus were called "disciples." They were not his students who went through his school, but they were his apprentices who lived with their master and did everything he did, as well as listening to his teaching. Jesus said that "A disciple is not above his teacher, but every one when he is fully taught will be like his teacher" (Luke 6:40). He did not say that the disciple will know the same information that he knows, think like him, or teach like him, but that he will *be* like him. This kind of relationship is reflected throughout the whole New Testament in a diversity of ways.

We are to "put on the Lord Jesus Christ" (Romans 13:14). Of God the Father, the apostle Paul exhorted us to "be conformed to the image of his Son" (Romans 8:29). Then in many more specific ways we are told to imitate him, to take him as an example and do things as he did them. The form it takes is consistently reflexive. We are to treat others as he treated us. In the way he lived, he was all that a human being is meant to be, the final standard of human excellence—not in the sense of being a "superman" but in the sense of being a restored man, someone who was fully human.

There are two common misunderstandings of the imitation of Christ. One is that we imitate Christ in order to merit his grace and acceptance; the other is that we imitate all the outward actions that we see him doing in the gospel accounts. Both confusions have profound practical consequences.

Imitation of Christ for Merit

Think first of the imitation of Christ for *merit*. The idea is that one imitates Christ in order to be found worthy of the forgiveness of God through Christ. Communion with Christ comes finally at the end of long striving to imitate him.

Seen in this way, the imitation of Christ has been a moral bludgeon, bringing guilt and discouragement to those unfortunate enough to take it seriously. One who pursues God sincerely by this path will always be confronted with ways in which he or she falls short of being Christlike, as in the experience of the young woman just mentioned. If receiving the grace of God depends on matching Jesus' life, there can be no peace or joy, only anxiety and fear, because you never know how close you have to get to Christlikeness to be accepted. Anyone with moral sensitivity can see that he or she falls well short of Jesus' standard.

In fact, this sort of imitation negates the whole New Testament idea of grace. Grace means unmerited favor and blessing. Its essence is that it is *not* deserved, so that when it is promised only at the far end of a difficult path of moral improvement, it has lost its identity and is no longer grace at all.

There is a wonderful English Christmas carol called "Once in Royal David's City"—wonderful, that is, apart from one verse, which I always eliminate when singing it. It goes like this:

And through all his wondrous childhood
He would honor and obey
Love, and watch the lowly mother
In whose gentle arms he lay. Christian children all must be
Mild, obedient, good as he.

First of all, this verse seems to sentimentalize the childhood of Jesus. The only information we have of his childhood is when, as a twelve-year-old, he stayed in Jerusalem discussing the law with the priests in the temple after his family had started home. This left his parents looking for him for three days (Luke 2:41-51). *Mild* is not the first word that springs to mind. But it is misleading in a far more profound sense. Do Christian children really need to be as good as Jesus was when he was a child? Have you ever known a child that *was* as "mild, obedient, good as he"? I haven't. Not even my own. Are they therefore no longer eligible for God's grace (whatever "grace" might mean in that context)? I would suggest that a morally sensitive child would be terribly discouraged by this sort of teaching.

The imitation of Christ to merit God's forgiveness turns the Christian message on its head. It puts acceptance with God at the distant end of a steep path of fearful moral effort—fearful because we never know if we will be accepted or rejected at the end. In fact, the whole point of Jesus' coming was that we can be accepted by God as we are, despite all of our imperfection, if we come to him and trust him for his mercy. We can imitate Christ not out of a spirit of fear but in a spirit of gratitude for a gift already received. Jesus is not like a perfect marble statue high on a faraway hill that looks down from his heroic height, but is an older brother who walks through life with us.

Imitation of Christ's Outward Actions

The second common confusion of the imitation of Christ is *the idea that we should imitate his outward actions, circumstances, and the details of his life.* For example, I know of a man who decided to spend forty days fasting in the desert in southern California but died of starvation trying to do it. He did it out of a desire to imitate Christ.

There seems to be a tendency when one is close to those who are considered great to copy the trivial details of their lives. It is said that Alexander the Great had one shoulder slightly higher than the other, and that he carried his head a bit to one side. Evidently, his generals began to tilt their heads to one side and carry one shoulder higher than the other. One piece of Islamic literature records that Muhammad ate watermelons, but no one knew whether or not he spat out the seeds or swallowed them. One scholar wrote that it was better not to eat watermelons at all in case you did the wrong thing with the seeds. I do not offer this as typical of Islam. It does, however, point to a broader human inclination to trivialize the lives of those we admire, instead of letting them challenge us more deeply. The imitation of Christ as taught in the New Testament has nothing to do with this kind of imitation.

Less extreme but equally misguided are those who say being celibate is higher and more spiritual than being married because Jesus never married. Others might say the same thing about Jesus not owning a house or having a regular job. These things are not virtues in themselves just because they might have been true of Jesus. Individuals might well take any of those paths in the course of serving God, but they are not the highest standard for all Christians because they were supposed to have been true of Jesus.

More obvious still is that much of what Jesus did was unique, once for all, and not intended to be followed, repeated, or imitated. For example, we are not meant to be messiahs, or saviors of the world. God did not intend us to be omniscient or to call all people to ourselves. To attempt to repeat some of the things he did would be both to blaspheme him and to forfeit one's sanity.

The focus of the imitation of Christ in the New Testament is that *we are to imitate Jesus' quality of life.* This is specifically described in the New Testament teaching that we are to imitate the heroic virtues we see in Jesus' life, like humility, love, willingness to suffer unjustly, forgiveness, courage, servanthood. Our motivation for following them is gratitude, having been forgiven and accepted by him when we did not deserve it. We are called not to imitate just anything in the life of Christ but to imitate the way he treated us. We are those for whom he suffered and was humiliated, whom he loved, forgave, and came to serve.

FOUNDATIONS FOR THE IMITATION OF CHRIST

Behind the very possibility of imitating Christ is our creation in the image of God. This image has to do with who we are, and also with how we live. It means that the word *image* is a noun (you are an image of God), but it also can be expressed as a verb (you can image God).

In the Old Testament we are called to imitate God himself—to be like God. God tells the people of Israel, "You shall be holy; for I the LORD your God am holy" (Leviticus 19:2). Because the personality of human beings corresponds in some mysterious way with the personality of God the Creator himself, the term "image of God" is not just an empty figure of speech but tells something profoundly true about human nature and value. Since we are images of God and created to image him, the more closely we reflect the character of God, the more we become our true selves, the people we were created to be.

Into the flow of the history of the Roman Empire, the New Testament tells us that God became a human being in the form of Jesus of Nazareth. This was not just a visible appearance of God, but his coming as a full human being. He lived his life story on earth. In that story he lived out the excellence of character that reveals the glory of God. The writer of Hebrews said Jesus "reflects the glory of God and bears the very stamp of his nature" (1:3). The apostle Paul wrote that we learn of the glory of God from the face of Christ (2 Corinthians 4:6). When God became a man, he set aside his splendor and status as God, but not his divinity itself or his excellence of character. It is not that we are permitted to observe the glory of God in Christ from a distance passively, as spectators. It is far more. As we imitate Christ we can actually acquire something of that glory ourselves. Paul described it this way: "And we all, with unveiled face, beholding the glory of the Lord, are being changed into his likeness from one degree of glory to another" (2 Corinthians 3:18). Here is the outline of true heroism. Our transformation into the likeness of Christ will be imperfect in this life, but it will involve growth toward what is really heroic, the glory of God.

We must remember that we are speaking of excellence of character, not of the externals of life. It was said about Christ long before he came to earth that he would have "no form or comeliness that we should look at him, and no beauty that we should desire him" (Isaiah 53:2). He was despised and rejected by men. He did not have those powers of attraction that would have made him a male model, film star, or presidential candidate in the United States in the late twentieth century. His excellence was an excellence of character that enabled him to show the glory of God in the way he lived out his story to death and beyond. Ever since the first century, people have been divided over whether these qualities were truly heroic or the marks of a loser or charlatan.

WHO IS THIS HERO FOR US?

If someone is our hero, it matters a great deal who that person is to us. Is our hero a parent? A friend? A celebrity that we have only seen on television or screen? Someone who despises us? A figure out of past history? A fictional character? What is his or her relationship to us?

When we speak of Jesus as hero, we are not talking about someone we first saw on television or in the newspapers, then sought out as a fan. If you are a follower of Christ, he first sought you out. You are not part of an anonymous mass of admirers to him. He knew your name well before you knew his.

He is also the one who "for the joy that was set before him endured the cross, despising the shame, and is seated at the right hand of the throne of God" (Hebrews 12:2). What joy could possibly make one willing to be crucified? It was a means of torture and execution ghastly beyond imagination. For Jesus, because of the unique character of his death, it meant hell on earth, quite literally. Yet there was joy about some future event that enabled him to endure it. What could that event have been? The joy that was set before him could only have been the joy of knowing and redeeming us, of reconciling us to his Father. There was nothing else that he had to gain from it. He already had everything else before coming to the earth in the first place. His joy was the joy of the father of the prodigal son. He rushed down the driveway to welcome his rebellious son who had come home after squandering the family fortune. He embraced him, reinstated him, and held a banquet. The love that he has for each believer took him to the cross of his own volition. It is no small thing to think of your hero serving you in that radical a way.

The author of Hebrews wrote that Jesus was "not ashamed to call [us] brethren" (2:11). Think for a minute how easy it is to be ashamed of people with whom you are identified. Americans can be ashamed of their fellow Americans when they see them doing foolish things in public abroad. Perhaps it is easiest to be ashamed of the members of our own family, bearing our name, when they behave in ways that embarrass us. Yet Jesus was not ashamed to call us his brethren—in other words, to welcome us into his own family, to call us "My sister," "My brother." This is personal acceptance, to willingly be identified with us.

God even named himself with the names of some of his very imperfect servants. He called himself the God of Abraham, Isaac, and Jacob, even though all those men fell short of his moral law in spectacular ways.

The point is that if we imitate Christ truly as hero, he is also our brother by adoption. He has laid down his life for us. He also walks beside us through life, not as a remote hero on a faraway hill but as one who has promised to help us imitate him and to never abandon us even to the end of the earth. What a contrast to most modern heroes! Our top cast of public heroes don't know the names of the vast majority of those who adore them. How could they? Many want to know as few as possible of their fans and admirers, and as little as possible about those few.

Think of the Rolling Stones in concert scorning the whole business by spitting on the screaming, adoring, hero-worshiping—and horrified—crowd. Think then of the contrast to Jesus Christ, who was willing to endure being spat on and scorned for the sake of those whom he had come to save (and being spat on was only the beginning). In Christ we have a unique and revolutionary hero.

WHY IMITATION?

A valid question is raised by those who would ask why, since we have the teaching of Christ in words, do we also need to imitate his life? Don't his words tell us all we need to know? It is not as if there is new information included in the imitation of Christ that is missing from his teaching. The same truths are taught, but they are taught through a different medium. His life is a story showing his teachings lived out in a flesh-and-blood narrative.

In three out of the four gospels, Matthew, Mark, and John, we have the accounts of those who lived alongside Jesus as his apprentices.[5] Their records enable us to see Jesus in moments of victory and tragedy, pleasure and pain, hope and regret. Although we do not have him with us bodily, we have the account of his life from those who were closest to him.

The New Testament writers tell us that he is to be an example or pattern for our lives. This is not some abstract standard, as if he were a blueprint on the wall or a checklist to measure ourselves by. It is rather his life story engaging our imaginations. We begin to project the way he lived into the many possibilities of our own lives. We wonder what it would be like to respond as he did to other people's hostility, and what kind of story our lives would make if patterned after his. We begin to hunger to be like him as we meditate on the wholeness of his life as a model of excellence. If the imitation of Christ works this way in us, it starts to work against one of the central problems of our moral life — that we can know a great deal about what we ought to do, and yet not do it. Part of that problem is a sheer lack of motivation. Wanting to do the right and good does not usually come as the result of learning new information, even if it is in the form of grim warnings about the consequences of doing wrong. One of the main ways most cultures have communicated their values to their children has been through the telling of stories. Good stories shape our moral character by creating in us an attraction to the heroic, which if the hero is good, means an aspiration for goodness and an aversion to evil.

In stories we see individuals' choices and their consequences in narratives. They are concrete, not abstract. It is hot or cold, things smell a certain way. People have pasts that include pain and triumph, regret and joy. They fear and hope, they long to be able to see the future but can only guess about it.

Good stories engage our imaginations because they are about people who are believable. We can picture them in the world we know around us. We have seen people respond in the same ways, or felt that way ourselves. We can therefore place ourselves in their shoes. We can understand their ideals, see those ideals come under pressure, and either crumble or hold up under the weight. We gain a sense of what it might be like to be Hamlet caught in fatal indecision, Raskolnikov beneath the hammering of guilt, or Ivan Denisovich in ecstasy over a bowl of watery soup. Through good stories, we build visions of what human glory or excellence is, which translates into the desire to "be like" one character and to "be unlike" another.

The story of the life of Christ is distinctive in many ways, one of them being that at almost every turn and anecdote the largest issues of life, death, good, evil, belief, and unbelief are raised. At the same time, the characters of the New Testament story do not have the one-dimensional quality of some mythologies, in which individuals are incarnations of single virtues but not the sort of people we would ever expect to meet on Main Street.

As we read the life of Christ, we meet contemporary people and contemporary problems. We see the well-meaning bluster of Peter, the mother of James and John wanting reserved seats in the kingdom of heaven for her boys, and the distracted anxiety of Martha, who felt abandoned with more than her share of housework. We see the agony of parents with sick children, the unimaginative pessimism of Thomas, and the brilliant vision of a blind man. Through the whole, we see the majestic figure of Jesus, who, even at his moment of greatest weakness, somehow mysteriously towered over his accusers, judges, and executioners.

The imitation of Christ is a lifelong task of extraordinary difficulty, if taken seriously. Yet at the same time, if rightly understood, it will expand the life of any aspirant. This is because Jesus is the perfect reflection of God, of which we are only pale and warped reflections. But it is also because he is at work in us, enabling us to grow in correspondence to the original.

Insofar as Christ is our hero, we have a powerful imaginative vision of moral excellence. This is going to shape our own life stories in profound ways. And all the while, this hero is not remote but is our adoptive brother. He who loves us intimately, ultimately, and unconditionally is not ashamed to be numbered with us. It is to his heroic virtues that we now turn, that we might learn what it means that Christ can be formed in us.

THE IMITATION OF A HUMBLE PERSON

❧

No silly notion of playing the hero—what have creatures like us to do with heroism who are not yet barely honest?[1]
GEORGE MACDONALD

❧

To know oneself is, above all, to know what one lacks. It is to measure oneself against Truth, and not the other way around. The first product of self-knowledge is humility, and this is not a virtue conspicuous in any national character.[2]
FLANNERY O'CONNOR

❧

If anyone would like to acquire humility, I can, I think, tell him the first step. The first step is to realize that one is proud. And a biggish step, too. At least, nothing whatever can be done before it.[3]
C. S. LEWIS

❧

He who ignores instruction despises himself, but he who heeds admonition gains understanding. The fear of the LORD is instruction in wisdom, and humility goes before honor.
PROVERBS 15:32-33

I t is a popular notion that the Christian faith and heroism have little to do with each other and that their quarrel is over humility. Some ideas of heroism focus on human greatness to the point of nearly deifying overconfident, high-performance individuals. A hero is a super-man or superwoman, one who is bigger than life. The Christian faith, on the other hand, affirms human greatness in imaging God, but it also finds that image to be tarnished and terribly twisted. It evaluates the human race with a brutal honesty, unable to ignore our self-deception, hypocrisy, arrogance, and cruelty. A person is a magnificent creature, yet one who is bent out of original shape.

The Christian is likely to say that the bigger-than-life hero will be "discovered" among us only if he or she is inflated by hype and sustained by illusion. The Christian faith and heroism can coexist only if we rad-ically break from modern consciousness about heroism—to realize that humility itself is heroic.

Many who have written about heroism have taken one heroic virtue to be the most basic and all other virtues heroic to the extent that they exemplify that one. In the past, courage or fortitude was often seen as the essence of heroism. Although fragmentation and diffusion of heroic visions characterize modern society, sensitivity, openness, and psychological transparency have recently become admired as the most basic virtues.

The Christian faith, by contrast, does not isolate one single heroic virtue. Human excellence is far too diverse and rich for that. Humility is not the most basic virtue in the sense that all other virtues can be reduced to it. But it does stand in a special place in Christian charac-ter. It is a gateway virtue. It stands at the gateway to a relationship with God and is vital for Christian conversion and growth. Without humil-ity we do not know God, we relate only poorly to one another, and we take our stand knee-deep in self-deception. Without humility, any hero-ism—no matter how extraordinary—falls short of Christian heroism.

Since we have taken Jesus as our model for excellence, let us start by looking at his life as a paradigm. The first Christmas is the most nat-ural place to begin.

GOD JOINS THE HUMAN RACE

From the very beginning, the central Christian claim has been about an "incarnation"—the word coming from "in flesh" in Latin. The idea of the Incarnation means that God actually came in flesh and blood. C. S. Lewis called this the "Grand Miracle," dwarfing all others.[4] The claim was that God had entered history in a once-for-all way in the person of Jesus of Nazareth.

He did not come in a blinding flash, brighter than a thousand nuclear explosions. He did not come as a figure fifty feet high in order to inspire awe and veneration. He did not even come as a new Alexander the Great or Judas Maccabeus to provide the needed military leadership to his embattled nation.

Humilty in Action

Jesus did come in the form of a tiny baby who probably weighed about six pounds and who was born just like any other baby, except that the delivery room was inadequate even by first-century standards. He was just as helpless as you and I were as babies. He could not roll over in his borrowed manger without assistance, and he could not hold up his head without a supporting hand. He had to have his swaddling clothes changed for him and dared to put himself at the mercy of first-century pediatric medicine.

Although Jesus was the only one who ever got to decide what family he would be born into, he did not choose the Roman royal family, nobility, or even the Jewish priesthood. He was born into a poor carpenter's family amid rumors of illegitimacy that persisted all his life.

If we understand it, the first Christmas should boggle our minds because it was God himself who came in this way—the King of kings, Lord of lords, the One through whom creation was made. The apostle Paul tells us that he did not count "equality with God a thing to be grasped" (Philippians 2:6). He left behind his glory and status as God. It was the Great Descent.

Sometimes Christians, grasping for an analogy adequate for the job, compare the Incarnation to a human being voluntarily becoming an insect to accomplish some necessary task that insects could not do for themselves. But this analogy falls far short of the extremity of the Incarnation. The Incarnation was eternal, uncreated God becoming a finite, mortal man and finally even submitting to death. In the words of hymn-writer Graham Kendrick, "hands that flung stars into space—to cruel nails surrendered."[5] The Christmas story is not first of all something quaint and sentimental. It is an astounding and mind-jarring event. The world has not been the same since. Some recent theologians are offended at the ascension of Jesus to heaven after his death and resurrection. It seems crude and embarrassing to their educated sensibilities. Actually, the Ascension was the most natural event in the whole

New Testament story. If the "Grand Miracle" is true, the Ascension is only Jesus going back where he came from.

The Incarnation was humility in action, and Paul drove the point home to us:

> Have this mind among yourselves, which is yours in Christ Jesus, who, though he was in the form of God, did not count equality with God a thing to be grasped, but emptied himself, taking the form of a servant, being born in the likeness of men. (Philippians 2:5-7)

Jesus was willing to let go what was his—his glory and status at the right hand of God the Father, where no creatures were able to hammer nails into him. At his descent he made himself vulnerable to rejection, scorn, and ultimately to the nails that killed him.

Our Humility—The Same But Different

Our humility images Jesus' humility. We, too, are to be free enough from egotism to serve others, to build them up, to live fully even when that means sacrificially. We are called to be free from the interference of gigantic, bumbling, and vicious human pride. This means free to honor God without letting our vanity get in the way—demanding recognition, admiration, and the inflation of our own egotism. Our humility is to imitate the humility of Christ.

But our humility is also different from that of Christ. Jesus let go what was really his—his glory and status as God. We are called only to let go what is not ours anyway—our illusions of divinity, self-importance, self-sufficiency; our pretended autonomy; and our supposed innocence. Jesus forfeited what had been his for eternity. We are asked to let go our self-deceptions, our attempts to cash in on the promise of Satan in the garden that we might "be like God" (Genesis 3:5). God asks us to relinquish only those attitudes and commitments that would ultimately destroy us.

WHAT IS HUMILITY?

It is easiest to define humility negatively. It is freedom from pride, arrogance, conceit, and vainglory. The humble person is not dominated by the need for self-exaltation, self-advancement, self-justification, or dedicated to establishing his or her own heroism before the eyes of a watching society. But what is humility positively?

Humility—Vice or Virtue?

Humility is not universally agreed to be a virtue, let alone a heroic one. It was not one of the cardinal virtues of the Greek philosophers, although perhaps prudence came the closest. Many have criticized it as too negative and weak. Let us begin with the German philosopher Nietzsche, for whom it was not a virtue at all, but a vice. "When it is trodden on a worm will curl up. That is prudent. It thereby reduces the chance of being trodden on again. In the language of morals: 'humility.'"[6]

In Nietzsche's view, humility is for the worms of human society, the compliant, obsequious, and cowardly who in their prudence avoid conflict and let the powerful run the world for them. The humble are wise in that they know how to save their own skins. But for Nietzsche they are despised. One can think of the many parallels in today's popular thought. The world is seen as a place of limitless possibilities for the one with limitless self-confidence. Excellence is rooted in unshakable self-esteem, is expressed in competitive success, and is measured in youth, beauty, dollars, and power.

Iris Murdoch, a British novelist and philosopher, saw humility differently: "Humility is not a peculiar habit of self-effacement, rather like having an inaudible voice, it is selfless respect for reality and one of the most difficult and central of virtues."[7] Here is a different idea entirely—not only a different meaning of the word *humility*, but a different view of life. In her view, humility is associated not with cowardice but with courage, especially the courage to see and grasp what is real.

Humility as a Recognition of Truth

In Christian thought, humility has far more to do with recognizing the truth than with compliance or obsequiousness. In the words of philosopher Joseph Pieper, "The ground of humility is man's estimation of himself according to truth. And that is almost all there is to it."[8] It is grasping the implications of two foundational truths in particular—the Creation and the Fall.

From the truth of creation we know we are extraordinary and valuable creatures, made in the likeness of the Creator God himself. However, we are still creatures, derived, not the Original. We are not self-caused, self-sustaining, or self-sufficient. We are still utterly dependent on the Creator for breath and life.

We are also fallen. Sin is an ever-present reality in all of human existence. It touches our motivations, our plans, our attitudes, our imaginations, along with our words and our actions. It also has a great deal to do with what we leave undone.

We have mentioned Francis Schaeffer's description of a human being as a "glorious ruin." This is an apt term because there are marks of both creation and fall on each of us. This requires us to acknowledge two things. First of all, we need to acknowledge our finitude, helplessness, and dependence on God. Second, we need to admit that our moral guilt before him is serious enough that we must seek his forgiveness, which he in fact offers us through Christ. Without his mercy we are without hope.

This response is "merely" bowing before what is true, giving up illusions of self-sufficiency and moral superiority. Humility is making contact with reality, not retreating from it. Here is where Nietzsche was so sadly wrong.

True humility is not learning to be obsequious, to grovel and crawl before the beautiful, powerful, and rich. Humility is not making a virtue out of that most popular of modern nightmares, "low self-esteem." Nor is it false modesty. False modesty is a form of gamesmanship, being a moral hustler, fishing for praise and self-promotion. Humility is learning to relinquish self-deception in thought, word, and deed. In the terminology of Iris Murdoch, humility is being able to deny the outsized demands of the "fat, relentless ego," which, if allowed to have its way, will shrink and shrivel our humanness itself.

We see this illustrated in Jesus' parable of the prodigal son (Luke 15:11-32). A younger son demanded his inheritance, left the country, and squandered it so completely that he was reduced to near starvation. He then changed his mind, returned, apologized to his father, and was welcomed home with great celebrations. His change of mind had everything to do with humility. What was his choice? He could have tried to keep up the self-deceiving illusion that he was both self-sufficient and innocent, hanging on to that mirage out of pride, and into the teeth of his own poverty and hunger. The other choice was to simply admit what he had done and ask forgiveness from the one he had wronged. Jesus described the choice not as self-flagellation, groveling, or cringing, but that he simply "came to himself." It is as if he finally woke up after a long sleep in the dreams of his vanity.

How to Stand

The Christian challenge to humility is well captured by the apostle Paul's words to the Christians in Corinth: "Let any one who thinks that he stands take heed lest he fall" (1 Corinthians 10:12). The person who "stands" refers to someone who has achieved something or who has been successful in some important way. What is that person's attitude to be? He or she is not meant to deny that success, to pretend it did not happen, in false modesty. The intelligent are not told to believe that they are stupid, or the beautiful that they are ugly. But nor is the person who stands meant to go into an orgy of self-celebration and praise, reveling in his or her inevitable continued success.

Paul calls the one who stands *to simply have a sober and truthful awareness of himself or herself,* knowing his or her vulnerability as a broken person in a broken world. This is humility. In this response you see not low self-esteem but a realistic recognition of dependency on God for the future. You see the failure to do precisely this in the rash promise of Peter to Jesus: "Though they all fall away because of you, I will never fall away" (Matthew 26:33). He was surely a brave man, and had already shown more courage than some of the other disciples. But he was inflated with ideas of his superiority over them that left no room for realism about his own weaknesses. Falling down in his area of strength was probably unthinkable for him. This naiveté made his fall all the harder when, under pressure, he denied Jesus in a way that the other disciples did not.

The Gateway Virtue

Humility is a gateway virtue. We need humility to enter the kingdom of God, and also to grow in it. It is the foundation under the first steps we take. It strikes at the root of the primordial sin of pride—attempting to be "like God" ourselves, arbitrating good and evil to our own design and liking.

Negatively, the lack of humility stands as a barricade between us and God. Paul pointed out that God's kingdom is so designed that "no human being might boast in the presence of God" (1 Corinthians 1:29). No one has ever boasted in the presence of God and nobody ever will. That is because if you are boasting, you are by definition not in God's presence, and if you are in his presence, you are by definition not boasting. You will not find a proud person in God's presence anymore than you will find water boiling at minus 10 degrees Fahrenheit. The apostle summarizes a long passage about the nature of salvation with a question, and then provides his own answer. He asks, "Then what becomes of our boasting? It is excluded" (Romans 3:27).

It is not that we do only bad things, or that the good things that we might do, do not matter. But we are not to fool ourselves into believing that the good things that we do can earn us the acceptance of God. Jesus told of those who would come to him and recite all the marvelous things they had done in his name, expecting to be received because of their performance. He told them, "I never knew you; depart from me" (Matthew 7:23). Jesus' ministry is characterized by offering more hope to the outcasts of society—the tax collectors, prostitutes, and derelicts—than to the respectable religious establishment. Why was this? Was it not that the outcasts were willing and able to see *their* need for salvation in a way that the respectable, by and large, were not?

We have seen that the lack of humility is a roadblock to a relationship with God. On the positive side, humility opens the door to this relationship because it displaces the very pride that isolates us from him. God dwells in a high and holy place, and therefore with high and holy people, right? Wrong. Isaiah puts it the other way:

> For thus says the high and lofty One
>   who inhabits eternity, whose name is Holy:
> "I dwell in the high and holy place,
>   and also with him who is of a contrite and humble spirit,
> to revive the spirit of the humble,
>   and to revive the heart of the contrite." (Isaiah 57:15)

He makes his home with those who are humble and contrite, who can see themselves as they are, admit their need for mercy, and therefore see God as he is. The prophet Micah makes the same point in the form of a question:

> What does the LORD require of you
> But to do justice, and to love kindness,
>   and to walk humbly with your God? (Micah 6:8)

It is not as if we are offered different attitudes to choose from as we walk with God. If it is really *God* that we are walking with, it *is* going to be in *humility*. Jesus said that "every one who exalts himself will be humbled, but he who humbles himself will be exalted" (Luke 18:14). He lays this down as a spiritual law more solid than the law of gravity.

If we have no humility, Jesus might be a distant hero for us, but he would always be a stranger. If we are looking for, or trusting, in our own glory and status first, then we are not followers of the one who set his own glory aside for us.

Humility as an Unnatural Virtue

Humility is an unnatural virtue. Let us be clear. In the midst of our brokenness, humility does not come easily or naturally to us. By contrast, self-praise, self-excuse, self-justification, and standing on our own dignity all come to us without much effort. How often are our society's public heroes known for humility?

Howard Cosell evaluated himself in this way: "I really believe I'm the best. My relationship with the men who play the games—all the games—is probably unparalleled in this country." Joan Kennedy, now the ex-wife of Senator Edward Kennedy, reflected on her own attributes: "I have talent. I know I'm smart. I got straight A's in graduate school. I've still got my looks. I know I've got all these terrific things going for me. I mean, my God, you are talking to, I think, one of the most fascinating women in this country."[9]

These testimonies stand out more for their lack of subtlety than for their qualitative difference from the way many of us, at times, think of ourselves. So many great men of the world have spent extraordinary time and energy to make sure that their greatness was noticed.[10] When we see this in a person, we realize that we are looking not at real greatness but at human shrinkage—the bleating and braying of egotism. The denial of faults and the inflation of imagined virtues—when it is unmasked enough so that we can see it for what it is—does not inspire aspiration, but aversion.

Humility And Self-Deception

Humility stands against the awesome power and inventiveness of human pride and self-deception. You can possess many virtues (for example, courage or determination) and be proud of them without destroying them by that pride. Not so with humility. The moment you are proud of your humility, you have lost it. The minute you reflect with satisfaction on how free you are from the vanity you perceive in others, you have joined ranks with those others, and your prized humility has vaporized.

Self-deception is so slippery that it is probably not wise to strive for humility directly. If we do aim at it directly, we are too likely to conclude that we have "arrived" and finally gotten over our arrogance. We sometimes feel deep satisfaction that we are no longer conceited. Of course, we have only embraced another more dangerous form of pride, which had crept in the back door unnoticed.

I find that if I happen to catch myself at this trick, still another voice is quick to suggest, "But not many people would be as morally sensitive as you are, to even notice such a contradiction. You must *really* have a well-developed sense of moral awareness!" And so it goes. I suspect that the more we mature, the more disguised and respectable are the forms of pride that we must combat.

If it is too dangerous to pursue such an unnatural virtue as humility directly, what can we do? *Perhaps the most reliable strategy is to simply strive to believe and live what is true.* If we do this, we will be growing in humility without so much danger of being overly aware of it.

The unnaturalness of humility is ironic, given its many advantages. Chesterton wrote, "On practical grounds the case for humility is overwhelming."[11] Without some level of humility, close relationships are extremely difficult and cooperation is impossible. Without humility it is very hard to learn from another person (who would be qualified to teach you, after all?). In Chesterton's words, the "divine glory of the ego is a great nuisance."[12]

The great Welsh preacher, Dr. Martyn Lloyd-Jones, used to tell a story of a minister who had prayed for years that God would do a great work in his church, deepening the commitment of those who were already there and leading many in the town to turn to Christ in faith. His prayer was answered, and there was a powerful work of God in his church, but when it happened he was furious. You might well ask why? It was because when it began he was not there. He was on vacation. He rushed home to take charge, but was himself humbled by God's Spirit. How our lack of humility works against the best things we might want to do with our lives! Our own vanity seems to be self-evidently "for us," but it works at a much deeper level against us. It will shrink and shrivel us as human beings. Again, it's better to simply live and believe what is true.

HUMILITY AND HEROISM

Humility is closely linked to courage. It takes great courage to see the truth. Honesty can be terrifying. When we are faced with the truth about ourselves in a way that would threaten the security of our well-constructed self-images, we may want to deny the truth, ignore it, or fight it—as a conditioned reflex.

Humility or Our Preferred Self-Image

How do we respond when someone laughs at us? Let us say that we have just done something stupid and someone jokes about it at our expense. What do we do? We have only one or two seconds to make up our minds about how we are going to react. Perhaps it was unfair and was said in a spirit of meanness. It is hard to let that pass, even if others are laughing with the joke. Will we take offense ("Well, if that's how you feel . . . !"), get angry, retaliate? Or, will we let it go, laugh along with the joke, and laugh at ourselves in the process?

This is an intentionally trivial example, but it illustrates in a small way an important dynamic. Are we able to step outside of our preferred self-images to see ourselves in an unflattering light for a moment? To do this we need a certain self-transcendence and freedom from the demands of our fat, relentless egos. To do this we need the courage to face the great unknown—experiencing ourselves without wearing our familiar, comfortable version of ourselves.

If we are in a marriage that is deadlocked in resentment, how easy it is to dig in our heels, taking our stand on where we have been right and our partner so inexcusably wrong. To openly admit our part in the problems requires the courage that only comes with humility. It means that in the interest of what is true, we need to be willing to forsake the psychological safety of our preferred self-image reflected to ourselves, and displayed to the outside world. If we possess some measure of humility, we will be able to risk acknowledging unflattering things about ourselves and admitting them to even a spouse whose failures "far outweigh" our own. Humility of this sort is very difficult. It feels safer to stand on our innocence and condemn our partner. Humility demands that we have the courage to step into new territories of honesty and openness. It also means that reconciliation becomes a possibility.

Humility and Our Relationship to God

We confront some of the same dynamics in our relationship with God, where the stakes are even higher. If we come to believe in the existence of God, and take that seriously, it radically reorients our picture of ourselves and of the world. We have already mentioned what is involved in no longer seeing ourselves as self-caused and self-sufficient, no longer righteous and deserving of God's rewards or acceptance. Believing in him presses us to acknowledge ourselves as dependent on his care and in need of his mercy. Here, too, the courage of humility is necessary to dare to see ourselves as God actually sees us.

It may be that there is a pride in us that makes it impossible to reach such a conclusion. Through the eyes of pride, this belief in God seems demeaning, catering to the helpless who are willing to be treated as cases for charity, or to those who are overly pessimistic about the whole human project. Pride does not want to admit dependence for knowledge or help in living on anyone, much less on God. Pride would rather reflect on its own power, sufficiency, resources, and goodness. It would rather think about the phenomenal breakthroughs in science and technology that seem to make religion superfluous or obsolete. It does not want to admit guilt and the need for forgiveness or the brokenness that surfaces in every human relationship. It would rather reflect on its own superiority to most of the other people walking on the planet and on its strategies for overcoming all frustrations.

Stepping outside of the confines of this pride is called repentance, literally a "turning of the mind." It is analogous to our decision about whether to laugh at ourselves or to take offense at someone's joke about us. Are we able to see the truth of the unflattering verdict that God would deliver about our lives, or is that too threatening? Are we able to receive the gift of God's reconciling us to himself through Christ, or is that too demeaning? The courage of humility makes those realizations open possibilities rather than closed doors, locked long ago, when God was thought to have fled in front of the advance of modern knowledge.

Subverting Self-Deception and Pride
Humor, like honesty, is on the side of humility, not against it. Humor thrives on exposing incongruity. Not all incongruity is funny, but all that is funny is incongruous in some way. Pomposity, pretension, and respectability are hopelessly vulnerable to humor, because humor can force us to see the incongruous shortfall between the proud posture and the real truth. This is why those institutions of society that are visible symbols of authority and respectability are such good quarries for humor. Without psychiatry, politics, the clergy, the police, and the military, cartoonists would be unemployed.

One of the greatest incongruities in the world is human pride. A human being lives in God's world, walks on his ground, and is able to breathe his air because of God's sustaining and preserving power and love. People break his laws repeatedly. In an uncertain world, one of the few great certainties is that each one of us will die. The Christian claim is that all of us will then appear before God for evaluation. The incongruity of human pride is that it cannot tolerate this future but builds alternative, distracting scenarios.

Pride focuses on human independence, resourcefulness, self-sufficiency, power, and progress, not on the fragility of health and the inevitability of death. It dwells on many reasons why we can be sure that we are good at heart, and why the bad things that we did could not have been helped. It does not consider that the moral catastrophes of the twentieth century might have something to do with the human nature that we all share. The incongruity is that as dependent creatures we claim independence and self-sufficiency; as those who are morally flawed, we claim innocence from guilt, if not positive goodness.

We know that conquering Roman generals were given the right to have a parade in their own city to celebrate each triumph. With this privilege, there was always a slave provided who would ride in the same chariot with the great man. The slave's unenviable job was, throughout the length of the parade, to say continually to him, "Reflect, victor, that you are mortal." The Romans evidently thought that the conqueror deserved a reality check as part of the celebration of his success. They showed greater sensitivity than the modern world to the destructiveness of pride's illusions.

Many of the writers of the Bible used humor to deflate pride's posturing. Vanity is the most vulnerable to satire of all vices. Jesus was a master at the use of preposterous and absurd images about swallowing camels, logs in the eye, and blind tour guides. He broke through pretense and masks to expose reality and lead his hearers into truth. He used the leverage of humor to push his contemporaries toward the courage of humility.

Trusting God to Take Care of Glory

If we seriously follow the God of the Bible, it means that we trust this God with the matter of our own glory. We must let God deal with our personal reputation, success, and heroic status. Our job is not to establish our own glory on earth, but it is to obey God, wherever that might lead. God is to be our primary audience. He will give true glory where it is due, but he has told us that the first will be last and the last first. That is to say, our human means of keeping score of success is likely to be badly skewed, even upside down.

Dietrich Bonhoeffer wrote of a Christlike person, "Often there is little to distinguish him from the rest. Nor does he attach importance to distinguishing himself, but only to distinguishing Christ for the sake of his brethren."[13]

Here we see something of the radical nature of Christian humility. The most important questions of life are not, How can I be a success? How can I be heroic? or How can I distinguish myself above others? It is rather, How can I imitate the hero in such a way that he will be known to others? Needless to say, it takes courage to live this way in a world where so many spend so much time and energy trying to distinguish themselves by other means. Ironically, one of the most universally acknowledged public heroes in our generation never set out to be a hero in the eyes of the world. Mother Teresa set out to follow Jesus as the hero, doing menial work in a city of teeming millions. Yet she ended up living a life of integrity and inspiring attractiveness to the world.

HUMILITY AND STRENGTH

Humility is strength. If we see humility as it is found in the Bible, there is no danger of confusing it with weakness, low self-esteem, or covert self-promotion. Instead, it is grasping reality in attitude and action. Remember the prodigal son who "came to himself" and, so, came home apologizing to his father and resigning his sonship? The father in the parable granted him only half of his request. He forgave the son, accepting him back with joy. That was the first half. But then he refused to accept his resignation from the family. He was not allowed to resign as a son just because he had failed. He was recommissioned. His identity was to be rooted in being a member of his family, not in his previous mistakes.

In a similar way, the followers of Jesus who were the first to hear this parable did not sit and whimper about what failures they had been, or how helpless they felt. Even after Peter's denial of Jesus, he was welcomed back and commissioned with leadership in the church. Through the power of God, the early Christians took the gospel of Christ to what is now England in one direction and possibly as far as India in another— *within the first generation.*

Jesus' use of the word *meek* is often misunderstood. "Meek" sounds too much like "weak" for its own good. In fact, it has nothing whatever to do with weakness. The word *meek* was used of horses that were able to use their great strength with precise control and even with gentleness. A Christian idea of meekness, which is humility before other people, does not commit us to a limp life of passivity, resignation, or ineffectiveness. It is quite the reverse. A life of true humility is a life unencumbered with the endless obstructions, distractions, demands, and harassments of the "fat, relentless ego." Humility enables us to expend life's energy on what has real and lasting significance. I have written in praise of humility that we might love humility and hunger for it, finding it attractive wherever we see it and having an aversion for arrogance and vanity. If our imaginations are engaged in the heroism of humility and the foolishness of vanity, then with God's help we will become humbler people from the inside out. In Jesus himself we have the archetype of humility. We are called to imitate him.

There are countless examples of Jesus' humility in action while dealing with people. In them we can see the excellence of the way he lived. In a society preoccupied with respectability and hierarchy, Jesus deliberately associated with the outcasts, even when it caused many "respectable people" to disapprove, and discredit his teaching. He was strong enough not to have to fight back when he was scorned and despised. He remained undistracted from his task of service. However, the main demonstration of the humility of Jesus was that he was here at all, that he became a human being, and that he gave his life in our service.

As we struggle in our battles with self-deceit and vanity, we can acutely feel our failure. The task seems too great, our pride too deeply rooted. The apostle Paul wrote to the Philippians, "Have this mind among yourselves, which you have in Christ Jesus" (2:5). This is the great call to imitate a humble person, Jesus of Nazareth. But it seems so difficult.

Notice that Paul began by saying, "Have this mind among yourselves, which you *have* in Christ Jesus." Lest we should get too discouraged by our failures, Paul is not telling us to strive for something beyond our reach and receding into the distance. He is telling us that if we are followers of Christ, we have this mind in us in some way already. If you have trusted in Christ, you have the mind of Christ at work in you, not as a result of your efforts, but because of the work of God that the Holy Spirit has begun in you. He who has begun a good work in us will bring it to completion at the day of Christ Jesus (Philippians 1:6).

Although humility is often scorned, and is rarely associated with our public heroes, it is in fact a necessary part of true heroism. To reject it may have its immediate rewards, but it is also to reject self-understanding and embrace self-deception. Humility requires courage at a deeper level than a single act of bravery. It requires courage in our inmost evaluation of ourselves. In Christ we have the pattern of heroic humility and also the promise to share it with us.

CHAPTER NINE

THE IMITATION OF CHRIST: THE BREADTH OF HEROISM

*The real man is at liberty to be his Creator's creature.
To be conformed with the Incarnate is to have the right
to be the man one really is.*[1]
DIETRICH BONHOEFFER

*For to this you have been called, because Christ
also suffered for you, leaving you an example,
that you should follow in his steps.*
1 PETER 2:21

*And we all, with unveiled face, beholding the glory
of the Lord, are being changed into his likeness
from one degree of glory to another.*
2 CORINTHIANS 3:18

Although Christian heroism begins with humility as its foundation, it does not end there. The Christian faith has a wide vision of what it is to be human. Excellence is very rich and diverse, yet it is not made up of haphazard and fragmented attributes and values. The coherence of Christian excellence is the life we see in the person of Jesus himself. True heroism is found in imitating him.

Jesus' quality of life can work in us like white light entering a prism. Its different virtues are like colors refracted into each human personality in as many different patterns as there are individuals. It is not a process of cloning or mass production, but of individual growth into excellence.

Having focused on one of those colors, the humility of Jesus as it was shown in Christmas, let us look at some of the virtues shown in his three-year ministry. We will then focus on his death, around which biblical writers build so much of the shape of Christian character.

JESUS' LIFE AND MINISTRY
It is impossible to restrict heroic qualities exclusively to certain periods in Jesus' life. For example, humility is seen not just at his birth but throughout his life and at his death. Yet it is still useful to organize our discussion around stages in his life. We will look at the imitation of two aspects of his active ministry—his sense of purpose in life and his love.

Having a Purpose
Jesus always spoke of having come to the earth for a very specific purpose. He did not suffer from a lack of a sense of direction, from aimless wandering or self-appointed crusading. He knew who he was, where he had come from, where he was going, and why. This is because his coming to the earth was the result of the plan of the whole counsel of the Trinity, a plan made in eternity and unfolded in the "fullness of time." He often spoke of how he was fulfilling his Father's will for his life, but he also made it clear that it was his own plan too. He spoke of intentionally laying down his life, "No one takes it from me, but I lay it down of my own accord" (John 10:18). Although it included much suffering and times of apparent helplessness, his daily life was part of a larger plan.

After Jesus' resurrection, the disciples were not sure what to do apart from waiting. They were together, behind locked doors, when the risen Jesus appeared among them. He told them, "Peace be with you. As the Father has sent me, even so I send you" (John 20:21). Just as he had been sent with purpose, so he would send them with purpose, and so he would send us. Their lives would be an imitation of his, in that they too were to be directed in a calling from beyond this world. Our identity as imitators of Christ is to be people with purpose in our struggles, sufferings, joys, and victories.

This is something quite radical in our century. It means that our highest purpose is not manufactured from within us individually, nor is it conferred on us by any human institution (such as the state or the media). It is from God himself.

This may sound strange to modern ears. It is a claim that flies into the face of today's secular orthodoxy. In its most common form, this orthodoxy holds that although there is no objective meaning for human life as such, each of us creates his or her own private meaning for himself or herself. A good example of this creed is in the promotional material of one of the better liberal arts colleges in the United States:

> We live in a vast and random world. The more closely we
> observe, the more complex it becomes. For each of us the
> challenge is to develop a personal understanding of life, and to
> learn to act upon that understanding. A satisfying and mean-
> ingful life must follow.

Although the world is random and without any ordering intelligence, the individual can generate the meaning for his or her life as an exercise of private enterprise. It is not seen as an obstacle that human existence itself is random and without meaning. Satisfaction is assured.

The contrast between this secular creed and the Christian faith is stark. In a Christian worldview, the meaningfulness of both human existence and our individual lives is integrated in God himself. The verdict about the purpose of human life must come from beyond human experience if it is to have any authority. If our purpose is only self-generated, then it has all the authority of a student who makes up an exam, takes it, and then grades himself on it. Without God, there would be no meaning at any level. There would only be the illusions of meaning generated by the hopeful individual or society, private or collective projections into a world with a dead God and the value-horizon missing.

God does not call us to generate our own meanings like alchemists, out of the thin air of an empty universe. But meaning and purpose on both larger and smaller scales are implicit in Jesus' statement "even so

I send you." He has called us all alike to serve him in the general sense of being his followers, but then he sends each one of us out with a vocation or calling to serve him in a way that is specific to us as individuals.

Allow me to reiterate. Jesus told his disciples, "Peace be with you. As the Father has sent me, even so I send you" (John 20:21). He was sent by the Father with a task to accomplish. We are to imitate him by living purposeful lives ourselves, and his peace will be with us.

Jesus' Love

One of the main themes of Jesus' three-year ministry, and one of the overarching categories of human excellence, is love. He described his relationship to his people as that of a shepherd to his sheep. A paid hand will care for the needs of the sheep until he is in danger personally, then he will run for his life, leaving the sheep to fend for themselves. But the good shepherd loves the sheep and chooses to make their welfare his commitment, even to the point of death. Jesus called himself the "good shepherd" in just those terms (John 10). The love of the good shepherd is one of the most basic virtues held before us for imitation. We are called to imitate his love for us personally, love that we have first received from him.

On the last night of his life on earth, Jesus met with his disciples. He knew that the mob coming to arrest and kill him were already on their way, yet he gave some of the most profound and expansive teaching of his whole life that night. He told them, "This is my commandment, that you love one another as I have loved you. Greater love has no man than this, that a man lay down his life for his friends" (John 15:12-13). They were not meant just to love each other, but to love each other as he had loved them. They were to imitate his love.

Jesus' teaching about love was one of the most distinctive themes in his whole ministry, especially given the way he demonstrated it in action. His love stretches from his concern for the smallest details in the lives of individuals to actions that have cosmic and eternal significance for all people. Let us look at how he treated some of the people in his path.

At the start of his ministry, Jesus went to a wedding at Cana of Galilee (John 2:1-11). A couple, who must have been friends of Jesus and his family, invited Jesus and his disciples to their wedding reception. In the middle of the feast, the caterer ran out of wine and seemed to have no way of getting more. This would have been a painful humiliation for the couple at the start of their married life. Jesus changed six very large jars of water into wine so that the party could go on, much to the consternation of two groups of present-day Christians (some are offended that he made a drink with alcoholic content, and others are embarrassed that he seemed not to have respected the laws of science).

In this first miracle, Jesus showed his commitment to the start of a marriage, that it might be a properly festive occasion. But he also showed his concern for the feelings of these "little people," whose names we do not know, that they be saved from embarrassment. What an extraordinary thing that the Lord of lords, the King of kings went out of his way to keep this couple from humiliation!

Jesus had already tangled with the religious leaders on one of their "sacred-cow" issues—an overly restrictive Sabbath observance—when he walked into their synagogue in Capernaum. It was a Sabbath day. He had broken their Sabbath rules before without apology. On the Sabbath you were allowed to take measures to keep some wound or sickness from getting worse—for example, to put on a bandage to stop someone from bleeding. But you were not allowed to do anything to make it get better, such as putting ointment or salve on the bandage. That was work, and therefore prohibited on the Sabbath.

On earlier occasions, his Sabbath healings had taken them by surprise. This time they were waiting for him. Sure enough, there was a man there with a withered hand. Would Jesus heal him or not? Since healing on the Sabbath was against their law (although not against the law of God), the leaders watched him intently. Jesus said to the man with the withered hand,

> "Come here." And he said to them, "Is it lawful on the sabbath to do good or to do harm, to save life or to kill?" But they were silent. And he looked around at them with anger, grieved at their hardness of heart, and said to the man, "Stretch out your hand." He stretched it out, and his hand was restored. The Pharisees went out, and immediately held counsel with the Herodians against him, how to destroy him. (Mark 3:3-6)

Think about the way Jesus' love for the man drove him to anger with those who would have, in the name of God, prevented the healing. His love was not sentimental or soft. It led him to a defiance against evil that was a great risk to himself, ultimately leading to his death. Jesus seemed to make a point of Sabbath healing in the temple and in synagogues. I often wonder if he did not intentionally heal on that day, and on their own "religious turf," in order to challenge the religious establishment with a different gospel—because he loved them, too.

We are given the direct command to love one another as Jesus loved us, but we are also pointed to Christ as the model of love in several other, more specific ways. The apostle Paul tells us, "Welcome one another, therefore, as Christ has welcomed you, for the glory of God" (Romans 15:7). Love is to be expressed especially to the stranger or newcomer, the one who is different from us. It will involve hospitality. Again, Jesus' life is the paradigm.

When he was encouraging the Corinthian church to finish taking a collection for poorer Christians, Paul gave them the reason why, "For you know the grace of our Lord Jesus Christ, that though he was rich, yet for your sake he became poor, so that by his poverty you might become rich" (2 Corinthians 8:9). We are to imitate the love shown in the Incarnation by having generosity to others. In doing that, we are reflecting to others what Jesus has done for us.

Last, Paul focused the imitation of Christ's love specifically on the quality of the husband's commitment to his wife: "Husbands, love your wives, as Christ loved the church and gave himself up for her" (Ephesians 5:25). The love of Jesus in his willingness to die for us is the pattern here. Most husbands would at least hope that they would risk their lives for their wives if there was a lunatic running at her with an axe. But would as many be willing to take the lesser step of jeopardizing their careers for the growth of their wives? The imitation of Christ has far more to do with the daily issues of life than with dramatic, imagined events that are unlikely ever to occur.

As we think about imitating the love of Christ in all its diversity, we quickly realize that we are striving toward something that challenges us to the depths of who we are. There can be no little checklist to give us a satisfied assurance that we have "made it." Although the imitation of Christ's love necessarily involves action, it is not limited to easily measurable behavior. It reaches into our deepest convictions, motivations, and patterns of putting them into practice.

Jesus said, "This is my commandment, that you love one another as I have loved you. Greater love has no man than this, that a man lay down his life for his friends" (John 15:12-13). Here is the standard. The love of Christ requires even the ultimate self-sacrifice, and therefore, of course, everything short of that as well. But even on the extreme possibility of the sacrifice of one's life, the imitation of Jesus' love is not a matter of simple observable behavior.

Some few years after Jesus gave his life, Paul wrote a famous chapter on love in his first letter to the Corinthians. He introduced it by telling them, "And I will show you a still more excellent way" (1 Corinthians 12:31). He was leading their attention away from the competitive measuring of their respective gifts, toward true excellence. Paul began by reflecting on the problem of motivation: "If I give away all I have, and if I deliver my body to be burned, but have not love, I gain nothing" (1 Corinthians 13:3).

What was he saying? He meant that one can even go to the absolute extremes of generosity or self-sacrifice but do it without any love at all! It is therefore useless in its value to God's kingdom. This is because it is possible to do "heroic" things out of a spirit of pride, exhibitionism, the love of praise, or even in order to cause others feelings of guilt and inadequacy. We all know those whose generosity in "giving" money or material things is a means of controlling the one who receives them. The command to love as Jesus loved is a searching beam of light into the recesses of our inner lives, calling for profound resources of integrity, compassion, and humility.

Love, as much as any other single virtue, spans the entire scope of human excellence. Consider Paul's introduction, "I will show you a still more excellent way" (1 Corinthians 12:31). Jesus was able to summarize God's whole desire for our race with the word *love*. In answer to the question "Which commandment is the first of all?" he said,

> "The first is, 'Hear O Israel: The Lord our God, the Lord is one; and you shall love the Lord your God with all your heart, and with all your soul, and with all your mind, and with all your strength.' The second is this, 'You shall love your neighbor as yourself.' There is no other commandment greater than these."
> (Mark 12:29-31)

Love is the operative word of excellence here. Love, understood in all its height, breadth, and depth, satisfies the whole of God's law.

A person who loves in the way Jesus loved may well get stepped on, and may not be the center of attention as much as others more eager for that position. The one who mirrors Jesus' love will certainly get hurt and will probably get "taken in" occasionally—but will not be too shocked by that. He or she will also be thought foolish some of the time. But whatever else you might say of this person, do not make the mistake of thinking that he or she is weak. Think of the strength required to free yourself from your own concerns and reach out to see, hear, and meet the needs of the hardest-to-love people. Think of the strength it takes to keep on loving a person after he or she has rejected you.

Once we have understood something of the love of Christ, and have seen it as true excellence, we may then hunger to live out more of it. We will quickly discover that we fall far short of his love, and that even some of our best efforts to love those most lovable and closest to us are shot through with selfish motivations and manipulative strategies. If we see this, we have come to a fork in the road. Some will back off from the whole project because of the pain of facing failure. Others will dare to experience the self-awareness that confronts them if they understand their failures with humility. If we do risk this self-awareness, then we are in a position to call on the God of love and mercy for the strength to grow toward excellence.

JESUS' DEATH

Much of the explicit teaching about the imitation of Christ in the New Testament centers around his crucifixion. This is because Jesus' purposeful self-sacrifice brings many of the Christian heroic virtues together. The writers of the gospels invited us to meditate on the cross by letting the last week of his life take up a disproportionate amount of the space in their telling of his story. The writers of the epistles also spend much of their time reflecting back on the cross and its significance. When Jesus told his disciples to take up their cross and follow him (Matthew 10:38), he meant the cross to be an integral part of the way we lead our daily lives.

The eleventh chapter of Hebrews gives an account of some of the heroes of the Old Testament and tells us to run the race of faith that is set before us. The climax of the passage says we are meant to run it "looking to Jesus the [hero] and perfecter of our faith, who for the joy that was set before him endured the cross, despising the shame, and is seated at the right hand of the throne of God" (12:2).

That is to say, there are many heroes of faith who can inspire us, but we are to live looking directly to the one who sacrificed himself for the joy of reconciling us to the Father. He is the ultimate hero of our faith. There are two heroic virtues that we are specifically called to "look to" in this verse—despising the shame of the cross, and the courage to endure the cross itself. We will then turn more briefly to three other virtues associated with the cross—the willingness to suffer unjustly, to forgive, and to serve.

Despising Unjustified Shame

What did it mean that Jesus despised the shame of the Crucifixion? Did it mean that he did not care very much about it, or feel the pain because it did not really hurt him? For example, Maharishi Mahesh Yogi claimed that "if we want to hold Christ as the Savior of mankind, then we are doing him the greatest injustice if we say he suffered."[2] This cannot possibly be meant, because all the accounts point to the terrible seriousness of the cross in Jesus' own mind, and the ghastly suffering that it actually caused him. There is no hint that for him it was "no big deal." All evidence points in the other direction.

Jesus despised the shame that his enemies—both Jewish and Roman—had tried to inflict on him. They exposed him to the most extreme torture available to their technology and the ultimate in shame according to their own standards of humiliation. He was tried as a criminal, spat on, beaten, mocked, and then nailed to a cross and left there. He was tortured to death slowly in a public place for all gawkers to see. In the Jewish mind-set crucifixion also marked one who is especially abandoned by God and under his curse.

Jesus did not merely brush this aside with indifference. But he despised the shame of all they could do to him in that he did not retreat from it, but willingly walked into it with his eyes open.

The greatest horror of the cross was invisible to most who observed him. It was the pain of alienation from his Father as he was cursed for our sin. He had contempt not for the people who crucified him but for their ideas of glory and for the power they thought they had over him. Their greatest threat had no leverage on him. He was not turned aside by Pilate's bewildered and exasperated question, "Do you not know that I have power to release you, and the power to *crucify* you?" (John 19:10, emphasis added).

We get a glimpse of his own ideas of glory as we listen to his words to his disciples the night before he was killed. Just after Judas left, he started telling them of his imminent death. He said, "Now is the Son of man glorified, and in him God is glorified; if God is glorified in him, God will also glorify him in himself, and glorify him at once" (John 13:31-32).

What a contrasting picture of crucifixion this is! From the point of view of his enemies, it was the ultimate shame that they could possibly heap on him. But Jesus saw it from a completely different perspective, and with the exact opposite conclusion. They thought of shame. He thought of glory, glory, glory, glory, glory—as he described the events of the next day to his friends, he used the word *glory* five times in this one sentence!

What kind of a bizarre attitude was this? One is tempted at first to see him as some kind of masochist or ascetic. In fact, the answer goes in a completely different direction. He promised the disciples that they would see glory, and that is exactly what happened. They would see glory because they were about to see into the character of God the way no human beings had ever been able to. To see the character of God is to see glory, excellence itself at its ultimate source. They would see the glory of the radical love of God in a way that had been hinted at but never before so fully revealed.

In the horror of the suffering of Jesus Christ, we, too, have the largest window into the glory of God's love for his people, a measure of the extent of God's commitment to us. It is the glory of radical love, which is not pretty in a fallen world desperately in need of redemption. In its very horror, blood, pain, and alienation is its glory. *God* was willing to do this for us! *He* went this far for love. "For God *so* loved the world that he gave his only Son, that whoever believes in him should not perish but have eternal life" (John 3:16, emphasis added). It was the just punishment for the sin of all who would ever trust in him that caused his suffering. It is glory because it provides the atonement for our salvation. In making that payment, God gave us this unique revelation of his character. If Jesus had contempt for the pseudohero systems of power and finery and the false shame that they would cause, how can we imitate that? It means that we need to emulate his freedom from the influence of fools and false hero systems, and his loyalty to the glory of love. In a world filled with dynamic and attractive fools and pseudoheroes, it means that having and living by true heroes is itself heroic. We are to imitate Jesus' example, who defied the power of his society to control him by shame.

If we emulate him it means that we are willing to undergo shame and humiliation in the eyes of the world around us. It is not that rejection will be painless. But it does mean that what we suffer for Christ is not justified shame in any true sense, but actually glory when seen from the eye of God.

As we imitate Jesus' ability to disdain the shame inflicted by the world on us, we are standing with imaginative moral vision against vast powers that would force us to conform. Think of the battles within any one of us who lives in a highly materialistic and consumer-oriented society. If God should call us to do so, can we live with a much lower income or standard of living than our peers—in order to follow Christ more single-mindedly? The real question is not whether we *can* do it, but whether we can do it joyfully, knowing that it is our glory to do it. If we can, it will not be only because we are critical of the world's materialism but because we have a positive and lasting glory to put in its place, the true glory of God in the face of Christ.

Courage and Endurance

One of the virtues almost universally associated with heroism has been courage. For example, it is almost impossible for most of us to consider its opposite, cowardice, as heroic. Although Christian heroism is far broader than courage alone, certainly courage is an indispensable part of it. The writer of Hebrews tells us to look to Jesus, who "endured the cross" (12:2), and to "consider him who endured from sinners such hostility against himself, so that you may not grow weary or fainthearted" (12:3). The endurance described here is courage over time. This is not the single-act heroism of a daring exploit that might be over in a few seconds. This is the long-term refusal to give in to fear, threat, discouragement, exhaustion, and pain.

We see this courage in Jesus' decision to "set his face to go to Jerusalem" (Luke 9:51), knowing full well what would happen when he got there. We usually think of courage as willingness to risk loss to reputation, career, life, or limb. Our courage is in proportion to how much we risk losing, and how great the risk is of losing it. The courage of Jesus goes the full distance. For him it was not even a matter of risk. It was a certainty, and what he would lose would be his life itself in the most painful conceivable way.

We do not know at what point in his life Jesus became aware of his eventual crucifixion, but by the time his public ministry began he was fully aware of it and lived with it for the next three years. Only by having courage over time was he able to resist the recurrent temptations to abort his mission and bypass the cross. He lived with death threats for the whole of those three years. Through courage he bore the scorn, misunderstanding, and rejection that labeled him an imposter and rebel against God and Moses. With courage he stood trial in a rigged court. Instead of trying to back down and keep a low profile to avoid their anger, he sealed his own doom by revealing himself clearly in his trial as the Son of Man who would be "seated at the right hand of Power, and coming with the clouds of heaven" (Mark 14:62).

What would it mean for us to imitate this courage of Jesus? Courage is a mysterious quality, easily confused with self-destructiveness, resignation, or foolish risk taking. It is not a devaluing of life or a negation of life's blessings, but it is to be free to respond to life's highest priorities. The words of Dr. Martin Luther King, Jr., are extreme as they stand, but are clearly backed by his life, and are in the right direction: "If a man has not found something he will die for, he is not fit to live." G. K. Chesterton has done as well as anyone at expressing its paradox:

> Courage is almost a contradiction in terms. It means a strong desire to live taking the form of a readiness to die. "He that will lose his life, the same shall save it," is not a piece of mysticism for saints and heroes. It is a piece of everyday advice for sailors or mountaineers. . . . A man cut off by the sea may save his life if he will risk it on the precipice. He can only get away from death by continually stepping within an inch of it. A soldier surrounded by enemies, if he is to cut his way out, needs to combine a strong desire for living with a strange carelessness about dying. He must not merely cling to life, for then he will be a coward, and will not escape. He must not merely wait for death, for then he will be a suicide, and will not escape. He must seek his life in a spirit of furious indifference to it; he must desire life like water and yet drink death like wine. No philosopher, I fancy, has ever expressed this romantic riddle with adequate lucidity, and I certainly have not done so. But Christianity has done more: it has marked the limits of it in the awful graves of the suicide and the hero, showing the distance between him who dies for the sake of living and him who dies for the sake of dying.[3]

Lest we should think that courage were demanded of us only on those rare occasions of high adventure, we must realize its importance in virtually all of life. This was well put by Yale theologian Paul Holmer:

> It is as if every person is being outfitted and made ready for the dangerous world and a world in which the qualities of the individual begin to count very much indeed. These qualities come very slowly and eventually become virtues or vices. . . . To take one example, courage is not . . . only "one" among several

virtues. Rather, it is the very form itself of any and every virtue at its testing point.[4]

What can any virtue mean if it is without courage? It means that it exists only until it is put to the test, then it crumbles. What is it worth? What is love that loves only until loving is difficult and then turns into hatred? We can see that courage is a hinge pin without which moral character does not hold together. Without it, all of our good qualities disappear in the face of fear, seduction, or discouragement. Being able to imitate Christ in his courage becomes necessary not just for the day when we might hear the sound of people's cries in a burning house, but for the growth of character itself.

J. R. R. Tolkien has given us a glimpse of the nature of heroism as it intersects our daily lives. The heroism of the Hobbits is not in the manner of Errol Flynn or John Wayne. They are creatures who enjoy their dinner on time and their evenings by the fire. They know about the paralyzing effect of fear. In fact, they do not go out of their way to look for adventure at all. Yet they are faithful in ordinary things, and when adventure does push its way into their lives, they rise to courage in remarkable and yet very believable ways. They often end up doing things that they themselves would never have thought possible before. Tolkien shows us a glimpse of the Christian idea of courage whose roots are less in high drama than in faithfulness and reliability in ordinary life. He offers us a picture of accessible heroism that can work in a real world.

I am often struck by the lives of those who have shown Christlike endurance-courage, doing the right thing in the teeth of great resistance, over a long period of time. It often follows the Hobbit pattern. Samuel and Pearl Oliner, in their study of those who helped Jews during the Nazi era, *The Altruistic Personality*,[5] record that most of the rescuers were not conscious of doing anything particularly courageous or heroic. It was the same with the residents of the French Huguenot village, Le Chambon, who together managed to save three thousand Jewish children during that same period. When asked why they helped those most dangerous guests, they replied, "What do you mean, 'Why?' Where else could they go?" "How could you turn them away?" "What is so special about being ready to help? There was nothing else to do."[6]

What kind of person cannot think of anything else to do in such danger? Most people in Germany and the occupied countries could and did think of all sorts of other things to do, things that were much safer. A person who cannot think of anything else to do in that situation is not lacking in intelligence or imagination, but has simply formed a deep habit of being a compassionate and courageous person when life was more "ordinary." The cowardice of noncompassion is not an option.

A Dutch watchmaker, Corrie ten Boom, wrote an autobiographical account of the same period called *The Hiding Place*.[7] She and her family ran a clock and watch-repair shop in Haarlem. Their lives were predictable to an extreme. Yet they were a family of deep compassion and commitment to Christ. Their home was a boundless source of hospitality and warmth, extended to everyone from fostered children to the hungry, poor, and needy. When the war came, they simply kept on doing what they had been doing all along—except that then those most in need of hospitality were escaping Jews. Corrie, though aware of the danger and no stranger to fear, was scarcely aware that she had gradually become a leader in the resistance movement. What unfolded was a hair-raising drama of escape, betrayal, concentration camps, and the death of several of her family members. But throughout, there was a sense that they were simply doing what had to be done in a broken world.

When people play down their own courage, it is easy to mistake it for false modesty. I suspect that, rather, there is a greater continuity of life between the ordinary and the extraordinary than we usually think. Patterns of character, whether vices or virtues, are formed in our normal, seemingly humdrum existence. Although they are not unchangeable, they usually follow us wherever we go. It means that the best training for courageous living may not be in the martial arts as much as in simply living with deep integrity.

Although we have focused on Jesus' long-term courage as he approached the climactic end of his life, we must not forget that he also lived out great courage all along the way. He was consistently unwilling to be compliant in the face of an evil status quo. He actively resisted injustice, lack of love, and hypocrisy countless times. He can therefore be emulated in our day-to-day battle to live faithfully as well as in the more dramatic events of life. The writer of Hebrews tells us to "consider him who endured from sinners such hostility against himself, so that you may not grow weary or fainthearted" (12:3). Considering Jesus' example is the place to begin if we want to overcome exhaustion and resist faintheartedness.

Suffering Unjustly

The command to imitate Jesus in his suffering is difficult to understand, more difficult to obey, and more difficult still to want to obey. Suffering has never been popular, and especially so when it is not deserved. The hedonistic priorities of modern Western culture create a deep tension with Christlikeness at this point. Jesus was the "man of sorrows," and if he is the model of human excellence, following him into his excellence will involve suffering. Love and courage demand willingness to suffer, but the imitation of Jesus' unjust suffering is taught so pointedly that it demands separate attention. In a section of his first letter telling servants to be submissive to their masters, the apostle Peter calls all Christians to follow Christ in this radical way:

> For one is approved if, mindful of God, he endures pain while suffering unjustly. For what credit is it, if when you do wrong and are beaten for it you take it patiently? But if when you do right and suffer for it you take it patiently, you have God's approval. For to this you have been called, because Christ also suffered for you, leaving you an example, that you should follow in his steps. He committed no sin; no guile was found on his lips. When he was reviled, he did not revile in return; when he suffered, he did not threaten; but he trusted to him who judges justly. He himself bore our sins in his body on the tree, that we might die to sin and live to righteousness. By his wounds you have been healed. For you were straying like sheep, but have now returned to the Shepherd and Guardian of your souls. (1 Peter 2:19-25)

Again we see the pattern, "Do this because I have already done it *for you*." It is as if Jesus had said, "The suffering that I suffered unjustly had your name on it and was due justly to you. I have borne it in your stead, that you not be destroyed by it. As I lived and died for you, let the willingness to suffer injustice from others and for others be part of your lives." We are expected to respond in kind to his sacrifice.

It is no secret that it is hard to suffer unjustly. I find that when my own reputation or future is at stake, my sense of justice is more fine-tuned than at any other time. I doubt that I am alone. We hate to be misunderstood, to be blamed for something we did not do, or to suffer for another's wrongdoing. One of the best ways of provoking a violent reaction is to blame someone for something that person did not do—and this starts at a very young age. Everything within us seems to call for vindication . . . now! Yet Jesus was not just willing to bear some misunderstandings and blame for the odd crime. He willingly bore the full judgment for all the sins of all of those who would ever trust in him. It was suffering unjustly on a cosmic scale.

The moment we grasp Peter's meaning here, all kinds of questions leap to mind. Am I ever allowed to defend myself? Is suffering good in itself? How would this be expressed today?

Although Jesus was for the most part silent before his accusers at his own trial, this was because of his submission to what he knew to be the will of God in his crucifixion. He had been far from silent at earlier times in his life as he was accused of heresies, blasphemy, and allegiance to the Devil. He repeatedly answered charges that were made against him and gave challenges back. The apostle Paul, who was quite willing to suffer injustice—and did, with many beatings and years of imprisonment—felt no obligation to suffer if he didn't have to. He never went looking for persecution. He appealed to the law protecting him as a Roman citizen to avoid being scourged without a formal trial (Acts 22:25). In the Bible, suffering is never seen as good in itself. Yet suffering must be born if we expect to honor God in a bent and twisted world that resists God's work. We will encounter it along the way of serving God, and do not need to look for it. God also can use it in our lives to make profound changes for the good, but this still does not mean that suffering itself is good. Aleksandr Solzhenitsyn claimed to actually be grateful for his imprisonment under Stalin—not because he thought concentration camps were nice, or ultimately good, but because it took that imprisonment to shake him free from his enslavement to Marxism.

The imitation of Christ in suffering unjustly will be increasingly radical in this world, and will put Christians on a different path from much of the rest of society. Willingness to suffer unjustly is the commitment to love uphill, against all the natural forces that would encourage us not to. Do we really believe that it is our *"glory* to overlook an offense"? (Proverbs 19:11, emphasis added). Jesus did, and he was as far from being a wimp as you can get.

Forgiving

Another side of the imitation of Christ in his death is the imitation of his forgiving. Forgiveness is central to all that Jesus came to accomplish. If you were to subtract forgiveness from it, there would be no Christian religion left. Paul stated our obligation clearly: "Be kind to one another, tenderhearted, forgiving one another, as God in Christ forgave you. Therefore be imitators of God, as beloved children" (Ephesians 4:32–5:1).

Here is the same dynamic as above. Paul did not tell us just to forgive, nor even to forgive because Jesus forgave. He told us to forgive others "as God in Christ" forgave us. Forgiveness is the reflex of redemption, our interpersonal response to God's freely given pardon.

One of the most instructive accounts of Jesus' forgiving is the story of his forgiveness and commissioning of Peter. Peter had just denied him three times. This was after boasting that even though all the other disciples might abandon Jesus, Peter would stand by him. But within hours, in the fear of being arrested himself, Peter swore that he did not even know Jesus although he had been his friend and follower for three years.

It would have been so "human" for Jesus to resent Peter for this betrayal at his time of great need. It is the sort of event that can end a relationship, with even family members not talking for years afterward. However, in the last chapter of the Gospel of John we read of Jesus' next meeting with Peter alone. He very gently made sure that Peter did not still think he was above all the other disciples, and then placed him in leadership in the church (John 21:15-19).

We often fear that if we were to live out this pattern of forgiveness, our life story would simply be that of a human doormat, always walked on and always saying, "Oh, that's okay." In fact, that is not what a commitment to forgiveness means. Jesus was far from being a doormat. His life changed the world more than any other single human life. His forgiveness never meant that he was too bashful to confront people, or afraid to resist evil around him. So it should be with us if we imitate him.

In fact, forgiveness is a doorway to growth and strength. Its only alternative is a dehumanizing and life-shrinking resentment. We sometimes experience this resentment as our "right" because we have been so clearly wronged. Yet it consumes us, narrowing our perception of the world and poisoning our other relationships.

Forgiving freely is tapping into Christlikeness. It is only when we stop resenting others that we can really take responsibility for our own lives. Forgiving is to give up blaming others for our frustrations, deprivations, and inadequacies. The forgiver does not need to say, "No one seriously hurt me," but rather, "All sorts of people have hurt me, some very seriously and painfully, but I refuse to hold it against them." With forgiveness comes greater freedom to focus on what we *can* do with our lives, instead of focusing on what we can't do because of what was done to us.

As with so many aspects of Christian heroism, we confront a paradox. Forgiveness appears to be a response of weakness or passivity. In fact, it is overwhelmingly an act that empowers us, freeing us to transcend injury as much as is possible as broken people in a broken world.

Service

Again we confront a paradoxical truth about human greatness. What seems lowly and demeaning turns out to be greatness on a larger scale of measurement. We are to imitate Christ in his role as a servant.

Let me begin with one of the more uncomfortable experiences that Jesus put his disciples through. He was with them at supper on the night he was arrested (John 13). Since they wore sandals, and the roads were dusty, it was the custom for a host to have a slave wash the feet of all guests who came to a meal. For some reason, on this occasion, it had not been done. During the meal, Jesus got up, put on the towel of a slave, and proceeded to wash all of their feet. One can imagine their confusion! Perhaps some of them had thought of doing it themselves, but it had been too humiliating a thought. Why should they do such a demeaning thing for those who were their equals, after all? But then Jesus, their master, the one whom they had come to believe was the Messiah of God himself, got up and did it! How much *more* humiliating this was! But Jesus asked them:

> "Do you know what I have done to you? You call me Teacher and Lord; and you are right, for so I am. If I then, your Lord and Teacher, have washed your feet, you also ought to wash one another's feet. For I have given you an example, that you also should do as I have done to you. Truly, truly, I say to you, a servant is not greater than his master; nor is he who is sent greater than he who sent him. If you know these things, blessed are you if you do them." (John 13:12-17)

In those few minutes during supper, Jesus set an example that for two thousand years has worked as a subversive time bomb in the swirling human passions for greatness. What becomes of our notions of success when the greatest of all behaves like this and tells us to imitate him?

It was not as if service had been a minor theme in Jesus' teaching. Earlier on, when James and John, with the prompting of their mother, were asking for specially reserved seats in the kingdom of heaven, Jesus called the disciples together and said:

> "You know that those who are supposed to rule over the Gentiles lord it over them, and their great men exercise authority

over them. But it shall not be so among you; but whoever
would be great among you must be . . . slave of all. For the Son
of man also came not to be served but to serve, and to give his
life as a ransom for many." (Mark 10:42-45)

The force of his words here are not just that we should serve, but that
we should imitate Jesus in his service. In that is real and true greatness.
But here again, we have a clear collision of heroic values. So often
greatness has been measured by the distance we are above menial service to others. It is more a question of how many people serve you or are
"under" you. If you are really great, there are servants by the thousands
whose careers are bent to the shape of your decisions and needs.

By comparison, Jesus shines a ray of light into the darkness. He
could have had a monopoly on high-visibility leadership. In fact, he was
offered just that by the Devil. He chose the way of service instead,
which took him to the cross. A hero of service is free from the addictive scrambling of self-serving greatness. According to Jesus, real greatness is measured less by how many people serve you than by how many
you serve. The greatest is the servant of all.

Places of visibility or leadership are not incompatible with a life of
service. Service is an attitude and root of motivation, and can be taken
into many different arenas of life, each with its occupational hazards
and opportunities. In fact, the higher our position in terms of human
authority, the more important it is that we are real servants in that position. The clear force of Jesus' words is that wherever we are, we should
be servants of all.

Having said that, we have a special obligation to serve the vulnerable—the widow, the orphan, the fatherless, the homeless, the poor, the
dispossessed. In the Old Testament, God judges nations not on how they
treat the rich and powerful but on whether they give justice and compassion to the defenseless. If you do not treat the rich and powerful well,
they have ways of getting even—a serious natural deterrent. The
defenseless, by definition, have no such clout. Therefore, the way these
people are treated is God's barometer of the moral quality of a society.

Jesus reaffirmed this Old Testament teaching as he offered the good
Samaritan as the model of how to care for our neighbor (Luke
10:30-37) and counseled that we especially direct our love toward those
who are unable to return it (Matthew 5:43-48). He taught that the way
we treat the least of the hungry, the naked, the imprisoned, and the
stranger, is the way we actually treat him (Matthew 25:42-45).

Service in the life and death of Jesus is heroic not just because it creates warm feelings and is socially redemptive. It is heroic because it is a way of living that corresponds to the truth about who human beings really are. It reflects the intrinsic value of all human beings, not just their positive value *for us* if we treat them well, or what they might do *to us* if we don't. We are all images of God. Our value does not come from our attractiveness, our wit, our wealth, our power, or any other distinguishing trait. By serving the vulnerable and helpless we live out the truth of creation in God's image in a way that nothing else does.

The work of Mother Teresa of Calcutta is a constant reminder and challenge that a life of radical Christian service is not a grim and joy-less process. All who visit her work are impressed by the alleviation of suffering, but also by the joy of those who spend their lives doing it. It is difficult to avoid the conclusion that she has hit on some values that really are valuable, and that hers is a life of excellence.

In the last two chapters we have discussed the imitation of Christ as it is explicitly taught in the New Testament. We have focused on eight virtues, or patterns of motivation and action: humility, living a purposeful life, loving, despising the culture's unjustified shame, courage over time, suffering unjustly, forgiving, and serving. This list is not meant to be exhaustive or definitive, but it does give a good picture of the Christlikeness that we are called to aspire to, the excellence that is to fire our imaginations.

It is intriguing that these patterns closely match both the description of Christian character given by Jesus himself in the Beatitudes (Matthew 5:1-12), and also the fruit of the Spirit as described by Paul (Galatians 5:22-23). We are given three complementary visions of human excellence: from the teaching of Jesus, the example of Jesus, and the working of the Holy Spirit within us.

The shape of Christian character described is unified, an unbreak-able whole. All aspects are damaged if even one is removed. What is love without courage? Courage without love? Any of them without humility? In this picture we do not have an odd collection of traits that some people happen to have found attractive. It is a unity, a coherence that is true humanness in the eye of the Creator of humanity.

Given the sheer height of this standard, we must remember that humility is included as an integral, foundational part. If this high stand-ard is not to lead to despair, it must come with the honesty, courage, and humility to recognize our sin and our need for God's grace. That grace, mercy, and love are open to all who turn to God in humility.

Jesus aimed his most searing satire at those who had seen the standard of God, thought they had lived up to it, and so concluded that they had no need of God's forgiveness. At the same time, his offer of unconditional love and forgiveness was always there for those who were free enough to make that admission.

Before we end the discussion of imitating Christ, there is one more angle that the writers of the Bible point out. It is the imitation of Christ indirectly through the imitation of other people who are Christlike in the past, present, or in fiction, and who can therefore be heroes to us in a qualified sense. We will turn to those people now.

CHAPTER TEN

HEROES NEW AND USED: IMITATING CHRISTLIKENESS IN OTHERS

≋

We come from the creator,
each of us trailing wisps of glory.[1]
MAYA ANGELOU

≋

But the effect of her being on those around her
was incalculably diffusive; for the growing good of the world
is partly dependent on unhistoric acts; and that things are not
so ill with you and me as they might have been, is half owing
to the number who lived faithfully a hidden life,
and rest in unvisited tombs.[2]
GEORGE ELIOT

When you ask people who their heroes are, if they can think of any, they might give you the names of a few people whom they have known personally. They might describe a few great figures from the past or even from fiction. We are all exposed to and surrounded by exceptional people from past, present, and fiction. We do not need to be caught in the swirl of the heroes of the month produced by the media. In it, whoever happens to appeal, excite, and delight is inflated for our entertainment pleasure but is liable to disappear from view and be replaced by another before aspiration can even take aim.

We have seen the heroic virtues of Christ as the measure of excellence. Does that mean that it is a mistake to even see other people as heroic? No, but it is worth thinking carefully about how to do it. We can look to Jesus and also emulate other heroic people who are closer to us in space, time, and circumstance. But we must see them in our peripheral vision. We can imitate Christ indirectly by imitating Christlikeness in other people. It is Jesus' qualities of character that are still the center of our vision.

We will never find a person, past or present, who is heroic in the same sense that Jesus was. But we will find "partial" heroes who live out elements of Christlikeness in marvelous and inspiring but nonetheless imperfect ways. In this way, contemporary, past, or fictional figures can become indirect but powerful ways to imitate Christ. This possibility opens the Christian life to enormous imaginative input.

"BE IMITATORS OF ME, AS I AM OF CHRIST"

People often take offense at these words of the apostle Paul (1 Corinthians 11:1). They consider it the height of conceit that Paul should call attention to himself in this way. Actually, it is not conceit at all. He is not putting himself forward as the human ideal. Notice that he did not just say, "Be imitators of me." The phrase "as I am of Christ" limits the statement drastically. He is saying, "*Insofar* as I am Christlike, imitate me." Any Christian ought to be able to say the same thing. "When and if you see anything in me that is Christlike, take note of it, watch carefully, and make it your own." In Paul's case, this was perfectly consistent with his painful awareness of his failings. He simply recognized that we are all surrounded with people who, despite their failures, still do Christlike things, and that we can learn a good deal by watching them.

An Accessible Heroism

Some object that having another person as a hero is a recipe for frustration and for warping our personalities out of shape. Often those who attract us as heroes are so different from us that we fruitlessly try to force ourselves into a mold that we were never meant to fill. I suspect we have all done this at one point or another. Heroism then becomes the vehicle not for enlargement but for a personal narrowing that brings frustration, shame, and self-hatred.

The answer to this problem is the subject of this chapter. We are to see other people as partial heroes, not total heroes. People who live in Christlike ways are living visual aids for us, not pointing to themselves as ideals of humanity but pointing by the way they live to the character of Jesus.

The writer of the letter to the Hebrews had some very shrewd counsel on this point. He wrote, "Remember your leaders, those who spoke to you the word of God; consider the outcome of their life, and imitate their faith" (13:7-8). The lives of our leaders have made a difference to us. Think about the fruit that their lives have borne. Then imitate their *faith*, not their *lives*. That is, we should not try to imitate their vocation, their vocabulary, their gifts, their opportunities, their physical appearance, their mannerisms, their wardrobes, their education, their property, or their economic status. Although all these things may be attractive, they are likely to distract us from what God does want us to learn from that leader.

When Paul told the Corinthians to imitate him as he imitated Christ, he did not want them to become traveling missionaries, tent makers, or Roman citizens. He did not care if they wore his brand of sandals. If they had all followed Paul in becoming missionaries, it would have emptied and ruined all the churches he had started. They were meant to imitate not his life but his faith, his relationship of trust to God. We, too, are to emulate the faith of those who are Christlike as they live out humility, love, courage, service, and forgiveness in this broken world. If we are to imitate the heroes' faith and not their lives, it makes heroism accessible to us in a way that most modern heroism is not. Modern heroism typically focuses on fame, exceptional talents (especially of leadership), wealth, beauty, and power. The winners are the "beautiful people," and the rest of us are pressing our noses against the glass, observing a heroism that is beyond our reach.

By contrast, heroism as Christlikeness is immediately open to us in hundreds of choices, words, and actions that we make each day. This is not to say that perfection is attainable, or that we could be acceptable to God by means of our own virtue. Rather, it simply means that opportunities to express humility, love, forgiveness, service, and courage surround us all the time. Nobel prizes, vast wealth, beauty, and acclaim are simply not available to us in the same way.

God's standard of excellence is so high that as we try to live up to it, we are faced with our inability to do it. To try is to be reminded again of our ultimate need for the mercy of God. One might think that if we strive toward a standard that we will never actually reach in this life, we would be guaranteed frustration.

Our inability to live completely Christlike lives raises two vital points. First, the entire Christian faith hinges on the promise of God, in Christ, to forgive those who come to him in humility and faith. This is promised from start to finish, and without it, the Christian faith would not exist. This is no small matter. It means that the Christian attitude toward God need never be fear that if we are not good enough we will be rejected. We know from the start that we are not good enough, never will be, and that we fully deserve to be rejected. But the Christian stance toward God is gratitude for having already forgiven us. This is not because we deserved it, but because of what Jesus did on our behalf, and which we received by accepting it as a free gift.

Second, even though we will inevitably fall short of the standard of Christlikeness, the closer we move toward it, motivated by thankfulness, the more we will be enlarged and stretched as human beings. Who was ever constricted by love, courage, or forgiveness, as these virtues are biblically understood? It is just the reverse. They draw us out of our shrunkenness and mediocrity to a greater humanness. The two sides are also inseparable. We must trust in God's mercy—but also in thankfulness—to strive, with his help, to grow toward Christlikeness.

Remember that neither leadership nor publicity is ever essential for heroism. Actually, we know that the first will be last and the last will be first. This means that our cultural scorekeepers, such as *Fortune*, *People Weekly*, *Rolling Stone*, *Sports Illustrated*, and their competitors (all with their different currencies of visible success), are very likely to have gotten the whole thing upside down about who is praiseworthy or important. It is not that leadership or publicity is bad or unheroic. In fact, if we have leadership or publicity, our obligation is all the greater to lead lives that are heroic in order that we would lead well. It is that leadership and fame are not the focus of what God counts as excellence.

For example, one day at the temple, Jesus called the disciples' attention to someone who had gone unnoticed. Probably most people had been impressed by the heavy hitters who contributed to the temple treasury. The Gospel of Mark tells us

> Many rich people put in large sums. And a poor widow came, and put in two copper coins, which make a penny. And he called his disciples to him, and said to them, "Truly, I say to you, this poor widow has put in more than all those who are contributing to the treasury. For they all contributed out of their abundance; but she out of her poverty has put in everything she had, her whole living." (12:41-44)

Jesus wanted the disciples—and us—to notice her. Nobody else did. He wanted us to realize that what we keep back may be more important than what we give. She made a very small contribution to the bottom line, but she made the largest contribution of the day in terms of God's accounting. She was not invited to a special dinner with the high priests in charge of "development" to honor the patrons and patronesses of the temple in the "gold" or "platinum" clubs. Her name was not put on a brass plaque on the temple wall. But Jesus wanted the disciples to see her as a shining example, even though no one else saw her at all. Notice what this says about the accessibility of heroism. It is within reach of our daily choices. You do not have to be rich to be heroic in generosity, only generous with whatever you have.

OBSTACLES TO IMITATING OTHERS
There are more obstacles to imitating others than we could ever enumerate, let alone evaluate. We have already looked at the problem of imitating the wrong kind of people and also the right kind of people in the wrong way. We will look at three further obstructions within ourselves. They are self-deception, laziness, and fear of change. All three can prevent growth through imitating others.

Self-Satisfaction
The first and most obvious obstacle is self-satisfaction. Why should I imitate someone else? Wouldn't I be saying that I am not as good as that person is? Aren't we all equal? Why should I have to learn anything from her? From him?

Although there is some truth behind this objection, it rests on a confusion of moral character with democracy. In democratic nations it is true that individuals, for all their other differences, are (at least in theory) equal before the law. It is also true that as God looks at us, he sees that we are equally images of God by creation, and that we are equally in need of his mercy by sin. Paul even says that between us there is "no distinction" (Romans 3:22). He does not mean that moral distinctions cannot be made between people. He means that even with moral distinctions, everyone is still in the same boat of being helplessly in need of grace. For every single one of us, our dependence on grace is total.

Having said that, there is a standard by which we are measured, and although we all fall short, we are not all in the same place before it. By whatever means, and ultimately it is by God's grace, some have grown and matured in ways that others have not. Understood with these qualifications, we must say that some people simply are not "as good as" others in certain ways, even though it might grate on our democratic ears to say so. The principles of democracy do not commit us to anything so foolish as the idea that moral stature is uniformly distributed throughout any given population. Therefore it does not violate democratic or theological principle to say that some people are better examples of certain virtues than others. It is rather that some level of humility is a prerequisite for emulating any other person. I must be able to admit, "Here is a person whose qualities I have yet to learn. I want to grow in those ways." Without humility of this minimal sort, the dynamics of growth through heroism will lie dead in self-satisfaction.

Laziness

The second obstacle to imitation is laziness. Imitating another person involves the desire and willingness to change, and that in turn requires effort. We can listen again to the writer of Hebrews: "And we desire each one of you to show the same earnestness in realizing the full assurance of hope until the end, so that you may not be sluggish, but imitators of those who through faith and patience inherit the promises" (6:11-12).

Notice that the choice offered here is between sluggishness and imitation. Staying just as we are is often comfortable and always familiar. Changing will be unfamiliar for sure, and perhaps uncomfortable as well. The writer of Hebrews saw the danger of apathy stifling growth that imitation might have accomplished. This is a particular danger for us if we are surrounded by those whose only heroes are the minimal heroes of the hassle-free life. The tragedy of the person who is sluggish in this way is that imagination is disengaged from his or her future. Boredom and escapism are likely to be dominant themes.

Fear

The third obstacle to imitation of others is fear. Two kinds of fear can abort growth through heroism: fear that the person who seems heroic will only let us down; and fear that if we follow someone who is heroic, we will take risks that are too great for us.

The first objection is one of the most common of all, especially in a society steeped in cynicism. It is the fear of disillusionment. Why set yourself up for it? Look at the glorious cast of fallen heroes exposed as jerks and scoundrels! Most of us have had a hero who either betrayed us or the values that we respected him or her for. It is a painful experience that we do not want to repeat. There is always evidence at hand that seems to prove the cynic to be right. What can be said on the other side?

To start with, imitating others for their Christlikeness does not mean that we think they are Christlike in all areas, or even in one area all the time. If we imitate others insofar as they are Christlike, it is a carefully qualified imitation of *partial* heroes. This itself is a protection against disillusionment. We are all broken and imperfect people, but we can sometimes still do extraordinary things that others can learn from.

Although disappointment with a hero is painful, we may even be able to grow through those who ultimately disappoint us. I recently spoke with a man who, when he was a child, had been befriended by an older man. This relationship was a great source of strength and direction to him in the absence of a good relationship with his parents. He later discovered that this older man had less than pure motives for the friendship. This revelation was shattering at the time. However, as an adult, he now realizes that despite the disillusionment, he had benefited enormously from the relationship and hates to think of where he would be without it.

The second kind of fear is that a hero will lead us to make larger commitments than we want to make. This is fear of risk. Again we turn to Hebrews. The letter was written to Christians who were bracing to face persecution, and some of them seem to have been asking, "Is Christ really worth it?" They had not yet had to shed their blood for their faith (12:4), but that threat seemed imminent. A great temptation for them was to shrink back from their earlier commitment. To help them prepare for this trial, the author wrote the eleventh chapter to remind them of the heroes of the Old Testament who were heroes of faith in times of danger and difficulty, the "cloud of witnesses" that surrounds us (12:1). But just before he began this account, he set the stage with a warning:

For you have need of endurance, so that you may do the will of God and receive what is promised.

> "For yet a little while,
> and the coming one shall not tarry;
> but my righteous one shall live by faith,
> and if he shrinks back,
> my soul has no pleasure in him."

But we are not of those who shrink back and are destroyed, but of those who have faith and keep their souls. (Hebrews 10:36-39)

The warning is put in a stark way. The danger was that, through loss of confidence and endurance, they would shrink back and retreat in fear. The result was not that fear would just inhibit their growth but that it would destroy them altogether. It is for contrast to this that he wrote them the eleventh chapter, with the long list of those who did not shrink back. He numbered himself with the Christians to whom he wrote. He put his confidence in them by saying, "We are not those who shrink back."

It is easy to see how this kind of fear cripples imitation. It freezes the flexibility of the imagination into one mode—seeing only the vivid dimensions of approaching disaster. It does not allow the imagination to create and investigate possibilities that could be constructive and good. It sees only what it cannot do, things that will never work. If fear is in control, the fact that courageous heroes have lived before is no help. They were different. If, on the other hand, we have accessible heroes, then they expand our views of what is possible. They push back the "I can't do it" spirit, because they are real people working against what had *seemed* like fixed limits, but who went *through* those limits.

THE LIFE OF FAITH

The entirety of the eleventh chapter of Hebrews is devoted to heroes of faith. It begins with a reflection on faith itself:

> Now faith is the assurance of things hoped for, the conviction of things not seen. For by it the men of old received divine approval. By faith we understand that the world was created by the word of God, so that what is seen was made out of things which do not appear. (verses 1-3)

In describing faith here, the writer is not telling us how to become a Christian (even though that is done by a step of faith). He writes of the life of faith, how someone who is already a Christian lives out that faith. It is by "the assurance of things hoped for, the conviction of things not seen." The Christian is to live out the virtues of Christlikeness, conscious of the presence of God and God's truth, even though he or she cannot physically see God. In this passage faith is not one more virtue added to our list of virtues, but it is the ability to trust God where each virtue is tested. By faith, the Christlike virtues are put into practice in the struggles of life.

Different life situations put each of the heroic Christlike virtues to the test at different times. One time the battle of faith will be whether we will forgive someone who has seriously wronged us. The question might be, do we really have faith that God is there, that his word is true, and that he will one day stand and judge the living and the dead? And does that God, who says he loves us, really want us to forgo spite and revenge to reach out in forgiveness and love?

At another time we might be tested in whether we really have faith that God has a purpose for us when all we can see is the futility of shattered hopes and plans. Or can we stand suffering unjustly, when all we can see is injustice? The battle of faith is whether we can keep on trusting the living God, "that he exists and that he rewards those who seek him" (11:6), even when he and the fulfillment of his promises are invisible to us.

The life of faith rests on the "conviction of things not seen." This has nothing to do with that conviction being irrational or God himself being imaginary. The Christian faith is most certainly not, as the critic's cliché goes, "believing in your heart what your head tells you is not true." It is rather believing on adequate intellectual grounds, with head and heart, that it is true, even though (as with every other worldview) that truth cannot be proved unequivocally in the visible world.

The faith that we see in the lives of the heroes in this chapter goes well beyond the question of intellectual conviction of God's reality. But it is not less than that. It is the ability to live out that well-grounded faith under the enormous stresses that we must live through.

The people addressed in Hebrews faced the likelihood of losing their property, if not their lives. Quite possibly, they could avert this danger by renouncing faith in Christ. To encourage them, the writer turned their minds to heroes of courage and endurance.

We Are Future Blind

These heroes faced extreme uncertainty about their own futures. We read of Noah's faithful response to God's word about "events as yet unseen" (Hebrews 11:7), so that he built a huge boat miles from water. We hear of the faith of Abraham leaving his home and a sophisticated civilization in Ur to wander "not knowing where he was to go" (verse 8), as a nomad living in a tent. We are told of the faith of Moses as he obeyed the word of God against the mighty power of Egypt, ultimately freeing his people from slavery, because "he endured as seeing him who is invisible" (verse 27).

We can see a common thread between the lives of the Old Testament heroes and what we experience daily in (usually) less extreme circumstances. We are all future-blind. Our lives are profoundly affected by events completely outside of our control. Not only that, we cannot even begin to predict life-jarring events, or when they will happen. Think of changes in international economics, war, our physical health, choices made by members of our families, or of a drunken driver veering into our lane of traffic. We are future-blind. We have no way of anticipating these events.

Then we make decisions that affect our own futures and the futures of those around us. But even here, how much do we really know about how these choices will turn out? Of course we can anticipate, predict, plan, have hunches, and make guesses. In fact, part of wisdom is to be able to do this with some competence and accuracy. But another part of wisdom is to know how little we really do know about the ultimate effects of our actions. Wisdom is to be aware of the powerful law of unintended consequences. Here, too, we are substantially future-blind.

The letter of James insists that wisdom depends, at least in part, on the humility to be aware of our ignorance of the future.

> Come now, you who say, "Today or tomorrow we will go into such and such a town and spend a year there and trade and get gain"; whereas *you do not know* about tomorrow. What is your life? For you are a mist that appears for a little time and then vanishes. Instead you ought to say, "If the Lord wills, we shall live and we shall do this or that." (James 4:13-15, emphasis added)

Being blind to the future has always been a source of frustration. One can well imagine Abraham thinking, *If I have to leave Ur, at least I would like to know where I am going and what I am meant to be doing there, how my family will be provided for, whether I will ever come back*—and a few hundred other questions. People throughout history have gazed into crystal balls, examined the entrails of birds, attempted to contact the dead, used the *I Ching*, imagined time machines, and any number of other strategies, all to get a glimpse into the future. "If I take this job, will it be a dead end?" "If I marry this person, will his or her bad qualities grow or wither away?" "If I bet on this horse, will he win or will I lose my shirt?" How we would love to know! How much more peaceful we would be (we think) if we only knew the future!

Our attitude in facing the uncertainty of the future has a great deal to do with the way our futures actually turn out. How do we see the future? What visions guide our choices? The message of James is clear but usually unpopular. We do not need to know our immediate future. In fact, often it would be harmful to us if we did know it. We are to trust the *Person* who will take care of us, not what we think his program for us ought to be.

Faith and Expedience

With the future unknown, one of the most powerful competitors with faith is expedience. Expedience means living by my own ability to predict what will turn out best for me. There are two elements here. First, there is the confidence in my own judgment to determine what is likely to happen and to outwit the law of unintended consequences. Second, there is the assumption that I actually know what my own best interests are and that those interests are the most important things I need to worry about. There is no higher moral norm above my own judgment.

The alternative to expedience offered by the author of Hebrews is faith. Faith by no means excludes common sense, planning, and trying to predict the outcome of various choices as best we can. It certainly does not exclude doing things that are in our own interest. Is faith, then, significantly different from expedience? I think so.

Expedience leads us to trust in a certain predictable program of future events. Faith keeps a looser grip on the predicted program and puts final trust in a Person. This difference is substantial. Faith also predicts but does not rely finally on prediction. Faith chooses according to the word of God, which overrides the authority of our predictions. Would Noah have built the ark as a result of the local weather report? Would Abraham have ever left Ur because he could predict the successful outcome of his journey and the founding of a nation? Would Moses have left the court of Pharaoh with all its splendor because he could see his role as a national liberator? I doubt it. What intervened in all of these cases was God's word. They all could have refused God, and each one did blatantly disobey him at other times, but in the events recorded in Hebrews 11, they acted in faith.

Faith in God is trust in him and commitment to his work on earth. It means that we as individuals are not the center of the world, but we give ourselves to an agenda with goals beyond our own personal satisfaction. We learn to do that from the word of the God whose plan is unfolding.

For example, both Abraham and Moses stepped out in faith, not as a means to the end of self-fulfillment or self-actualization, but because God had told them they had vital roles to play in the nation for years to come. Moses made it very clear what his own interests were—as he understood them. He wanted to retire (Exodus 3–4). It took a great deal of argument, even from God, to pry him loose from this retirement plan. This raises the second problem that faith has with expedience. Given that we are substantially future-blind, do we really know what our best interests are? It seemed more expedient to Moses to grow old in Midian, leaving his people in their slavery.

Take the very common example of lying. People do not usually lie just for the fun of it. People normally lie because of the force of expedience. If I have made a mistake and my boss were to know the truth, my job might be in jeopardy. Expedience also tells me that it is certainly not in my best interests to even risk getting fired. I can predict what the outcome of different courses of action will be—telling the truth will mean a high risk of being fired, lying will mean that the whole matter will be put to rest and never be thought of again. Besides, everybody does it, sometimes. If I am governed by expedience, there is no moral dimension to the choice. My own interest is my highest standard of appeal. If I do not look out for my own interests, who else will?

By contrast, faith confronts the same choice. By faith I know perfectly well that I might be fired, but also that I cannot really know for sure how the boss will respond. I have known people who told the truth, expecting to be fired for it, but who were instead commended for their integrity. The Watergate fiasco was an example of lies not putting anything to rest. Contrary to the predictions of all those involved, the lie made things infinitely worse than an initial admission of the truth would have done. But if I approach the decision by faith, my own prediction of the outcome will not be the determining factor.

There is a word from God that tells me that lying in that situation is morally wrong. Faith means that I let that word be the determining factor. Faith also knows that there is a larger story of which I am a part. My own life's meaning comes from that larger story, not from my ability to fulfill my detailed plans for my life. If I meet this decision with faith, I will know that even if I do get fired and end up suffering for it, that God still loves me, is committed to me, and will see that I bear fruit for him in some way. Some of the heroes of faith led nations and conquered kingdoms, but others were brutally persecuted and killed. All of them were commended by God. Whatever my boss decides, it will be better, and ultimately better for me, if I tell the truth.

Faith is not obeying God because you know in your heart that if you are fired, a better job will be waiting for you. It might be, and it might not be. Faith is not a crystal ball to see into a guaranteed glowing future. That would be a bypass around faith. Faith is the willingness to walk into the future blind, but honoring a trustworthy God in our decisions, whatever the outcome.

Faith, Suffering, and Risk Taking

God never promised immunity from suffering for those who follow him. There is no guarantee of the fulfillment of the "American Dream." When the ten Boom family sheltered fleeing Jews during the Second World War in Holland, they did not do it because they knew they would all remain safe and sound. They did not remain safe or sound. Some of the family lived through concentration camp, others died, all suffered. Although they endured terrible anguish, they did not conclude that God had betrayed their faith but saw his hand in their daily lives.[3]

Although living by faith means taking risks, it is not simply risk taking. Faith is not just being daring. It is actually very shrewd living. Remember our earlier discussion of Jesus' parable of the rich fool (Luke 12:16-21)? Seen from the perspective of only the visible world, he was very wise, and his future was very prosperous and secure with its nest egg. His only problem was bad luck. Yet when seen from the perspective of the invisible world of the living God and future judgment, he was the classic fool. He took an insane risk to dare to be caught bankrupt where it mattered most. Think of Jesus' suggested cost-benefit analysis for us all, "For what will it profit a man, if he gains the whole world and forfeits his soul?" (Matthew 16:26).

The words of missionary Jim Eliot illustrate the shrewdness of faith: "He is no fool who gives up what he cannot keep to gain what he cannot lose." In these terms, what I have described as expedience is, at the end of the day, not very expedient.

Toward the end of Hebrews 11 there is an account of men and women, some named and others unnamed, who were heroic in faith. Let me mention some of my favorite heroic examples from the Old Testament who might have been included among those not named:

Shadrach, Meshach, and Abednego stand out as heroic for three words that they said. Their story is in the third chapter of the book of Daniel. They were ordered to fall down and worship a god made by Nebuchadnezzar, the king of Babylon—otherwise they would be thrown into a furnace. Expedience would have told them, "Oh, go ahead and worship it, it won't make any difference. It is just a religious rite and it will be over in a few minutes. If you don't, it will be certain death, and there is too much good that you could do with your lives to waste them in that way." But they knew that it was wrong to honor an idol as if it were God, and they also knew that the future under God might hold other possibilities, so that they did not rely on their own predictions. They put it this way to Nebuchadnezzar:

> O Nebuchadnezzar, we have no need to answer you in this matter. If it be so, our God whom we serve is able to deliver us from the burning fiery furnace; and he will deliver us out of your hand, O king. *But if not*, be it known to you, O king, that we will not serve your gods or worship the golden image which you have set up. (Daniel 3:16-18, emphasis added)

The essence of their heroism was in the three words "But if not." These words show that they did not know how it would turn out. Like us, they were future-blind. They knew that God was able to rescue them if he chose to, but they had no assurance that he would do it. They were not able to look back on it as a past event and say, "Of course God was going to rescue us." They had had no opportunity to read their story in Sunday school literature. For them it was the present moment, with the future a blank. They said God could deliver them, but even if he did not, they would still not worship the idol. They were the Rhodes and Fulbright scholars of their day, with full lives before them. Yet they were willing to stand against a vast, visible, military, and political power that had already ravished their country and refuse to obey because of their loyalty to an invisible God.

The story of Esther is also powerful. She was a Jew, but queen of

King Ahasuerus of Susa, who reigned from India to Ethiopia. There was a decree that all the Jews should be killed. Mordecai, her uncle, told her to plead with the king for the life of their people. But they both knew that anyone who appeared before the king without first being summoned by him, could be put to death. To persuade her to go, he said:

> For if you keep silence at such a time as this, relief and deliverance will rise for the Jews from another quarter, but you and your father's house will perish. And who knows whether you have not come to the kingdom for such a time as this? (Esther 4:14)

Esther sent back a message requesting that they hold a fast. "Then I will go to the king, though it is against the law; and if I perish, I perish" (4:16). She had no way of knowing how it would turn out. She was future-blind, like the rest of us. But she was willing to perish. As it turned out, she was the one by whom her people were saved, but she only knew that afterward.

At the very end of the eleventh chapter of Hebrews, the writer tells of those heroes who "became mighty in war, put foreign armies to flight. Women received their dead by resurrection" (11:34-35). Then he carries on with the unbroken list of heroes, but there is a change:

> Some were tortured, refusing to accept release, that they might rise again to a better life. Others suffered mocking and scourging, and even chains and imprisonment. They were stoned, they were sawn in two, they were killed with the sword; they went about in skins of sheep and goats, destitute, afflicted, ill-treated—of whom the world was not worthy—wandering over deserts and mountains, and in dens and caves of the earth. (11:35-38)

These were the heroes who risked death for their faith, not knowing whether or not they would be spared, and they were not spared. They suffered both appalling violence and also extreme poverty and homelessness. But we are told that they were "well attested by their faith" (verse 39), and that they were people "of whom the world was not worthy" (verse 38). Think of it. The world with all its power, palaces, armies and navies, wealth and finery was not worthy of those men and women of faith who lived in caves and dressed in animal skins. They were heroes who despised the shame of their society's humiliations and lived trusting a God they could not see. These heroes are an important corrective to anyone who tries to associate heroism with health and wealth. They had the approval of God in the midst of poverty, torture, and martyrdom.

Looking to Jesus

As a climax to the long line of Old Testament heroes, the writer finally tells us that we should "run with perseverance the race that is set before us, looking to Jesus the [hero] and perfecter of our faith" (12:1-2). The heroes in the eleventh chapter were heroic because they were Christlike in certain ways, often at important times for the whole people of God. Most were Christlike in courageous faith and endurance. Those times of faith are held before us for our inspiration and imitation. However, it is Jesus who is still *the* Hero, the paradigm of heroism. All of these heroes were heroic only insofar as they were Christlike. That is why we are told to look to Christ directly, and to all others with peripheral vision, even though others may be closer to us in space, time, or circumstance.

The men and women listed in Hebrews 11 all had feet of clay. They were failures, often appalling failures, in things that really mattered. If you look at their life stories, which were told in other places in the Bible, you will find that some of them murdered, committed all kinds of sexual sins, drank too much, and lied. They all had moments of profound un-faith when fear, greed, pride, and the seductive power of expedience got the better of them.

This is why we were never told to imitate everything about their life stories, especially not their clay feet. It is for the same reason that Paul said, "Imitate me *as I imitate Christ.*" Christ is the standard. But we can be inspired and stretched by past, present, and fictional people as visual aids—Christlike acts, words, and commitments made by extremely broken, fallible people. They show us that it can be done in our world, even by people like us.

The cynic has a quick and easy escape from the challenge of the excellence of another human life. He or she can simply find a major fault (usually not hard to find) and say, "So there! Look at that! Why should I look up to that person?"

A case in point is Dr. Martin Luther King, Jr., whose sexual sins and (more recently) plagiarism have come to light. What do we do with this knowledge? First, we can grieve, because what he did, if accurately reported, was really wrong. But should we then say that we can exempt ourselves from the uncomfortable challenge of his extraordinary commitment to justice and nonviolent social change? Of his enduring courage? Of his forgiveness? Of his willingness to suffer unjustly and without call for revenge? We certainly *can* sidestep his challenge. He has given us the perfect excuse with his failures. But if we do, we will probably also sidestep the challenge of most of the people in the eleventh chapter of Hebrews as well. Who will be the loser?

We have focused on Hebrews 11 because it invites us to imitate those who were heroic in faith. History abounds with fallible men and women who have nonetheless done extraordinary heroic things. We can either ignore these people, or let what they did inspire and extend us.

HEROISM AND THE DIFFERENCES BETWEEN US

As we look at the past or the present, we will see people who show us heroic Christlike virtues. Some, of course, will be easier to identify with than others. It is inevitable that people who have important things in common with us and who succeed in facing the same sorts of challenges that we face, can be especially powerful heroes for us.

A young person will be challenged especially by someone who is also young or just a little bit older. Often those of a racial minority group will find it especially helpful to find another person of their race who is heroic. Men may find male heroes of Christlikeness to be the strongest for them, and women, female heroes of Christlikeness. If there is someone like us in these ways, it is less of a stretch of our imaginations to put ourselves into their shoes. It may make it easier to break the "I can't do it" attitude.

Think of the reluctance of Frederick Douglass, having escaped slavery in the South, to take up the task of speaking against it to white people in the North in 1841. He was a natural orator and had moral passion and extraordinary gifts of intellect. Yet, William Lloyd Garrison described him as initially unwilling to consider this call because "the path marked out was wholly an untrodden one."[4] Or, as Douglass put it in his own words, "The truth was, I felt myself a slave, and the idea of speaking to white people weighed me down."[5] It demanded a momentous change for him, and no one had done it before him. But since he was able to do it, and to do it so well, he has been a hero to countless others who have faced similar obstacles.

Heroism Cuts Across Our Differences

But it is important to point out that *the heroic virtues themselves are the same for all of us.* They cut across all divisions—of sex, race, age, economic status, educational experience, nationality. Heroism is Christlikeness, whoever is living it out. None of these differences should block us from treating people who are different from us as heroes.

There are no distinct masculine and feminine heroic virtues anymore than there are certain virtues that apply to some races and not others. We are all called to imitate the same Christ, to live out the same Beatitudes, to bear the same fruit of the Holy Spirit, to put on the same armor of God. The excellence of Christlikeness is both powerful enough and broad enough to stretch and enlarge any human being toward greater humanness.

Think of how this idea was emphasized in Jesus' teaching. He called everybody to imitate him, not just young adult Jewish males of the artisan class. He expected everyone to transcend their differences to strive toward this goal with God's help.

Jesus seemed to make a point of subverting the pride of superiority that he found in the many hierarchies of his society. He would often challenge those higher on the pecking order to imitate or learn from those who were ranked lower and therefore assumed to be inferior. In a society in which men were assumed superior to women, Jesus often gave women as examples for all to learn from. Why not? There is no reason why the lives of women cannot be profoundly challenging to men, and vice versa. The only obstacle is a social ranking system that gets institutional support from human vanity. Think of the way Jesus held up children to be emulated by adults in all their adult authority, sophistication, and knowledge. He must have driven them wild when he said, "Unless you turn and become like children, you will never enter the kingdom of heaven. Whoever humbles himself like this child, he is the greatest in the kingdom of heaven" (Matthew 18:3-4).

To a society that held the Samaritans in racial, religious, and moral scorn, he told the parable of the good Samaritan. In it, a Samaritan alone exemplified the compassion of being a true neighbor while the officially religious priest and Levite failed. The lawyer to whom Jesus told the parable had been trying to "justify himself." After telling the story of the Samaritan, Jesus told him, "Go and do likewise" (Luke 10:37). He was sent off with instructions to imitate one of the despised race.

Heroism and Fiction

The universality of the heroic virtues of Christlikeness, and the power of the story to carry them, means that works of fiction, drama, or film may be very effective communicators of heroic character. The narrative arts offer an almost limitless resource of good stories at every level of sophistication and for all ages.

The glory and the danger of fiction is its ability to communicate profound truth—or untruth—in an imaginatively powerful way. The author of fiction, for example, gets to play God in the sense that he or she shapes the story in a way utterly impossible for any of us to shape our ordinary lives. Every author gets to decide what choices the characters will make and what the consequences of their choices will be. This power to shape the story in turn gives them great power to influence our minds as we read or see the story. A good question to ask of a narrative is not only "What is the worldview of the author?" but perhaps more to the point, "What does this story make me want to become? What does this story make me want to avoid?"

God's goal is the enlargement of each Christian by imitating Christ through others—in past, present, and fiction. God's commitment to work this in us is disconcerting and uncomfortable because it requires change. Change can be obstructed in many ways, whether our imagination becomes stifled by cynicism, frozen by fear, or atrophied by self-satisfaction. The apostle Paul's appeal to the Christians in Corinth is helpful here: "Our mouth is open to you, Corinthians; our heart is wide. You are not restricted by us, but you are restricted in your own affections. In return—I speak as to children—widen your hearts also" (2 Corinthians 6:11-13).

God's concern is to widen our hearts also. He has no interest in crushing or restricting us. This is why the centrality of the imitation of Christ is so important. It will enlarge us the way no other heroism can. Yet it can help us desire his qualities if we see them in others who become partial heroes in our peripheral vision while we focus directly on Jesus himself.

In an age of celebrity and triviality of public heroes, perhaps our best examples of Christlike heroes will be unsung heroes. Perhaps they will be unglamorous people doing unglamorous jobs. Perhaps they will be lonely and underpaid. They might have spent years in a wheelchair or hospital bed. Yet it may be these people who can inspire us toward greatness in a way that no celebrity can.

The important questions are not, Will I be well known? Will I delight the crowds? but rather, Will God delight in me? The psalmist puts it well:

His delight is not in the strength of the horse,
    nor his pleasure in the legs of man;
but the LORD takes pleasure in those who fear him,
    in those who hope in his steadfast love. (Psalm 147:10-11)

PART THREE

HEROISM AND THE YOUNGER GENERATION

CHAPTER ELEVEN

HEROISM AND
MORAL LEARNING

*The young no longer feel heroic in doing
as their elders did, and that's that.*[1]
ERNEST BECKER

*I am not wise enough to say where the young can find
what they need. Is it possible that all America can offer them
is a list of names and places, and a shopping bag of books
about the world as people conceived it in long ago places
and times? That, and the advice, "JUST SAY NO" to
drugs? Who will help them find out what they need
to say yes to? How can they be helped to read,
and write, a coherent story for our times?*[2]
NEIL POSTMAN

For some years I have lectured on the subject of heroism in the United States and in Europe. No matter what aspect of the subject I have spoken about, if those listening were in their thirties or older, the first questions asked have always been, "What about children?" and "How can we help children to have good heroes?" Heroes are most certainly not only the province of the young. Nevertheless, the flexible, expanding, and powerful imaginations of children make them especially moldable to the shape of people whom they consider heroic. Such malleability means vulnerability. Children form aspirations and aversions at an early age—both good and bad—which may shape the rest of their lives.

There is widespread concern for children in American society today. They are said to be "at risk," in "crisis," or "abandoned" in countless feature articles in our major newsmagazines and newspapers. We are told that children of middle-class parents are paying (without having been asked) the price for their parents' entry in the "rat race." Children of all economic backgrounds are said to be without heroes, and this is taken to indicate that they are alienated from life, especially from adult life. That is to say that while all children are vulnerable, it could well be that this current generation of children is especially vulnerable.

In the short range, there is already widespread misuse of drugs and alcohol, and the collapse of any guidelines for sexual life. The educational system is becoming more and more a source of frustration and disillusionment. The disparity between rich and poor is increasing. There is boredom, a need to escape, a sense of being disconnected from life, and increasing violence, especially in the cities.

In the long range, our children will face all these issues as well as problems on an even larger scale. Some of these challenges will come from inherited problems that today's adult generation has created but refused to face. Problems of national economic indebtedness and environmental irresponsibility will come home to roost within the next generation. American society is also becoming ever more fragmented, with less of a working public philosophy or common sense of the common good. In practical terms, this means that whatever problems we face, we cannot count on meeting them with a strong moral consensus.

Today's children need to be giants of faith and courage right now, but even more into the future. No one can predict how these forces will affect our children's lives. How is the adult generation preparing them for these challenges?

Here is the bad news. The children of today are getting less attention and care from their parents. It is not just that both parents are now working. Historically both parents working has been far more the norm than most people realize. But now both parents are working away from the home. This is a new development. And more and more often two parents are not part of the picture at all. A wise African proverb states that "it takes a village to raise a child." There is no village in the lives of most young people today, let alone one that takes an interest in their growing up. Also, powerful forces in the popular mind devalue children and the time spent caring for them. Social historian Peter Stearns observes,

> The competition demands that we be rational, orderly, forceful and efficient. Children are often non-rational, disorderly, powerless, and redundant. Though we may never have been guilty of physically abusing children, we have verbally abused or ignored them.[3]

We hear of the joys and virtues of being "child-free," especially among DINKs (double income, no kids), but also among those whose children are old enough to be out of the home. We are relentlessly reminded of what an economic liability children are, by voices that children can overhear.

The irony is that these changes are taking place just as psychologists are confirming the need for a high level of involvement of both parents in the lives of children from birth on, for healthy psychological development to take place. There seems to be an inverse relationship between what we know of the importance of parenting in the early years and the amount of time and effort parents are spending with their children. America is at this point doing significantly worse than other industrialized countries.

The scope of these chapters allows us to look only briefly at the child's experience (or lack of it) with heroes. We will start with a contemporary dilemma in the very idea of moral learning in a pluralistic society.

A CONTEMPORARY DILEMMA
One of the major dilemmas in moral education in a secular society starts with its relativistic assumptions about moral values. The relativist holds that since there are no absolute moral standards, all of our values are "relative to" the psychological profile, cultural background, economic

interests, and time in history of the one or ones who believe them. No one has the authority to impose his or her views on another. Because no transcendent standards command us, there is no way, finally, of saying one person's values are better or truer than another's.

What group could be more vulnerable to having values imposed on them than children? What groups would be more likely to do that imposing than parents and schools? Therefore, according to this view, utmost care must be taken not to interfere with the free development of a child's process of moral discovery.

The other side of the dilemma is that most people, even rigorous relativists, do not really live as if there were no final moral guidelines that stand over the individual. They want no absolutes, and they want each person to freely choose his or her own values, but within limits — their limits. They are not at all happy if the values freely chosen are ones that they themselves consider to be either barbaric or personally harmful to them.

The dilemma is experienced especially by the relativist who, despite his or her relativism, is horrified and indignant at Wall Street or Washington corruption, or the injustice of the caste system in India. It is hard to find the modern relativist who considers rape or racism to be simply valid lifestyle options or culturally valid expressions of individuality. One can think also of the confusion that has resulted in classrooms where it was taught that each person is free to choose any values, when students asked, "Then does that mean that I can choose to cheat in this class?"

There is a widespread and growing concern for the teaching of ethics in our society. Ethics is taught not as just an interesting academic subject but in order to teach young people to live lives that build a stable and just society rather than destroying it. The adult generation wants the younger generation to be ethical, for sure. Yet the adult generation does not want to specify exactly what that means, or how they themselves happen to know it. The outcome of the dilemma is that the younger generation is given a confused message: "Be a good person, but do not ask 'why?' or how we have determined 'good' for you, or for that matter, exactly what a 'person' is."

Any generalized plan for moral education faces extraordinary difficulties in a pluralistic society. This is because as soon as almost any value is affirmed, someone else stands up and says, "That is not what *I* believe! You can't teach that to my children with my tax money." Any such program must not be seen to teach specific moral requirements that people could disagree over. It must not seriously challenge relativism.

The Fear of Indoctrination

Let us first say that the concern not to indoctrinate children with prepackaged morality is certainly a valid one. Many people bear the scars left by parents who have tried to bypass their abilities of discernment and choice. Parents and schools have tried to impress their values directly into the minds of children, letting the children have as little to do with the process as possible.

Having said that indoctrination is both counterproductive and morally wrong, we must also say that it is impossible for a parent or school *not* to exert some moral influence in one direction or another. There is no neutrality. Trying to disclaim moral influence on a child simply confuses everybody. There are all sorts of ways that we morally influence any child that we care about. Even if we are parents trying to keep our child free from our own moral influence, *that attempt itself* exerts an immense moral influence from a certain philosophy. It assumes that a child has some innate system of moral direction that will flower if not interfered with by religious or philosophical ideas from others. This idea itself is far from being "objective" or "self-evident." It is made up of doctrines held by faith commitments. There is nothing neutral about it.

But if we try to separate moral choices from the religious and philosophical foundations of those choices, we tend to conceal from ourselves and the child the real issues that are involved in our own moral decision making. We never reveal how we have arrived at convictions about what is ultimately true and good, and how we know them to be true. We can thereby mislead the child to believe that learning to live morally is as disconnected from these larger issues as is learning the technical skills of using a word processor.

Therefore, young people get a message about morality that is confusing. It is as if moral categories were pulled out of some magician's hat. Almost one hundred years ago, G. K. Chesterton saw this coming in his study of both literature and popular moralizing.

> Every one of the popular modern phrases and ideals is a dodge in order to shirk the problem of what is good. We are fond of talking about "liberty"; that, as we talk of it, is a dodge to avoid discussing what is good. We are fond of talking about "progress"; that is a dodge to avoid discussion of what is good. We are fond of talking about "education"; that is a dodge to avoid discussing what is good. The modern man says, "Let us leave all these arbitrary standards and embrace liberty." This is,

logically rendered, "Let us not decide what is good, but let it be considered good not to decide it." He says, "Away with your old moral formulae; I am for progress." This, logically stated, means, "Let us not settle for what is good; but let us settle whether we are getting more of it." He says, "Neither in religion nor morality, my friend, lie the hopes of the race, but in education." This, clearly expressed, means, "We cannot decide what is good, but let us give it to our children."[4]

This vacuum at the "top end" of morality has a profound effect on the nature of moral life that is presented to the younger generation. Look, for example, at the way our society tries to teach specific behavior to the younger generation, such as saying no to drugs and alcohol abuse, sexual promiscuity, smoking, and fast driving.

Fear Is Not Enough
You will notice that the appeal is almost always to self-interest, and that it is usually negative. We are told in graphic detail about what will happen to us if we indulge in the forbidden behavior. We are all treated to photographs of girls with two hundred stitches in their faces, in the hope that we will drive slowly and wear seat belts. We are shown pictures of the tar-caked lung of the cigarette smoker to persuade us to chew gum. We are shown the solemn funeral of the promising athlete who was using cocaine, that we might stay away from the stuff. We see the emaciated body of an AIDS patient, and are told to use condoms.

Young people do need basic information. They cannot be expected to make good decisions about dangerous substances and behavior patterns without knowing some facts. But if the adolescent heroic ideal happens to be in seeing how close you can come to self-annihilation without actually succeeding, this kind of "education" can even be counterproductive. It can fuel the fire, making the dare more daring and well defined, and therefore more alluring. That is not to say that it does more harm than good. Happily, there are also other heroic ideals at work in the youth culture. More importantly, negative information alone has great limitations as a source of motivation.

Do we really think that the widespread abuse of drugs such as "crack" comes primarily from honest ignorance of its harmful effects? Is the spread of AIDS in this country primarily because people are uninformed about how the disease is transmitted? Is the high level of fatal accidents from drunken driving among teenagers really the result of unfamiliarity with the relevant traffic statistics? I doubt it. Most of the young people that I know already know far more gruesome factual information than their parents about all these hazards. Undoubtedly, a lack of knowledge is part of the problem. But far more serious is the problem that too few take what they do know seriously. It is not that all the efforts to educate the young in this way are useless. It is that they are insufficient. There are vital factors missing.

An Accessible Positive Ideal

One thing that is missing is a positive ideal that is attractive and will give the younger generation a powerful reason to live because there is something that they *want* to become. What is missing is a confident, moral, imaginative vision of life. Its absence is what Chesterton called the "great gap in modern ethics."[5] That is to say, there is no believable ideal or accessible heroism.

What is missing is also a sense of personal story—that an individual life, any life, can make sense in terms of a heroic ideal, and be a *good* story because it has a purpose within a larger story. Our potentially good stories can be instantly ruined or ended by any one of the killers that we mentioned; but that danger is unheard and unheeded if there is no awareness of having a good story to lose. Neil Postman, a communications professor at New York University, put it well:

> Children everywhere ask, as soon as they have the command of language to do so, "Where did I come from?" and, shortly after, "What will happen when I die?" They require a story to give meaning to their existence. Without air, our cells die. Without a story, our selves die.[6]

Moral education must acknowledge this need for and fascination with the story. Well-documented, extensive, factual accounts (complete with graphs, photographs, and tables) of what ought to be horrifying dangers may be motivationally feeble in the lives of those who most need to pay attention to them. Statistics do not do well when pitted against the powerful self-destroying heroic visions sustained by the youth culture through music and film.

Theories of Moral Development

It is little help that neither of the two leading theories of moral education, the "values clarification" approach and the "cognitive development" theory of Lawrence Kohlberg, pay any attention to the significance of the imagination and the need for a positive moral vision. They present not stories but only open-ended dilemmas and discussions in a historical and narrative vacuum, careful not to suggest that the parent generation has anything of moral legitimacy to pass on.

By contrast, the most skillful generators of motivation today are in the advertising industry. *They* are not ambivalent, confused, ashamed, or even shy about telling us of the ultimate good, and how to get it. Needless to say, the moral growth of our children is not at the heart of their agenda. They are effective because they are masters at engaging our imaginations to conform to their own commercial purposes.

Neil Postman has written an intriguing essay on television commercials as a new genre of religious literature, a development of the parable. He pointed out that we are often offered an entire commercial theology, including a fall into sin, redemption, a path of holiness, and in the final stages of the parable, a materialistic vision of eternal bliss. A genuine attempt is made to portray ecstasy (usually a honeymoon in Hawaii) as the soul is joined to the deity—the deity being the latest technology.[7]

The educational establishment's confidence in moral goodness is far more timorous than the ideas of goodness in the consumer culture. It is also less imaginatively expressed. We are left vulnerable to the seductions of the consumer world's powerful missionary arm, the advertising industry.

My point is that modern relativism introduces such uncertainty about ultimate goodness that there is a profound loss of confidence about what is right, good, and worthy to strive for. Relativism sometimes begins with a legitimate fear of imposing one's values unfairly on others. But it goes far beyond that. It is skeptical that there are any universal values, and so encourages the fear of passing on *any* values by *any means*. It undercuts the ability of the relativist to communicate even some of the very moral values that he or she relies on in neighbors.

Boston College psychologist William K. Kilpatrick argued that if we were anthropologists, we would not be at all surprised to find the elders of a remote tribe teaching their culture's values to their children, nor would we dispute their right to do it. If we noticed that the elders were not doing this, we would conclude that the culture was within a generation or two of collapse. He then concluded:

> This is easy enough to see for other cultures, but when it comes to our own, a certain inhibition against cultural transmission

sets in. A pervasive nondirectiveness and subjectiveness dictates that we don't have the right to impose our values on our children. And consequently we are forced to create the fiction that each child is in his own right a miniature Socrates—a moral philosopher, as Kohlberg would have it.[8]

The constraints that relativism imposes on the public teaching of morality are substantial. It may be that the public moral education of the younger generation will end up focusing largely on an appeal to fear before the court of the young person's own self-perceived self-interest. This is not bad in itself. The consequences of some choices certainly are fearful, so we are better off if we experience that fear than if we don't. But just as stiffening the punishment for a crime does not necessarily diminish the number of offenses, moral education is severely limited if fear is its main focus.

There must also be the component of obligation, that we are answerable to and loyal to something or someone greater than we are. We are not alone in the world. Finally, there needs to be a powerful component of aspiration, a positive sense of the heroic. There must be an awareness of an excellence that is actually worth pursuing, even sacrificing for. We turn now to a more promising basis for moral learning, one that has a place for wider sources of motivation—fear, obligation, and aspiration.

THE CONTEXT OF MORAL LEARNING

A Christian approach to moral learning must take into account the two sides of human nature that we have already addressed. Each one of us is a "glorious ruin." We are made images of God, and yet we are fallen. Both of these sides are very close to the surface in the life of the child.

The Child as God's Image

Every child has the capacity to reflect something of the character and excellence of God in many forms. When Jesus taught that we all need to become as little children in order to enter the kingdom of God, he was not being cute or sentimental. He referred to an openness, a sense of wonder that he linked to humility. Perhaps it is an aliveness, an ability to learn new things without being threatened. Perhaps it is a freedom of the imagination that most of us have lost as adults in our supposed sophistication and in our felt need to be in tight control of our lives.

As images of the Creator God, we are both called and equipped to be creative. This imaging of creativity bursts out of a growing child in marvelous events of discovery, excitement with learning, and doing new things. A young child makes new sounds, shapes, and word combinations that have never been made in quite the same way before. One of the most exciting things about being a parent is witnessing these new dawns, to be ever surprised by original and unpredicted insights and actions. As soon as a child begins to develop a sophisticated use of language we are let in on extraordinarily creative pictures, trains of thought, and association.

I can remember vividly when one of our sons, at age four, announced to me, "Daddy, I am like God." I said, "Hmm . . . really? In what way?" while at the same time my mind was racing, wondering where in the world this idea had come from, and where it might be headed. He blindsided me with his response, "Yes, it's because I love you even when you're bad!"

It may be that in the love of a child we get one of our best images of the wholehearted, unconditional love of God. In the love of a child we can sometimes see love's uncomplicated, uncalculating, and passionate expression. Adult love is often so intertwined with the personal agenda of the one doing the loving that one longs for the unsophistication of the child's love.

The Child as Fallen

The child's ability to image God graphically is not the whole story, however. Just as creativity and love are played at high volume in the life of the child, so also is the fallenness of human nature. Sin is right on the surface, without the sophisticated and elaborate systems of covering up, the self-justifying and self-deception that we have learned to associate with adult sin. No one has to teach children to put themselves at the center of the universe—it comes quite naturally to them. But it does take some years for most children to transform raw selfishness into something that appears more respectable in society. Roger Gould, a psychiatrist studying the life cycle, pointed out that a two-year-old makes two demands of life—of omnipotence and absolute safety. He claimed that we spend the rest of our lives trying to disengage ourselves from those demands and the havoc that they cause.[9]

Children express anger much more freely than adults. In fact, when an adult goes into a blind fury, we often say that he or she is being childish. It sometimes appears to us as comical for that reason (if it does not do too much damage). A child's anger is often irrational rage, with no sense of the perspective of a long-term view of life, or the safety of any-one else who might be in the way.

The cruelty of children is also exposed right on the surface, with-out the disguises that make adult malice seem more genteel. Children can, at moments, be quite unashamed about the desire to hurt another person. It is for these reasons and others that the book of Proverbs says that "Folly is bound up in the heart of a child" (22:15).

The two sides of human nature, the glory and the ruin, make the attempt to raise children a daunting task. There is so much that is pre-cious, delicate, and potentially so powerfully good, that one does not want to crush it. On the other hand, there is so much that is wrong, destructive, and narrowing that one does not dare to leave it unchecked. The challenge is that we be able to provide moral leader-ship to our children but at the same time not constrict their curiosity, exuberance, and growth. Reminding ourselves of the high goal set by God for us all will make sure that we have the right picture in mind. God wants us to be able to discern right from wrong, but that is not all. He wants us to do the right. He is not so concerned that we be able to give correct answers as we sit in a classroom with a paper and pencil in front of us. He is not even particularly concerned that we use the "approved" processes of moral reasoning in solving morally confusing quandaries. He cares that we live out what is right, and he cares how we live it out. But even that is not all. God would have us *love* the true and the good, and delight in doing it. This is another dimension alto-gether, and the one that has been the preoccupation of this book.

How can we integrate this goal with an approach to children? How can we avoid invading a child's own private space if we try? Of course, the potential for manipulation and indoctrination is great, but not inevitable. Many parents have been so intimidated by the danger of indoctrination that they have allowed their children to flounder with no solid moral guidelines at all. Ironically, their children often interpret this not as welcome respect for their individual freedom but as the parents' neglect and indifference. This is not the only alternative to indoctrina-tion. Perhaps a better model is "stimulation." There needs to be explicit teaching, and there needs also to be discipline, but the major factor to encourage a delight in the true and the good will be the catalyst of exam-ple. The most important context for this catalyst is the family.

THE INTEGRITY OF THE PARENT GENERATION

❯❯❯

*I do not believe that anyone can teach us who we really are
more than our children. They expose our pretensions and our
limits with glaring clarity, because they so relentlessly push us
right up against them. And at the same time, our children
challenge and expand our strengths by expecting
(indeed, demanding) that we be better, stronger,
kinder, smarter, more patient than we are.*[1]

BURTON, DITTMER, AND LOVELESS

❯❯❯

*Self-giving, not self-fulfillment, lies at the heart
of the parents' vocation. If such a self-giving should prove to
be deeply satisfying, we have reason to be thankful.
But there are no guarantees of such symmetrically satisfying
results, and to seek them is not the best preparation for
parenthood. To give birth is a venture that should always be
carried out in hope and in faith that the Creator will
continue to speak his "yes" upon the creation.*[2]

GILBERT MEILAENDER

W hat are the most important factors in the development of a positive moral imagination in a child? If there had to be one theme, it would be the integrity of the family. The family is the most important influence by far, not just the nuclear family, but the extended family also, if there is one. Rabbi Jonathan Sacks put this well: "The family is the matrix of individuality. It is that enclosed space in which we work out, in relation to stable sources of affection, a highly differentiated sense of who we are."[3]

The family has always been the central institution involved in the raising of children, but it stands more alone now than in other times. In most of this advanced industrial society, the nuclear family no longer enjoys the support of the extended family, the church, synagogue, local community, or "village" to help in raising a child. The family alone, or what is left of it, stands between the growing child and the impersonal mass of society. If the Christian family is to nurture the moral imagination, it must itself have integrity. That does not mean that it must be perfect, but that it must stand with honesty about its failures before God.

What follows is in no sense a comprehensive treatise on raising children. I will only point to a few pressure points that are important to the growth of a Christian moral imagination.

I should say also that I come to the subject with a deep bias. Raising our own three sons has been one of the most exciting and fulfilling parts of my own life. I write, therefore, as an unashamed celebrator of children.

INTEGRITY BEFORE GOD IN QUALITY OF LIFE

Like it or not, parents have the major responsibility for raising their children. It is they who have the awesome task to reflect the glory of the character of God in their home. It is their example that will make more difference than anyone's, and will shape their children far more than their own lectures on any subject. This example is a twenty-four-hour-a-day exposure to the mixture of ideas, hopes, commitments, possessions, words, behavior, and emotions that make up the intangible but immensely powerful atmosphere of the home. What is communicated through example is, by definition, "caught" more than consciously taught. Children will simply adopt certain of their parents' behavior patterns or attitudes without knowing it or intending it. But children will also consciously emulate parents' strengths when they are admirable in their eyes, and distance themselves from, if not despise, what inspires aversion.

Educator Gilbert Highet described the inevitability of this process:

"It is impossible to have children without teaching them. Beat them, coddle them, ignore them, force-feed them, shun them or worry about them, love them or hate them, you are still teaching them something, all the time."[4]

Having a Good Story
If Christian parents want their children to want to be Christlike, the parents' lives must be "good stories." By this I mean not that they are successful in the eyes of their neighbors or their high school classmates, or even the people in their church, but that their lives correspond to the master story of life. Their lives might well involve much suffering, poverty, and disappointment—but health, wealth, and dreams-come-true are not necessarily what makes a life story good. Being Christlike in their own unique ways, perhaps in the midst of suffering, poverty, and disappointment, is what makes a good story.

The desire to have a child, of itself, implies some notion of life as a story that reaches beyond the life cycle of the parent. Having a child is not just a biological event. It is bringing into existence part of a new generation, those who will continue the story after we have had our crack at it. It is interesting how often parents in Old Testament Israel were told to answer their children's questions by telling the stories of God's past dealing with their people. The obligations and loyalties of the family were part of a larger ongoing history of tribe and nation.

What does it mean to have a good story? Negatively, it means that parents avoid life commitments to idols. A life story that is dominated or distracted by greed, the quest for fame, power, self-indulgence, respectability, or any other of the hundreds of modern idols, will not be a good story. These priorities will come between the family and God, confusing the story, perhaps even making the plot incomprehensible. Woody Allen once said middle-class people take life very seriously, and with equal seriousness, God and carpet. If this is so, it is not only an insult to God. It is also missing the point of life.

If this is true of us as parents, we will be transparent hypocrites in the eyes of our children. They will see that we have missed the point of our own faith. Children, especially our own, are experts in hypocrisy detection. Hypocrisy, next to cowardice, is one vice that most inspires aversion. When our children perceive us as hypocrites, our credibility and God's credibility through us are devastated. The God who shares his authority with a carpet invites not awe, but contempt.

Positively, our stories will be good stories if Christlikeness is our real goal. That will mean that we are unafraid to be individuals, that we are not clones of some Christian leader or group stereotype, but that our lives cohere around the qualities of character we see in Jesus. A child looks out at the many options that life offers, and compares stories. He or she wants to know what to do with freedom, with the open-endedness of the story. If the story our children see at home is over-whelmingly one of constriction, prohibition, and joylessness, how can the child want to walk in those footsteps? If there is much talk of the love of God, but little love between members of the family, how believ-able or attractive is the love of God?

Jesus was known for taking extremely hard and uncompromising stands on many issues. But he was also known—and criticized—for violating the establishment's rules and taking unheard-of freedoms. The religious leadership was outraged at him and called him a "glutton and a drunkard, a friend of tax collectors and sinners" (Matthew 11:19), because he enjoyed the good things of life too much, and cared too much for the people everybody else despised.

We must reiterate that the Christian faith, as expressed in the imi-tation of Christ, is life-affirming. This creates no tension with Jesus' com-mand that we should deny ourselves, take up our crosses, and follow him (Matthew 16:24). Denying ourselves, as Jesus meant it, is the way to affirm life. It is not that withholding pleasurable things and experiences from ourselves is a virtue in itself. Self-denial is first a commitment against what is evil and life-destroying within us. We must deny these things and their power in order to affirm the life God has given us to lead.

There are also some tasks in life so important that we must deny ourselves perfectly legitimate pleasures in order to fulfill them. The statement of Martin Luther King, already discussed, "If a man hasn't found something he will die for, he isn't fit to live," is not a negation of life. It is the reverse. It posits that there is something so important to life, so meaningful, that it is even worth giving up your own life to serve that purpose. The value and affirmation of life must be visible in the Christian home.

The Bible is notable for its consistent challenge to joy. This comes not from a denial of the existence of evil and suffering, nor from a dis-tancing from the battle against them, but from a God who has done something joyful in this broken world. Think of the festivals in the Old Testament to commemorate the great acts of God in the story of the people. God himself ordered feasts that would last for days at a time—

to remember, to worship, and to rejoice in as a community. Despite suffering and disappointment, life is good.

The New Testament picks up the same challenge. One thinks especially of the apostle Paul, while in prison and in danger of being executed, writing, "Rejoice in the Lord always; again I will say, Rejoice" (Philippians 4:4). The Christian church has continued the tradition in its celebration of Christmas, Easter, and Pentecost, also times for remembering, worshiping, and rejoicing together.

Our lives need to be attractive to our children in the ways that matter most. These ways do not involve our possessions or our professions as much as they do our allegiances. If we have ultimate allegiance to Christ, we will be far from perfect, but we will have integrity before him.

The goal of the Christian parent is not to so "protect" a child that he or she does not know any other way of life. Nor is it to so intimidate the child that he or she follows Christ only out of fear of stepping off a narrow path. The goal is that our children should say, "I really *want* to walk in those footsteps." This is why it is so vital that the atmosphere of a family, each in its own unique way, must capture Jesus' affirmation of life. When they have a choice about it, most young people will not decide to subject themselves to a grim and joyless existence.

Invested Identity

The integrity of the family before God depends on the life allegiances of the parents, but also on the specific attitudes of the parents toward the child or children. If parents think the success of their lives depends on whether their child turns out "well," then the child has become a God-substitute for the parents. This is a disaster for all concerned. As a parent I can have an "invested identity." As with a financial investment, I can expect an eventual return—here measured in increased self-esteem—for the time, money, and love expended on child raising over the years.

What a delicate balance this is! Of course, any parents who love their children will be proud of their children's successes and grieve over their failures. However, there is something more than this if we have invested our identity in our children. Russell Baker, in his autobiography *Growing Up*, described the role that his own future would play in the life of his widowed mother, who was determined to "come up from the bottom" in the Depression.

In this long, hard pull, I was now cast as the central figure. She would spend her middle years turning me into the man who would redeem her failed youth. I would make something of myself, and if I lacked the grit to do it, well then *she* would make me make something of myself. I would become the living proof of the strength of her womanhood. From now on she would live for me, and, in turn, I would become her future.[5]

It is easy to see both the pressures and constraints that this kind of a wager puts on a child. A child is not allowed to image God, but must instead image the parents' idea of success—whether that means being a successful athlete, movie star, professor, doctor, executive, statesman, or missionary. No matter how virtuous it is, the prescribed agenda becomes a straitjacket, and failure is a trauma of betrayal ("How could you do this to us?!"). No human being, let alone a child, is large enough to "become the future" for another person. A prepackaged agenda for a child's life is either a prescription for crushed and resentful obedience or an invitation to outright rebellion.

Nurture

God has told parents to nurture their children. Nurture is the wider context within which authority and discipline find their place. Discipline is vital, but it should not be the center of the parent-child relationship. Nurture requires time, a lot of time. There is the contemporary myth that we can have quality time with our children and therefore do not need a large quantity of time. But good quality time does not happen without a large quantity of time. Harvard psychiatrist Armand Nicoli observed that time with both parents is like oxygen. The quality of the air we breathe is important, but we also need a fairly large quantity of it all the time as a matter of life or death. A little bit of even very high quality oxygen occasionally, dispensed at times convenient to someone else, will not keep us alive.

Too often parents, especially fathers, decide to spend time with their children only after one of them has gotten into trouble. The father will decide to take the son on a fishing trip after the son's first arrest. Of course, by that time the son might well not be too excited about a week alone with his father, and the father himself might dread the long silences. Both can easily think of places they would rather be. The problem of parents' time with children demands a great deal of creativity in the complex working world today. It also requires the ability to see that life comes in chapters, not in one uniform piece. With growing children, and a changing working world, no one arrangement can last for long.

One of the vital keys is that raising children is not "women's work." In fact, the biblical teachings about raising children are usually addressed to both fathers and mothers, and many to fathers alone. The mother and father are both needed and must both be deeply involved. The abdication of fathers is one of the most destructive aspects of the modern family. If both father and mother are fully involved, it creates many more possible combinations of timing and division of labor. It also suggests an unrealized responsibility of the church in the case of single parents.

Will these priorities impinge on the career of a parent who is living in the fast lane? Of course they will. He or she is sure to be competing with people who either have no children or who spend no time with the children they do have. There will always be people whose job owns all of their time and possibly their souls as well. But career sacrifices made for the sake of raising children is one of the wisest tradeoffs one can ever make.

I remember hearing a U.S. Senator say, after resigning from the Senate for family reasons, that he had never heard a person on his deathbed say, "If only I had given more time to my job." But he had many times heard people say, "If only I had given more time to my children." The problem is that the children can "always wait." Time spent with them never seems as urgent as other pressing matters and deadlines. Yet time passes and is lost. We can never get the stages of growth of our children back. Each chapter is different, and we only get it once.

We need to be friends with our children. We need to enjoy their company. If we (fathers are especially guilty here) start befriending our children only when they become teenagers, we have waited too long— although it is never too late to start. We need to be friends from the earliest days. Those friendships need to have the depth, substance, and momentum of many shared memories by the time our children hit adolescence.

There ought to be plenty of laughing together in the family. What a wonderful, positive, and vital gift humor is! How much can be shared through it! I am not speaking here of humor misused to punish or control family members by its power to humiliate. (It is hard to see that this is ever legitimate.) But humor can disarm and defuse all sorts of potential or actual conflict—especially if parents are able to laugh at themselves. I sometimes seriously consider that if we had been deprived of humor in our family, we would all now be either in jail or dead.

Another key element in parents' nurture is that they must realize that their children are created by God to have dominion in the earth. By God's design, they have an increasing mastery over themselves and their environment. As they grow, they are able to responsibly cope with more freedom from parental discipline and supervision. This is what God is doing in the life of the growing child. It is vital that parents are working with God's program rather than butting their heads against it.

What happens when a seventeen-year-old is not allowed to choose her own clothes? If she has not been entrusted with that weighty responsibility, how is she likely to function at eighteen when she decides to leave home altogether and live on her own? It is a great struggle for some parents to trust their children to grow up. "But they might make bad decisions, and we can prevent that!" Of course children *will* make bad decisions, but they will never learn to make good ones if they are not allowed to make decisions at all. If parents are not willing to take risks in this area, they will either impede their children's growth or force rebellion — or both.

Our children must experience that we are *for* their growing up, not against it, dragging our feet at every new freedom. They must know that we are in favor of their actually becoming adults, and that our goal is that they be able to cope with all that life has for them by the time they leave home. If we, as parents, do not convey that message, we will be found helplessly tilting against the windmill of time itself, God's time.

Inevitably, tensions will arise over how much freedom should be enjoyed how soon, and with what level of proven responsibility. However, these tensions are minimized when children are confident that their parents really welcome their increasing freedom and have their complete independence as a goal. Some families have found it helpful to set up a time schedule of increasing levels of freedoms and responsibilities, so that both parent and child can look into the future and see where they are headed.

An important question for Christian parents is whether their children share their belief in Christ. This is one of the most delicate areas of all. Christian parents will want to encourage their child to trust in Christ, but the trust must be the *child's* trust, not the parents' imposed veneer. That means that parents must encourage freedom of thought, welcoming questions, doubts, and difficulties by taking them seriously. Taking them seriously means hours of listening, admitting when they do not know an answer, and trying to discover answers together.

They must make it clear that each of us must make our own

choices, and that the faith of the parent never substitutes for the faith of the child. One of the hardest things for parents is to give their children space in this area. Yet space is exactly what is needed if we expect our children to be able to look into the future and say, "I can see myself following Christ, and I *want* to live this way."

INTEGRITY BEFORE BIBLICAL ETHICS

Francis Schaeffer used to say that there are two equal and opposite ways to destroy the authority of the Bible. One is to deny or contradict clear biblical teachings. The other is to take our own traditions and treat them as equal in authority to the Bible. This second option can actually be more dangerous than the first because it usually lives under the umbrella of piety and spiritual maturity.

There are few issues so important for parents as having a clear picture of the difference between the absolute values of God's truth and the relative values of specific cultures and subcultures. Without clarity of vision here, parents can either fail to provide the real and important boundaries to moral life for their children, or they can fossilize their children in restrictions that seemed wise to their grandparents but are unworkable or even laughable today.

Especially in a time of accelerated cultural change, if parents get stuck making absolutes out of the last generation's judgment calls, their children will be forced either to become living anachronisms or to bolt in rebellion. The following illustration comes from a diatribe against the evils of drink in nineteenth-century England:

> It must be evident to everyone, that the practice . . . must render the frame feeble and unfit to encounter hard labor or severe weather. . . . Hence succeeds a softness, an effeminacy, a seeking for the fireside, a lurking in the bed, and . . . all the characteristics of idleness. . . . (Drinking) fills the public house, makes the frequenting of it habitual, corrupts boys as soon as they are able to move from home, and does little less for the girls, to whom the gossip of the (drinking place) is no bad preparatory school for the brothel. At the very least, it teaches them idleness.[6]

The interesting thing is that the drinking referred to was the drinking of tea. This warning appeared at the start of a twenty-page instructional booklet for the making of home-brewed beer, the nutritious family drink. Why should tea be the object of such dire moral dangers? My own guess is that in that part of England it was new.

This should function as a warning to us. Time plays funny tricks on us. What appears self-evident or axiomatic to one generation may seem outrageous to the next, and vice versa. If there is no word from a God who transcends human cultures and history, we can be blown about by the arbitrariness of moral speculations and passionate ideologies. In our enlightened century, we have seen evil located in such things as the wearing of short skirts, long hair, racial impurity, and the private ownership of property.

But if God has spoken, we have a standard to discern between what needs to be affirmed because it is of God, what is negotiable because it is culture-specific (to either the present generation or previous ones), and what needs to be resisted in God's name.

Think of some of the things that Christian parents can make a moral issue about: exact parameters about clothes to wear and music to listen to, length of hair, beards, King James Bible translations, exact male-female role descriptions, prohibition of dancing, and drinking of alcoholic beverages. I know a pastor's son who was told to leave home because his hair was too long and he asked too many questions. He was told that for these reasons he "compromised" his father's ministry. For the parents of another high school student it was a moral issue to keep a Bible at all times on top of all his other books at school.

Jesus warned against making void the commands of God for the sake of traditions of men. How long do you suppose *his* hair was? Do we really know that the wine he made (John 2:1-11) and drank was unfermented? This seems a bit farfetched since it made the heart glad, and if you drank too much of it, it made you drunk. What about the command to praise God with dancing (Psalm 150:4)?

The apostle Paul carried on the same theme of freedom in his letter to the Romans as he pled with his readers to give each other space for different views on all sorts of things that were not essential to Christian ethics. He was not threatened by differences. "One man esteems one day as better than another, while another man esteems all days alike. Let every one be fully convinced in his own mind" (Romans 14:5). Both Jesus and Paul outlined a path of freedom within a structure of essentials, in contrast to the rules and regulations orientation of both the Jewish and Gentile cultures of that time. There is no more sure way of discouraging our children from wanting to follow Christ than by adding the restrictions of human traditions to the real absolutes of God's Word. They will project their imaginations into the future and say, "I cannot live that way," "I cannot walk down that road," "There is not enough room for me in that way of life." Living out the moral teachings of Jesus is difficult enough without adding more rules to them.

Just as destructive is subtracting from or ignoring the teaching of Jesus. It is always the path of least resistance to do what everyone around us is doing and raise our children as they raise their children. But a powerful relativistic mind-set in our society suggests that parents have no right to influence their children's values, tendencies, or behavior at all. The results of this practice have led some teachers of moral education to ascribe to their students such phrases as "moral illiteracy."

We may also disregard the values of Jesus by accepting the ideas of success that surround us. It is important to remember the distinctions made in the first chapter, between heroism, talent, and celebrity. A hero shows Christlike virtues of moral character. A talent can do something well, whether it be in sports, academics, the arts, business, or leadership. A celebrity is someone who is well known. For the good of our children, if for nobody else, we must have these categories of exceptional people prioritized as God does.

How easy it is in our society to get confused and communicate to our children that excellence is found in competitive success or high visibility. The drive to make it to Wimbledon, Wall Street, or Carnegie Hall or even to a prestigious college can overshadow what matters far more in life. If our highest notion of excellence is of talent or celebrity, that priority becomes a cruel and tyrannical master. A child pressed into this mold is often made into the image of high family expectations and oversized psychological needs rather than into the image of God.

INTEGRITY BEFORE THE GOSPEL IN SIN AND FAILURE
We have stressed at length the importance of the imitation of Christ, that our lives would be good stories, and that we might reflect Christlikeness to our children. However, if our hope as parents is in our own perfect success in imitating Christ, it is slender hope indeed. What parents can boast of freedom from all idols and hypocrisy? It is all fine and good to have an ideal of Christlikeness, but both parents and children are bent and broken people in need of God's forgiveness and help, living in a bent and broken society that often pulls hard in wrong directions.

Parents' Failure
You may have noticed how children love to hear stories. They have a special love for stories about their parents when they were children. No sooner does the parent tell one story than the child will say, "Tell me

another" or "Now tell me about the time you . . ." or "Tell it to me again." It is important that children know their parents' stories. It is part of the way they place themselves in a larger story of the family, to establish a sense of boundaries for their own lives.

When we as parents tell stories about ourselves to our children, it is intriguing which ones we select. I find it fascinating that most of them seem to lean heavily toward the "success literature" genre. At one point with our children, I realized that they were getting a very warped picture. It was easy to tell stories about my failures, or about the trouble that I had gotten into, if in some mysterious way it was "cool" to get in trouble in that way. It was daring when I broke the rules. In this mythic past, I was somehow respected or admired for it all. In other words, despite or even because of failures, I ended up the hero. For some reason, the stories that ended with me feeling stupid, compromised, ashamed, inferior, homesick, helpless, or feeble were never told.

This is no help to our children. If they look at us and think that when we were their size, we landed miraculously on our feet at the end of every disaster, what will they conclude? First of all, the picture that we have given them was a lie. Second, and worse, they may not realize that it was a lie. Third, they know for sure that they do not always land on *their* feet. As they project themselves into their parents' shoes, they see that they will never make it.

It discourages them into thinking that they will never be capable of competence in the adult world. They will look to the future and be tempted to say, "I give up," "I can never be good enough, strong enough, smart enough to make it in their world." It builds discouragement and fear of failure, instead of a sense that although I will certainly fail, that will not end the world.

The question of parents' sin and failure in the present is also important. The parents' authority is a derived authority. It is not that parents are bigger, smarter, older, or stronger and therefore have unlimited authority. Their authority is from God, and it comes along with daunting responsibility for the welfare of the children that God has entrusted to them. This is actually a great freedom because it means that their authority does not rest in never making mistakes, always being right, or never changing their minds.

That in turn means that when parents do make mistakes and hurt their children through their own faults, they can be honest about it and apologize without jeopardizing their authority. In fact, for their authority to have any credibility, they *must* apologize and ask the forgiveness of their children when they have sinned against them. This is one of the most important things of all when we are talking about integrity. It points to the difference between having integrity and being perfect. Being perfect is being perfect. Having integrity is aiming at perfection but being honest and open about our failures to reach it.

If we as parents are free to apologize to our children, and to let our children see us apologizing to others we have wronged, we are sending a vitally important message to them. It is that we, too, really stand under the eye of the living God, we bow to a truth that is bigger than we are. We fail before that truth. We are not just into some "power trip," enjoying bossing our children around and controlling them. On the other hand, if we refuse to apologize, we expose ourselves as hypocrites and God as just a marginal presence in our lives, to be used when needed for pushing others around. In short, being willing to ask for forgiveness establishes both our credibility and God's. Refusing to do it undermines both.

Children's Failure

We have spoken of our sin and failure as parents. What happens when the child fails? This is one of the most important times of all. It raises the unsettling and challenging question, Is the gospel of Jesus Christ alive in our home or not? Do we as parents reflect the forgiveness and unconditional love of Christ, or is it guilt and recrimination time?

If the parents have invested the whole of their identity in their child, it will be very difficult for them to show Christ's love when the child fails. They will experience the failure not for what it is but as a personal betrayal against them. Their child was meant to be a credit to them, to enhance the family name, but now this!

While giving a lecture on this theme, I mentioned the example of a father coming to pick up his son from the police station, the son having had his first brush with the law. The father walked into the police station and shouted, "Now look at what you've done to us! After all we've done for you! You'll never know how much you've hurt your mother!" A police officer in the audience told me that was what nine out of ten parents do. If our identity is overinvested in our children, we are not free to see and respond to the suffering that *they* are enduring in the midst of their failure. We cannot see through their eyes. All we can see and feel is our own broken dreams, and a psychological investment gone bad.

Parents are responsible to discipline their children. Of course, this is more necessary for some children than others, and for each child more necessary at certain stages. Discipline is not a refusal to forgive. Discipline, as it is conceived in the Bible (Hebrews 12:11), involves pain but is not primarily a question of punishment. Punishment is to establish justice after some past transgression. Discipline is future-oriented and is training for the days to come. While it should never be less than just, the purpose of discipline is not in itself justice, but moral learning. Discipline must be clear, carefully thought out, and consistently administered by the parents. It must be predictable, and therefore able to be anticipated by the child.

Discipline should not involve humiliation, especially public humiliation. I find that for many parents, one of the main means of shaping the behavior of their children is putting them down verbally in public. This is not discipline in any remotely Christian sense. Too often parents discover that the pain of public humiliation adds motivation for the child not to repeat the offense. This may be true in a very limited way, but it adds a lot more as well, and it is habit forming for the parent. It is read as a personal rejection and a reveling in parental power. As such it undercuts both the love that we need to show our child in the midst of his or her failure, but also our authority under God. If discipline is done in this way, most children eventually conclude that they are more on the receiving end of their parents' ego inflation than of God's disapproval.

Every effort must be made to enforce discipline in private. Perhaps this is part of what Paul had in mind when he wrote, "Fathers, do not provoke your children to anger, but bring them up in the discipline and instruction of the Lord" (Ephesians 6:4). Provocation and discipline are distinguished here. It was obviously an important point for Paul. In the parallel passage in his letter to the Colossians, he wrote, "Fathers, do not provoke your children, lest they become discouraged" (3:21). Of course, some children will be provoked or discouraged no matter how carefully their parents discipline them. However, parents are called to take great pains to avoid what will predictably produce provocation and discouragement.

Discipline is necessary because it adds negative motivation to the positive motivation to live a good life. It reinforces the aversion/aspiration dynamics that have been our concern. It also teaches a child that there are boundaries in the world, which are stepped across only at cost.

But all this is in the context of the parents' forgiveness and love. They can reflect the unconditional love of God, or they can make it clear that there are mysterious conditions attached to that love and acceptance. Jesus has given us a marvelous picture in the parable of the prodigal son (Luke 15), a picture of a father's acceptance of his son after the son has squandered half the family fortune. The father did not demand an accounting of the losses, or a program for repayment, but ran out to meet him, hugged him, brought him in, and had a banquet. Although discipline will sometime be necessary with our children, the moral context should be that of the parable of the prodigal son.

The occasion of sin and failure is one of the most important times to affirm our love and acceptance of our children. We do not need to love and accept the things that they have done wrong, but we must love and accept them as persons, and let them know it. Children will remember for years the way they are treated by their parents in their moments of extreme vulnerability in failure and humiliation. They are likely to draw deep conclusions from the responses — both about their parents and about reality itself. If they meet only conditional love, we are hiding from them the power and the joy of the gospel of Christ itself as it can work in the home. We also inflict on them a fear of failure and a conviction of not being good enough to follow Christ.

We have looked at the family as the setting for a child to develop a moral imagination, and at some of the pressure points in family dynamics. But the family itself is in the wider setting of society. We turn to some of the distinctive aspects of modern society that bear on this same character formation.

CHAPTER THIRTEEN

CHILDREN
IN SOCIETY

≋

*More and more adults are very much in the business
of giving youth the means to show how different they are
from older people. In the past, youth typically had to
"generate" their own values, beliefs, and practices.
Now, however, corporate North America has found
that encouraging relatively distinct generational groups
helps the proverbial bottom line. Since you like to be
different, these corporations have decided to heighten
that sense of distinctiveness. Why not sell them their
"own" music, clothing, films, TV shows, radio stations—
whatever sub-group product the youth market will buy.*[1]

ROY ANKER

The family is the most important influence on a child, for both good and bad. But as the family becomes both weaker and less supported by other institutions, society at large has an increasing role in shaping the lives of young people. From a vast array of influences affecting the growth of the moral imagination, we will look at two formidable forces in modern society—the role of television and the phenomenon of a youth culture.

TELEVISION

Despite choruses of protest and condemnation, television is certainly here to stay. I will not attempt to join the acrimonious debate about its benefits and liabilities as a medium of communication, or the arguments about the moral virtues and vices of its programming. What television does best is to provide entertainment, and that it does well. It can be a good educational tool, but the jury is still out about whether its blessings are outweighed by the unintended consequences of its trivialization and deterrence to reading.

Television can certainly stimulate us and introduce us to new information, new places, new stories, and vicariously to many new experiences. Who can argue with these benefits? But the question in our present discussion is about its role in the lives of children who watch hours of it each day.

We have already spoken of children bearing the image of God, part of which includes the capability for dominion in this world. The growing sense of mastery in ever-new areas of life is one of the most exciting things both for children and any adults closely involved with them. It is in this area that my own anxiety about television begins.

Television seems to be a passivity-producing medium for those who watch it for long hours. There is what one could call the "dislocated lower jaw syndrome," the symptoms of which are glazed eyes and mouth hanging open for long periods of time. For the many hours spent in front of it, the child spends his or her time in the role of a spectator. With the added availability of cable television, MTV, and video, we are the most thoroughly entertained people in world history. Full-color, twenty-four-hour entertainment is available.

My concern is not just for what is happening as children watch television, but for what is not happening. Think of all the other things that children could be doing, but are not doing, while they are watching television. Children could be drawing, making music, playing games and sports, investigating the world, talking, walking, reading out loud, or

staging any one of the thousands of pretend dramas that children create. They could be working, playing with animals, climbing trees, argu-
ing, fighting, or laughing. All are active pursuits that demand an effort
of concentration and an engagement of mind and body. Television
demands only that we sit relatively still and do not close our eyes.

Television entertains, but your imagination is passive. Everything
is provided by the screen. You do not even need to visualize anything—
it is all there in front of you. The only effort asked of you is that you do
not fall asleep. If you are reading a story, or even listening to someone
else reading one, your imagination is active. You must create a vast,
technicolor visual picture of the story with all the characters and landscapes to go with what your ears are hearing. Watching a lot of television can provide a deadening effect to the imagination and may contribute to an imaginative disengagement from life.

This tendency to passivity is increased by commercial television's
preoccupation with the idealized and the sordid. The idealized people
of television are more perfect in appearance and coordination than most
of the people we normally meet, and many appear more perfect than
anyone who exists on this planet. The sordid also are more sordid than
most of the people we meet. It is only the very exceptional people who
are sufficiently newsworthy to make it on television—not just the murderer, but the bizarre mass murderer. It shows us a world that rivets our
attention, but it is a world that is quite unlike our own. The television
world claims to be the world where the real action is happening, but it
is not the world that we walk around in. This creates a sense that we are
disengaged from the world that really matters—the world on the screen.

Television also exposes us to hundreds of crises and disasters in the
world about which we can do nothing. There are earthquakes, wars,
dangers of wars, famines, typhoons, floods, economic disasters, all well
beyond our powers to understand, let alone respond to in caring or constructive ways. There will be a whole new set next week. Its overall
impact for those who watch it in large doses from an early age may well
be to encourage both passivity and a sense of fatalism. What can I do
about it, after all? There is talk of media-created "compassion fatigue."

I was recently rereading *The Adventures of Tom Sawyer* and was
struck by the life of the imagination of a boy of that time. In the famous
account of whitewashing the fence, Tom was able to barter the privilege of doing his chores with passing boys for all sorts of valued objects:

There was no lack of material; boys happened along every little while; they came to jeer, but they remained to whitewash. By the time Ben was fagged out, Johnny Miller bought in for a dead rat and a string to swing it with; and so on, and so on, hour after hour. And when the middle of the afternoon came, from being a poor poverty-stricken boy in the morning, Tom was literally rolling in wealth. He had, besides the things I have mentioned, twelve marbles, part of a jew's harp, a piece of blue bottle-glass to look through, a spool-cannon, a key that wouldn't unlock anything, a fragment of chalk, a glass stopper of a decanter, a tin soldier, a couple of tadpoles, six fire-crackers, a kitten with only one eye, a brass door-knob, a dog collar—but no dog—the handle of a knife, four pieces of orange-peel, and a dilapidated old window-sash. . . . If he hadn't run out of whitewash, he would have bankrupted every boy in the village.[2]

Compare Tom's wealth with what constitutes wealth for his contemporaries today. The equivalent valued possessions would have been bought at Child World or Toys "R" Us, selected from their acres of plastic. There would be army missile launchers and troop carriers molded to exact scale, down to the rivets on each component, which would shoot scale-model missiles that stick to the refrigerator. Lights would flash and appropriate grinding noises would be made. They might even be operated by remote control. The interesting question to ponder is not the progress of toy technology but the difference in the involvement of the imagination. Without question, Tom was way ahead. With the modern toy, there is nothing left to the imagination to create except the size. It is all there. With Tom Sawyer, almost every part of his fortune demanded a formidable effort of the imagination to enjoy it or even to value it at all. Most children today would put his whole fortune in the trash as quickly as possible, except perhaps the one-eyed kitten.

The imagination, when it fastens on accessible heroes, has the potential to push people through barriers and limitations that they would not have thought possible themselves. The medium of television itself, when it swallows up a young person's free time, can rob him or her of such an active imagination.

The role of good literature is very different. As children read or are read to, they are more active. Their imaginations must visualize the narrative, creating portraits, landscapes, and sequences of action. A novel, a biography, or autobiography can also reflect far more deeply on life than is possible with television. It is not that the purpose of a narrative should be primarily didactic, but that it can arouse excitement, delight, admiration. It can create a hunger to follow one pattern of life rather than another.

If parents want their children to delight in living as Christians, they should be good storytellers, or at least get good stories to their children somehow. The ideals of Christ must be incarnated in narrative for us to be able to apply them to our lives and to motivate us to follow them.

YOUTH SUBCULTURE

It is not new to be worried about the younger generation. Some people in every generation, going back at least to Socrates, have believed that the younger generation has abandoned the foundations of a good society and that profound social collapse was imminent. We may debunk all those generations as historically naive doomsayers. But we would be historically naive ourselves if we forgot that a few of the doomsayers actually turned out to be right. Civilizations have fallen.

My intention here is not to continue the checkered tradition of this debate. It is instead to reflect on some of the changes from the adult side that have dramatically altered the experience of growing up today. Many of the most serious changes are less the result of outrageous choices, ideas, or actions of young people themselves than of changes in the social context that they have stepped into. These have had a profound effect on the development of the moral imagination.

Age Segregation

I will generalize about modern North American and European society at this point, so it would be easy to find exceptions to every aspect of this change. Take the rise of "age segregation." Young people today are age-segregated in a way that makes positive identification with adults difficult. This, in turn, makes the whole transition into adulthood a greater leap into insecurity and the unknown than it has been at other times.

As we look at the history of youth and the family, this change has come in many stages. In early American and European history, the economy was largely agrarian. Children were an economic asset, to help work the farm. There was no sharp division between the child's and the adult's sphere of activity, and they might have been within earshot of each other much of the day. Education took place at least in part in the home.

Two factors here are important to our discussion: first, young people had significant social relationships with people both older and younger than themselves; second, they did economically useful work that was often essential to the family's well-being. This meant that they were exposed regularly to older people, often of two generations, with whom they could identify, as well as younger children for whom they had responsibility. It also meant that from an early age they could begin to understand how the adult world worked, and how their own work mattered in it. The adult world was not some distant, mysterious time of testing on the far side of the chasm of adolescence and formal education.

Industrialization brought profound changes into this world, from the early-nineteenth-century migration to the cities, to the increased occupational choice that resulted. The public school system arose, bringing great educational benefits to more people but removing education from the home. In the early twentieth century, new theories arose about childhood, and especially adolescence. In fact, the word *adolescent* only came into currency less than one hundred years ago. There had been no word that was needed to describe the stage between puberty and adulthood.[3] It became fashionable to believe that the storm and stress of sexual maturation was such an unsettling time that the adolescent should not have other expectations put on him or her during that period. It was also believed that growth was best accomplished when young people were kept largely to their own age group. These ideas have profoundly shaped the modern experience of growing up. In the words of social historian Joseph Kett, "Adolescence was essentially a conception of behavior imposed on youth, rather than an empirical assessment of the way in which young people actually behaved."[4]

Kett observed that the result was a social revolution of rare completeness. We have "segregated young people from casual contact with adults."[5] Instead, contact with adults took place increasingly in formal contexts, such as classrooms where the adult was the expert or specialist.[6] The major social relationships of young people were with each other. With industrialization and a high level of prosperity, work was predominantly outside the home, education took much longer, and the young became important as consumers rather than integral parts of the labor force.

A New Youth Culture

By the mid-1950s another ingredient was added—the youth subculture. The structures of society had been intentionally shaped to keep young people relating mainly to each other, but in the 1950s the teenagers began to develop a subculture of their own.

The main elements making this possible were from the adult world—music and film, aided by television. There developed an awareness of a group identity, a sense of unity and solidarity across the whole country with other teenagers, fed and sustained primarily by rock-and-roll. In its first generation, it was music about school, cars, love, and the difficulty of getting along with parents who didn't understand. It was powerful music that gave young people something vital as a bond between them. Chuck Berry, in "Sweet Little Sixteen," sang about rock and roll uniting young people from Boston to San Francisco and in many of the cities in between. This song claimed the existence of a youth subculture—across the nation. A common music was the bond that tied it together. They were beginning to dance to the same songs.

While at first rock-and-roll did not deliberately exclude adults, it was a side benefit if it shocked them. Chuck Berry's advice was "Roll over, Beethoven." Part of any group identity is always the exclusion of those outside the group. This became a conscious side of rock music in the more politically oriented 1960s. Bob Dylan's "The Times They Are A-Changin'" became a rallying cry. The adult generation's advice seemed irrelevant to the needs of the subculture. But more than that, as Dylan charged, they were actually obstructing the ill-defined dream held out as a carrot in front of the younger generation in the 1960s.

By calling attention to a youth subculture, I do not mean, of course, that it was or is a self-sufficient, separate culture. It has always been entirely dependent economically on enough adult prosperity for adolescent leisure. It has become interdependent with the adult world in the form of a multibillion-dollar entertainment industry, aimed at exploiting this age group.

On the other hand, it is a separate culture in the sense that it has its own values and heroes, formed in interaction with the entertainment industry. The values and heroes of the adult world seem disconnected from the new and fast-changing scene. What do parents know about the latest dances, fashions, or drugs, or how to avoid being a social misfit in high school? It is a self-authenticating subculture. It does not appeal beyond itself for legitimacy. Authority that really matters is peer authority. The music and films of the youth culture do not, for the most part, deal with the world that the teenager is growing into, or has grown out of, but the world that he or she is in at that moment.

Age Segregation and Heroism

It is not my purpose to evaluate the youth subculture, but rather to call attention to one aspect of it—age segregation—and its impact on heroism. Insofar as the generalized picture that I have painted of young people in modern society is true of individuals within that society, they will have greater difficulty making the transition into adult life than their counterparts one hundred years ago. Yale historian John Demos puts it in this way:

> In cultures where a prolonged period of adolescent crisis *is*, more or less, a normal part of development two kinds of social factors seem broadly responsible: (1) There are major "discontinuities" between the generations; the common experiences of children and adults are radically different from one another. (2) The culture itself is enormously varied and complex. Thus the young person approaching adulthood confronts a bewildering array of alternatives as to career, values, life style and so forth.[7]

First of all, not all cultures *do* have adolescent crises as a normal occurrence. Our society does, and certainly qualifies on Demos's two factors. It is both age-segregated and extremely complex.

Young people are facing this "bewildering array of alternatives" with less experience of having rubbed shoulders with adults than before. Because of high mobility, there are fewer grandmothers and grandfathers who are willing and able to take an active part in the growth of their grandchildren. There are fewer aunts and uncles who are willing and able to be involved. Since most parents work outside the home, children have little exposure to the working world of their parents.

Work that adolescents do, such as it is, usually gives them little meaningful time with adults who are doing the kind of work that they might aspire to themselves. Because of the breakdown of the family, and less family time spent together generally, young people see less of families working together, building one another up, resolving conflict, planning together, or making marriages work through hard times.

If the adult views adolescence as only a period for biological maturation and socialization with peers, then that becomes a self-fulfilling prophecy. It lowers adult expectations for significant interaction with young people through a vast potential range of human activities and interests. The youth subculture in its many variations is likely to confirm adults in the conviction that they have little in common with young people "these days." The youth culture, of course, returns the compliment.

All of this makes it difficult for young people to identify with adults in a way that will encourage their imaginative development, to find shoes that they might like to walk in. If this general age segregation is true of any young person, he or she has not thought together, worked together, suffered together very much with adults as fellow human beings. Perhaps he or she has related to adults formally, as educational or social-service experts, but not as "fellow travelers to the grave." This pattern is a hindrance to having real-life heroes to look up to. It is harder for young people to reference themselves forward in age, to place themselves into their own futures with a sense of positive expectation and hope. If there is little involvement with children younger than they are, then they are separated also from their own past, the sense of being part of a life story, as well as from roles of responsibility for others. Age segregation seems to invite boredom and alienation, as well as being ill-prepared for responsibilities of both family and work.

Needless to say, I have not introduced the issue of age segregation in order to provide the adult generation with another way to blame the younger generation for the ills of society. Certainly, young people make choices, and some of those choices are very bad ones. But *they* did not create the world they stepped into. The adult generation and its predecessors did. But the question is, What, if anything, can be done about its destructive side?

Thinking of John Demos's two factors for prolonged adolescent crisis, there is little that Christians can do about the complexity of society—apart from attempting to withdraw from it. That would only make matters worse. We can, and many of us should, lead more simplified lives, but this will not significantly change the structure of the society into which young people must step. At least it will not change it quickly enough to be of benefit to their children. But is there nothing we can do about the radical discontinuity between generations? There are some things that would be wrong or foolish to try to change, but there might be others that could at least be resisted. Too often, Christians have simply accepted the results of industrialization as given, part of the nature of things, when in fact they are relatively recent and may still be changeable.

Railing against the youth subculture and its obvious excesses cannot be the *whole* solution. It has at times even unwittingly been counterproductive and helped to establish the worst in that subculture more firmly, by strengthening its internal identity through providing it with a "usable" enemy.

What we can do is to make efforts to build bridges positively between generations in family, church, and working worlds—and make that a priority. We can lean against age segregation in as many areas as possible. Time spent with adults whose priorities and lives of faith they can respect will in the end be far more effective than attempts to censor young people's heroes in music and film.

The most important area is the immediate family, and the way to pursue age integration is through time spent together in a wide variety of different activities. But mothers and fathers could make an effort to take their children to their workplace, so that they can see what happens there. They can also make an effort to enable their children to have a wide circle of adult friends of all ages. In short, to include their children as much as possible in their lives. They can help one another's children by giving them real work to do for pay, so that their work is valued.

The church has great untapped potential for encouraging age integration. Unhappily, the church too often has simply duplicated the age segregation of society at large, with its separate groups and programs for each age group—junior high, senior high, college, singles, young marrieds, divorced, older marrieds, older singles, and so on. Of course, in a society that is already age-segregated, it is much easier to do things this way, and any church concerned mainly with numbers is unlikely to risk change at this point. However, the church could be a place where these segregations are broken down through common service projects of people of all ages. It is not that all age-stratified groups should necessarily be abolished; it is that age-integrating priorities should be added.

THE SCULPTOR OR THE GARDENER?

The common line in these chapters has been how to encourage the younger generation to have vital, Christlike heroes. Although I have made some suggestions, it may well be that the most important part is that we be able to keep out of the way of what God is doing.

We can think of two images of child raising, the sculptor and the gardener. The sculptor, let us say, starts with a shapeless piece of marble or lump of clay, and with skill and creativity shapes out of it a form that he or she had in mind. The success or failure of the final product has to do almost entirely with the patience and skill of the sculptor.

By contrast, the gardener starts with a seed that has a life of its own once it germinates. It has a certain genetic code of its own. The gardener who plants an acorn does not expect it to produce tomatoes, nor the tomato seed to produce an oak tree. The gardener must prepare the soil, provide nutrients, water, and sunlight. A fruitful harvest will be in part due to the gardener's efforts, but also due to the original seed and many aspects of the environment that were outside of the gardener's control. There is a great deal that a gardener can do to encourage or discourage healthy growth, but the gardener is an observer to something that God is doing in a way that the sculptor is not.

Raising children is more like being a gardener than being a sculptor. Children are not the products of their parents' proficiency, but are first of all images of God, entrusted to the parents' care. God gives the growth. God would not have us abandon them to their own devices, nor would he have us forcibly mold them into a shape that pleases us.

We parents need to look to other parents of older children who have exemplified these attitudes. Look for people whose children really want to follow Christ and do it joyfully. We all need heroes, and people who are heroic as parents are some of the most worth watching.

The task to live out true glory or human excellence is certainly a daunting one, and it is even more daunting to have the responsibility to influence young people toward this goal. It could well be that the most significant influence that any one of us has in this world—for good or evil—is on a child or children, on our own or on the children of others. Whether we are parents or not, if we are in any way involved with young people, we must say with the apostle Paul, "Who is sufficient for these things?" (2 Corinthians 2:16). Our ultimate hope is the grace of God.

NOTES

⌇

Chapter One: Who Needs Heroes?
1. Ernest Becker, *The Denial of Death* (New York: Free Press, 1973), page 4.
2. William James, *The Varieties of Religious Experience* (New York: New American Library, Mentor Books, 1960), page 281.
3. Ray Browne and Marshall Fishwick, *Heroes in Transition* (Bowling Green, OH: Bowling Green University Press, 1983), page 288.
4. Philip Hallie, *Lest Innocent Blood Be Shed* (New York: Harper & Row, 1985), pages 1-4.
5. Hallie, page 2.
6. Jonathan Swift, as quoted in M. Thomas Inge, "A Hero in Our Eyes," *World & I*, vol. 66, no. 11, November 1991, page 571.
7. G. K. Chesterton, *The Napoleon of Notting Hill* (New York: Paulist Press, 1978), page 87.
8. Daniel Boorstin, *The Image* (Harmondsworth, Middlesex, England: Pelican Books, 1963), page 67.
9. Elizabeth Kastor, *Washington Post*, June 20, 1990, page C1.
10. Mark Gerzon, *A Choice of Heroes* (Boston: Houghton Mifflin, 1982), pages 32ff.
11. Lawrence Shames, *The Hunger for More* (New York: Times Books, 1989), page 101.
12. Thomas Peters and Robert Waterman, *In Search of Excellence* (New York: Harper & Row, 1982), page xxiv.
13. Jeffrey Sonnenfeld, *The Hero's Farewell: What Happens When CEOs Retire* (New York: Oxford University Press, 1988).
14. Helen Lynd, *Shame and the Search for Identity* (New York: Harcourt & Brace, 1958), pages 27-73.
15. *A Mind Awake, An Anthology of C. S. Lewis*, Clyde Kilby, ed. (New York: Harcourt Brace Jovanovich, 1968), page 42.
16. Blaise Pascal, *Pascal's Pensees* (New York: E. P. Dutton, 1958), number 404.

Chapter Two: Heroism and Cynicism
1. F. Scott Fitzgerald, as quoted in Paul Johnson, *Modern Times* (New York: Harper & Row, 1985), page 222.
2. James Patterson and Peter Kim, *The Day America Told the Truth* (New York: Prentice Hall, 1991), page 208.
3. David Daiches, "The Possibilities of Heroism," *American Scholar*, Winter 1955–56, page 106.

4. Richard Purtil, *J. R. R. Tolkien, Myth, Morality and Religion* (New York: Harper & Row, 1984), page x.
5. Peter Kreeft, *Knowing the Truth About God's Love* (Ann Arbor, MI: Servant, 1988), page 97.
6. Sam Shepard, "Fool for Love," *Fool for Love and Four Other Plays* (Toronto, New York: Bantam Books, 1988), pages 32-34.
7. Theodore Gross, *The Heroic Ideal in American Literature* (New York: Free Press, 1971), page 238.
8. Bertolt Brecht, *Galileo*, trans. Charles Lawton (New York: Grove Press, 1966), pages 114-115.
9. E. Merrill Root, *America's Steadfast Dream* (Belmont, MA: Western Islands, 1971), page 20.
10. G. K. Chesterton, *Heretics* (Bodley Head, London: John Lane, 1938), page 29.
11. Robert Nisbet, *The Twilight of Authority* (New York: Oxford University Press, 1981), pages 109-110.
12. Donald Richardson, *Peace Child* (Ventura, CA: Regal, 1983).
13. Ernest Becker, *The Birth and Death of Meaning* (New York: Free Press, 1971), pages 119-126.
14. C. E. M. Joad, as quoted in Orrin Klapp, *The Collective Search for Identity* (New York: Holt, Rinehart & Winston, 1969), page 60.
15. Patterson and Kim, page 208.
16. Robert Nisbet, *Prejudices* (Cambridge, MA: Harvard University Press, 1969), pages 152-158; see Ernest Jones, *The Life and Work of Sigmund Freud* (Harmondsworth, Middlesex, England: Penguin Books, 1961), as a case in point.
17. Erik Erikson, *Insight and Responsibility* (New York: Norton, 1964), page 112.
18. Michael Lesy, *Rescuers, the Lives of Heroes* (New York: Farrar, Straus & Giroux, 1991), page 43.
19. Lesy, page 63.
20. Lesy, page 106.
21. Joyce Carol Oates, as quoted in James Atlas, "Speaking Ill of the Dead," *New York Times Magazine*, November 6, 1988.
22. B. F. Skinner, *Beyond Freedom and Dignity* (New York: Alfred A. Knopf, 1971), page 110.
23. Skinner, page 111.
24. George Sheehan, *Running and Being* (New York: Simon & Schuster, 1978), page 10.
25. Jules Henry, as quoted in Christopher Lasch, *The Culture of Narcissism* (New York: Warner Books, 1979), page 157.
26. Francis Schaeffer, *How Shall We Then Live?* (Old Tappan, NJ: Revell, 1976).
27. Robert Bellah, et al., *Habits of the Heart* (New York: Harper & Row, 1985).
28. Russell Baker, "Taking Heroes Seriously," *New York Times Magazine*, December 20, 1981, page 17.

29. Logan Piersall Smith, as quoted in Orrin Klapp, *Heroes, Villains and Fools* (Englewood Cliffs, NJ: Prentice Hall, 1962), page 170.

30. Arthur M. Schlesinger, "The Decline of Greatness," in *Representative Men*, ed. Theodore Gross (New York: Free Press, 1970), page 22.

31. David Houston, *Science Fiction Heroes* (New York: Starlog Press, 1980), page 7.

32. Gertrude Himmelfarb, *On Looking into the Abyss* (New York: Knopf, 1994), page 27.

33. Gertrude Himmelfarb, "Of Heroes, Villains and Valets," *Commentary*, vol. 91 no. 6, June 1991, pages 20-22.

34. George Hegel, as quoted in Himmelfarb, *Looking into the Abyss*, page 27.

35. G. Himmelf, "Of Heroes, Villains, and Valets," *Commentary*, vol. 91 no. 6 (June 1991), page 22.

36. Rollo May, *Psychology and the Human Dilemma* (New York: D. Van Nostrand, 1967), page 4.

37. Oates, as quoted in Atlas, page 40.

38. See Samuel and Pearl Oliner, *The Altruistic Personality* (New York: Free Press, 1988).

39. Robert Coles, "How Do You Measure a Child's Level of Morality?" *Learning*, July/August 1981, pages 70-73.

40. Thomas Keneally, *Schindler's List* (New York: Simon & Schuster, 1993), page 14.

41. Blaise Pascal, *Pascal's Pensees* (New York: E. P. Dutton, 1958), number 418.

Chapter Three: Heroism and Triviality

1. Marshall Fishwick, *The Hero: American Style* (New York: David McKay, 1969), page 2.

2. Daniel Boorstin, *The Image* (Harmondsworth, Middlesex, England: Pelican Books, 1963), page 76.

3. Richard Pryor, as quoted in Leo Braudy *The Frenzy of Renown* (New York: Oxford University Press, 1986), page 548.

4. Norman Corwin, *Trivializing America* (Secaucus, NJ: Lyle Stuart, 1983), page 17.

5. Ernest Becker, *The Structure of Evil* (New York: Free Press, 1968), pages 50-51.

6. See Boorstin.

7. Boorstin, pages 7-8. In fact, the paper did not even appear for a second edition; evidently the Governor and Council did not welcome its promise to combat the spirit of lying and villainous crime in Boston. See Neil Postman, *Amusing Ourselves to Death* (New York: Viking Penguin, 1985), page 36.

8. Arthur MacEwen, as quoted in Boorstin, page 8.

9. Braudy, page 71.

10. Braudy, pages 59-60.

11. Braudy, page 3.

12. Braudy, page 584.

13. Michael Kelly, "David Gergen, the Master of the Game," *New York Times Magazine*, October 31, 1993, page 97.
14. Postman, pages 99-105.
15. S.L.A. Marshall, "We Must Have Heroes," *The Hero and Heroic Ideal*, in *The Great Ideas Today, 1973*, Robert M Hutchins, Mortimer Adler, ed. (Chicago: Encyclopedia Britanica, 1973), page 41.
16. Postman, page 7.
17. Boorstin, page 4.
18. Erving Goffman, *The Presentation of Self in Everyday Life* (Garden City, NY: Doubleday Anchor, 1959), pages 230-232.
19. Christopher Lasch, *The Culture of Narcissism* (New York: Warner Books, 1979), page 170.
20. Andy Warhol, as quoted in Lasch, page 170.
21. Warhol, in Lasch, page 170.
22. Kenneth Gergen, *The Saturated Self* (New York: Basic Books, 1991), pages 139-170.
23. Boorstin, page 57.
24. Roger Rollin, as quoted in "The Lone Ranger and Lenny Skutnik: The Hero as Popular Culture," *The Hero in Transition*, Ray Browne and Marshall Fishwick, ed. *Heroes in Transition* (Bowling Green, OH: Bowling Green University Press, 1983), page 14.
25. Rollin, page 15.
26. Rollin, page 25.
27. *Heroes of Popular Culture*, Ray Browne, Marshall Fishwick, and Michael T. Marsden, ed. (Bowling Green, OH: Bowling Green University Press, 1972), page 7.
28. Cutty Sark advertisement, *Time*, November 14, 1983.
29. Lenny Skutnik, as quoted in Browne and Fishwick, page 111.
30. Susanna McBee, "Heroes Are Back," *U.S. News and World Report*, April 22, 1985, pages 44ff.
31. John Skow, "Modeling the Eighties Look," *Time*, February 9, 1981, page 82.
32. Ron Suskind, "The Power of Political Consultants," *New York Times Magazine*, August 12, 1984, page 35.
33. Suskind, page 35.
34. Kiku Adato, "The Incredible Shrinking Sound Bite," *New Republic*, May 28, 1990, pages 20-23; see also Kiki Adato, *Picture Perfect* (New York: Harper Collins, Basic Books, 1993).
35. Earl Blackwell and Cleveland Amory, as quoted in Boorstin, page 58.
36. Boorstin, page 58.
37. Braudy, page 3.
38. Boorstin, page 4.
39. Blaise Pascal, *Pascal's Pensees* (New York: E. P. Dutton, 1958), number 418.

Chapter Four: Heroism and the Person in the Street

1. A. M. Schlesinger, Jr., "The Decline of Greatness," *Representative Men*,

Theodore Gross, ed. (New York: Free Press, 1970), page 22.

2. Orrin Klapp, *Symbolic Leaders* (Chicago: Aldine, 1964), page 26.

3. Ernest Becker, *Escape from Evil* (New York: Free Press, 1975).

4. Country singer Waylon Jennings in an interview.

5. Klapp, *Symbolic Leaders*, page 26.

6. Leo Braudy, *The Frenzy of Renown* (New York: Oxford University Press, 1986), page 3.

7. James Thurber, *The Thurber Carnival* (Harmondsworth, Middlesex, England: Penguin, 1977).

8. Orrin Klapp, *The Collective Search for Identity* (New York: Holt, Rinehart & Winston, 1969), pages 212ff.

9. Klapp, *Collective Search*, page 213.

10. Braudy, pages 589-590.

11. Klapp, *Collective Search*, page 239.

12. *New York Times Magazine*, December 4, 1983, page 120.

13. Michael Novak, *Ascent of the Mountain, Flight of the Dove* (New York: Harper & Row, 1978), page 52.

14. Braudy, page 579.

15. Orrin Klapp, *Heroes, Villains and Fools* (Englewood Cliffs, NJ: Prentice Hall, 1962), page 168.

16. John T. Molloy, "Executive Style, the Inestimable Impact of Image," *Success*, September 1986, page 50.

17. Klapp, *Heroes, Villains and Fools*, page 220.

18. Erving Goffman, as quoted in Christopher Lasch, *The Culture of Narcissism* (New York: Warner Books, 1979), page 165.

19. William Kirk Kilpatrick, *Psychological Seduction* (Nashville: Nelson, 1983), pages 120-121.

20. Theodore Gross, *The Heroic Ideal in American Literature* (New York: Free Press, 1971), page 280.

21. Eric Russell Bentley, *A Century of Hero-Worship* (Philadelphia: J.B. Lipincott, 1944), page 34.

22. Becker, page 164.

23. G. K. Chesterton, *The Everlasting Man* (Garden City, NY: Doubleday, 1955), page 245.

Chapter Five: A Foundation for Heroism in the Twentieth Century

1. Joy Gould, "Heroes in Black and White," in *The Hero and the Heroic Ideal*, in *Great Ideas, 1973*, Robert M. Hutchins and Mortimer Adler, ed. (Chicago: Great Books Publications, Encyclopedia Britanica, 1973), page 59.

2. Daniel Boorstin, *The Image* (Harmondsworth, Middlesex, England: Pelican Books, 1963), page 76.

3. Orrin Klapp, *Heroes, Villains and Fools* (Englewood Cliffs, NJ: Prentice Hall, 1962), page 173.

4. Klapp, page 176.

5. Norman Corwin, *Trivializing America* (Secaucus, NJ: Lyle Stuart, 1983), page 292.

6. Corwin, page 293.
7. Joseph Campbell, *The Hero with a Thousand Faces*, Bollingen Series (Princeton, NJ: Princeton University Press, 1972), pages 43-49.
8. Campbell, page 30.
9. Power, page 130.
10. Campbell, page 387.
11. Christopher Lasch, "The Mismeasure of Man," *TNR* (April 19, 1993), page 34.
12. Lasch, page 34.
13. Power, page 211.
14. Power, page 148.
15. Ernest Becker, *The Denial of Death* (New York: Free Press, 1973).
16. Becker, *Denial of Death*, page 26.
17. Gerard Manley Hopkins, J. Sire, page 42.
18. Leo Braudy, *The Frenzy of Renown* (New York: Oxford University Press, 1986), page 3.
19. Friedrich Nietzsche, *Thus Spoke Zarathustra* (London: Penguin Books, 1988), page 297.
20. Dietrich Bonhoeffer, *Letters and Papers from Prison* (New York: Macmillan, 1962), page 221.
21. Braudy, page 58.
22. Becker, *Birth and Death of Meaning*, page 124.
23. Becker, pages 124-125.
24. Pascal, as quoted in Becker, *Birth and Death of Meaning*, page 123.
25. Sidney Hook, *The Hero in History* (Boston: Beacon Press, 1955), page 13.
26. William Barrett, *The Illusion of Technique* (Garden City, NY: Anchor Books, 1979), page 154.
27. James Fowler, *Stages of Faith* (San Francisco: Harper & Row, 1981), page 279.
28. C. S. Lewis, *The Weight of Glory* (Grand Rapids, MI: Eerdmans, 1979), page 10.
29. Becker, *Denial of Death*, page 91.
30. Thomas Merton, as quoted by L. Morrow, "Have We Abandoned Excellence?" *Time*, March 22, 1982, page 90.

Chapter Six: Fools and Foolworship: Knowing the Pseudohero

1. William Gaddis, as quoted in Lawrence Shames, *The Hunger for More* (New York: Times Books, 1989), page 237.
2. Dietrich Bonhoeffer, *Letters and Papers from Prison* (New York: Macmillan, 1962), page 22.
3. Augustine, *The City of God* (Garden City, NY: Doubleday, Image Books, 1953), page 238.
4. Erasmus, *In Praise of Folly* (New York: New American Library, Mentor-Omega Books, 1964). See also 1 Corinthians 1–2.
5. Orrin Klapp, *Heroes, Villains and Fools* (Englewood Cliffs, NJ: Prentice Hall, 1962).

6. Konrad Kellen, in Introduction to Jacques Ellul, *Propaganda* (New York: Vintage, 1973), page vi.
7. See chapter 2.
8. Peter Sloterdijk, *Critique of Cynical Reason* (Minneapolis: University of Minnesota Press, 1987), pages xi, 4.
9. Dorothy Sayers, *Christian Letters to a Post-Christian World* (Grand Rapids, MI: Eerdmans, 1969), page 152.
10. Gaddis, in Shames, page 237.

Chapter Seven: True Heroism: Why the Imitation of Christ?

1. Robert Stone, "The Reason for Stories," *Harper's Magazine*, June 1988, page 75.
2. G. C. Berkouwer, *Faith and Sanctification* (Grand Rapids, MI: Eerdmans, 1966), page 149.
3. Irenaeus, quoted in Douglas Hall, *Imaging God* (Grand Rapids, MI: Eerdmans, 1986), page 200.
4. Iris Murdoch, *The Sovereignty of the Good* (New York: Ark Paperbacks, 1970), page 56.
5. Luke alone had not known Jesus before the Resurrection, but he consulted with those who had.

Chapter Eight: The Imitation of a Humble Person

1. George MacDonald, *George MacDonald, An Anthology*, ed. C. S. Lewis (New York: Macmillan, 1956), page 59.
2. Flannery O'Connor, *Mystery and Manners* (New York: Farrar, Straus & Giroux, Noonday Press, 1992), page 35.
3. C. S. Lewis, *Mere Christianity* (Glasgow, Scotland: Collins, Fontana Books, 1975), page 112.
4. C. S. Lewis, *Miracles* (Glasgow, Scotland: Collins, Fontana Books, 1974).
5. Graham Kendrick, "From Heaven You Came," in *The Servant King* (Eastbourne, England: Kingsway Publications, 1985), page 17.
6. Friedrich Nietzsche, *Twilight of the Idols/The Anti-Christ* (Harmondsworth, Middlesex, England: Penguin Books, 1968), page 26.
7. Iris Murdoch, *The Sovereignty of the Good* (New York: Ark Paperbacks, 1970).
8. Joseph Pieper, *The Four Cardinal Virtues* (Notre Dame, IN: University of Notre Dame Press, 1980), page 189.
9. Howard Cosell and Joan Kennedy, as quoted in Frank Trippett, "On Leading the Cheers for Number One," *Time*, June 8, 1981, page 81.
10. Leo Braudy, *The Frenzy of Renown* (New York: Oxford University Press, 1986). This book is a history of the quest for fame.
11. G. K. Chesterton, *The Defendant* (London: R. Brimley Johnson, 1901), page 97.
12. Chesterton, page 97.
13. Dietrich Bonhoeffer, *Ethics* (New York: Macmillan, 1965), page 82.

Chapter Nine: The Imitation of Christ: The Breadth of Heroism

1. Dietrich Bonhoeffer, *Ethics* (New York: Macmillan, 1965), page 81.
2. Maharishi Mahesh Yogi, *Maharishi, the Guru* (New York: New American Library, A Signet Book, 1968), page 28.
3. G. K. Chesterton, *Orthodoxy* (Garden City, NY: Doubleday, Image Books, 1959), page 93.
4. Paul Holmer, *C. S. Lewis: The Shape of His Faith and Thought* (New York: Harper & Row, 1976), pages 53-54.
5. Samuel and Pearl Oliner, *The Altruistic Personality* (New York: Free Press, 1988).
6. Philip Hallie, "From Cruelty to Goodness," in *Vice and Virtue in Everyday Life*, ed. Christina Hoff Sommers (New York: Harcourt Brace Jovanovich, 1985), page 16.
7. Corrie ten Boom, *The Hiding Place* (Old Tappan, NJ: Revell, Spire Books, 1971).

Chapter Ten: Heroes New and Used: Imitating Christlikeness in Others

1. Maya Angelou, "That Which Lives After Us," in *Facing Evil* (LaSalle, IL: Open Court, 1989), page 28.
2. George Eliot, writing of Dorothea in *Middlemarch* (New York: New American Library, Signet Books, 1981), page 811.
3. Corrie ten Boom, *The Hiding Place* (Old Tappan, NJ: Revell, Spire Books, 1971).
4. Frederick Douglass, *Narrative of the Life of Frederick Douglass* (New York: Signet Books, 1968), pages vii-viii.
5. Douglass, page 119.

Chapter Eleven: Heroism and Moral Learning

1. Ernest Becker, *The Birth and Death of Meaning* (New York: Free Press, 1971), page 126.
2. Neil Postman, "Learning by Story," *Atlantic Monthly*, December 1989, page 124.
3. Peter Stearns, *Themes in Modern Social History* (Pittsburgh: Carnegie Mellon University Press, 1985), page 227.
4. G. K. Chesterton, *Heretics* (Bodley Head, London: John Lane, 1938), page 26.
5. Chesterton, page 20.
6. Neil Postman, "Learning by Story," page 122.
7. Neil Postman, *Conscientious Objections* (New York: Knopf, 1988), page 71.
8. William Kirk Kilpatrick, *The Emperor's New Clothes* (Westchester, IL: Crossway, 1985), page 84.
9. Roger Gould, *Transformations* (New York: Simon & Schuster, 1979), pages 17-42.

Chapter Twelve: The Integrity of the Parent Generation

1. Linda Burton, Janet Dittmer, and Cheri Loveless, *What's a Smart Woman*

Like You Doing at Home? (Washington: Acropolis Books, 1986), page 116.
2. Gilbert Meilaender, "What Families Are For," *First Things*, October 1990, page 38.
3. Jonathan Sacks, "Reith Lecture Number 3," *Listener*, November 29, 1990, page 17.
4. Gilbert Highet, *The Art of Teaching* (New York: Vintage Books, 1950), page 5.
5. Russell Baker, *Growing Up* (New York: New American Library, Signet Books, 1982), pages 121-122.
6. William Cobbett, "Beer," *Consumer Reports*, July 1983, page 342.

Chapter Thirteen: Children in Society
1. Roy Anker, ed., *Dancing in the Dark* (Grand Rapids, MI: Eerdmans, 1991), page 3.
2. Mark Twain, *The Adventures of Tom Sawyer*, in *The Family Mark Twain* (New York: Harper & Row, 1972), pages 295-296.
3. John Demos, *A Little Commonwealth* (New York: Oxford University Press, 1988), page 145.
4. Joseph Kett, *Rites of Passage* (New York: Harper & Row, Basic Books, 1977), page 243.
5. Kett, page 6.
6. Kett, page 3.
7. Demos, page 150.

BIBLIOGRAPHY

≫

Adato, Kiku. "The Incredible Shrinking Sound Bite." *New York Times Magazine* (May 28, 1990), pages 20ff.

Adato, Kiku. *Picture Perfect.* New York: Harper Collins, Basic Books, 1993.

Angelou, Maya. "That Which Lives After Us." In *Facing Evil.* LaSalle, IL: Open Court, 1989.

Anker, Roy, ed. *Dancing in the Dark.* Grand Rapids, MI: Eerdmans, 1991.

Atlas, James. "Speaking Ill of the Dead." *New York Times Magazine* (November 6, 1988).

Auerbach, Eric. *Mimesis.* Princeton, NJ: Princeton University Press, 1974.

Augustine. *The City of God.* Garden City, NY: Doubleday, Image Books, 1953.

Baker, Russell. *Growing Up.* New York: New American Library, Signet Books, 1982.

Baker, Russell. "Taking Heroes Seriously." *New York Times Magazine* (December 20, 1981).

Barrett, William. *The Illusion of Technique.* Garden City, NY: Anchor Books, 1979.

Becker, Ernest. *The Birth and Death of Meaning.* New York: Free Press, 1971.

Becker, Ernest. *The Denial of Death.* New York: Free Press, 1973.

Becker, Ernest. *Escape from Evil.* New York: Free Press, 1975.

Becker, Ernest. *The Structure of Evil.* New York: Free Press, 1968.

Bellah, Robert, Richard Madsen, William M. Sullivan, Ann Swidler, and Steven M. Tipton. *Habits of the Heart.* New York: Harper & Row, 1985.

Bentley, Eric Russell. *A Century of Hero-Worship.* Philadelphia: J. B. Lippincott, 1944.

Berkouwer, G. C. *Faith and Sanctification.* Grand Rapids, MI: Eerdmans, 1966.

Berkowitz, Bill. *Local Heroes.* Lexington, MA: Lexington Books, 1987.

Biallas, Leonard. *Myths, Gods, Heroes and Saviors*. Mystic, CT: Twenty-Third Publications, 1989.

Bonhoeffer, Dietrich. *Ethics*. New York: Macmillan, 1965.

Bonhoeffer, Dietrich. *Letters and Papers from Prison*. New York: Macmillan, 1962.

Boorstin, Daniel. *The Image*. Harmondsworth, Middlesex, England: Pelican Books, 1963.

Braudy, Leo. *The Frenzy of Renown*. New York: Oxford University Press, 1986.

Browne, Ray. *Heroes of Popular Culture*. Bowling Green, OH: Bowling Green University Press, 1972.

Browne, Ray, Marshall Fishwick, and Michael T. Marsden. *The Hero in Transition*. Bowling Green, OH: Bowling Green University Press, 1983.

Brownstein, Rachel. *Becoming a Heroine*. Harmondsworth, Middlesex, England: Penguin Books, 1984.

Burton, Dittmer, and Loveless. *What's a Smart Woman Like You Doing at Home?* Washington: Acropolis Books, 1986.

Campbell, Joseph. *The Hero with a Thousand Faces*. Bollingen Series. Princeton, NJ: Princeton University Press, 1972.

Carlyle, Thomas. *Heroes, Hero-Worship and the Heroic in History*. London: Chapman & Hall, 1904.

Chesterton, G. K. *The Defendant*. London: R. Brimley Johnson, 1901.

Chesterton, G. K. *Everlasting Man*. Garden City, NY: Doubleday, 1955.

Chesterton, G. K. *Heretics*. Bodley Head, London: John Lane, 1938.

Chesterton, G. K. *The Napoleon of Notting Hill*. New York: Paulist Press, 1978.

Chesterton, G. K. *Orthodoxy*. Garden City, NY: Doubleday, Image Books, 1959.

Cobbett, William. "Beer." *Consumer Reports* (July 1983), page 342.

Coles, Robert. "How Do You Measure a Child's Level of Morality?" *Learning* (July/August 1981).

Coles, Robert. *The Moral Life of Children*. Boston: Houghton Mifflin, 1986.

Corwin, Norman. *Trivializing America*. Secaucus, NJ: Lyle Stuart, 1983.

Daiches, David. "The Possibilities of Heroism." *American Scholar* (Winter 1955-56).

Demos, John. *A Little Commonwealth*. New York: Oxford University Press, 1988.

Douglass, Frederick. *Narrative of the Life of Frederick Douglass*. New York: Signet Books, 1968.

Dykstra, Craig. *Vision and Character*. New York: Paulist Press, 1981.

Edwards, Lee. *Psyche as Hero*. Middletown, CT: Wesleyan University Press, 1987.

Eliot, George. *Middlemarch*. New York: New American Library, Signet Books, 1968.

Ellul, Jacques. *Propaganda*. New York: Vintage Books, 1973.

Erasmus. *In Praise of Folly*. New York: New American Library, Mentor-Omega Books, 1964.

Erikson, Erik. *Insight and Responsibility*. New York: Norton, 1964.

Fishwick, Marshall. *The Hero: American Style*. New York: David McKay, 1969.

Fowler, James. *Stages of Faith*. San Francisco: Harper & Row, 1981.

Gergen, Kenneth. *The Saturated Self*. New York: Basic Books, 1991.

Gerzon, Mark. *A Choice of Heroes*. Boston: Houghton Mifflin, 1982.

Goffman, Erving. *The Presentation of Self in Everyday Life*. Garden City, NY: Doubleday Anchor, 1959.

Goode, William J. *The Celebration of Heroes*. Berkeley, CA: University of California Press, 1978.

Gould, Joy. *Great Ideas, 1973*. Great Books Publications, 1973.

Greene, Theodore P. *America's Heroes*. New York: Oxford University Press, 1970.

Gross, Theodore. *The Heroic Ideal in American Literature*. New York: Free Press, 1971.

Gross, Theodore. *Representative Men*. New York: Free Press, 1970.

Hall, Douglas. *Imaging God*. Grand Rapids, MI: Eerdmans, 1986.

Hallie, Philip. "From Cruelty to Goodness." In *Vice and Virtue in Everyday Life*. Christina Hoff Sommers, ed. New York: Harcourt Brace Jovanovich, 1985.

Hallie, Philip. *Lest Innocent Blood Be Shed*. New York: Harper & Row, 1985.

Hauerwas, Stanley. *A Community of Character*. Notre Dame, IN: University of Notre Dame Press, 1983.

Hauerwas, Stanley. *Vision and Virtue*. Notre Dame, IN: University of Notre Dame, 1981.

Highet, Gilbert. *The Art of Teaching*. New York: Vintage Books, 1950.

Himmelfarb, Gertrude. "Of Heroes, Villains and Valets." *Commentary*. Vol. 91, no. 6 (June 1991).

Himmelfarb, Gertrude. *On Looking into the Abyss*. New York: Knopf, 1994.

Holmer, Paul. *C. S. Lewis: The Shape of His Faith and Thought*. New York: Harper & Row, 1976.

Hook, Sidney. *The Hero in History*. Boston: Beacon Press, 1955.

Houston, David. *Science Fiction Heroes*. New York: Starlog Press, 1980.

Inge, Thomas M. "A Hero in Our Eyes." *World & I*. Vol. 66, no. 11 (November 1991).

James, William. *The Varieties of Religious Experience*. New York: New American Library, Mentor Books, 1960.

Johnson, Paul. *Modern Times*. New York: Harper & Row, 1985.

Jones, Ernest. *The Life and Work of Sigmund Freud*. Harmondsworth, Middlesex, England: Penguin Books, 1961.

Kantor, Elizabeth. *Washington Post* (June 20, 1990), page Cl.

Kelly, Michael. "David Gergen, the Master of the Game." *New York Times Magazine* (October 31, 1993).

Keneally, Thomas. *Schindler's List*. New York: Simon & Schuster, 1993.

Kendrick, Graham. "From Heaven You Came." In *The Servant King*. Eastbourne, England: Kingsway Publications, 1985.

Kett, Joseph. *Rites of Passage*. New York: Harper & Row, Basic Books, 1977.

Kilby, Clyde. *A Mind Awake, An Anthology of C. S. Lewis*. New York: Harcourt Brace Jovanovich, 1968.

Kilpatrick, William Kirk. *The Emperor's New Clothes*. Westchester, IL: Crossway, 1985.

Kilpatrick, William Kirk. *Psychological Seduction*. Nashville: Nelson, 1983.

Kilpatrick, William Kirk. *Why Johnny Can't Tell Right from Wrong*. New York: Simon & Schuster, 1992.

Klapp, Orrin. *The Collective Search for Identity*. New York: Holt, Rinehart & Winston, 1969.

Klapp, Orrin. *Heroes, Villains and Fools*. Englewood Cliffs, NJ: Prentice Hall, 1962.

Klapp, Orrin. *Symbolic Leaders*. Chicago: Aldine, 1964.

Kreeft, Peter. *Knowing the Truth About God's Love*. Ann Arbor, MI: Servant, 1988.

Lasch, Christopher. *The Culture of Narcissism*. New York: Warner Books, 1979.

Lesy, Michael. *Rescuers, the Lives of Heroes*. New York: Farrar, Straus & Giroux, 1991.

Levine, Arthur. *When Dreams and Heroes Died*. San Francisco: Jossey-Bass, 1978.

Lewis, C. S. *The Last Battle*. New York: Macmillan, 1976.

Lewis, C. S. *Mere Christianity*. Glasgow, Scotland: Collins, Fontana Books, 1975.

Lewis, C. S. *Miracles*. Glasgow, Scotland: Collins, Fontana Books, 1974.

Lewis, C. S. *The Weight of Glory*. Grand Rapids, MI: Eerdmans, 1979.

Lynd, Helen. *Shame and the Search for Identity*. New York: Harcourt & Brace, 1958.

MacDonald, George. *George MacDonald, an Anthology*. C. S. Lewis, ed. New York: Macmillan, 1956.

May, Rollo. *The Cry for Myth*. New York: Norton, 1981.

May, Rollo. *My Quest for Beauty*. San Francisco: Saybrook, 1985.

May, Rollo. *Psychology and the Human Dilemma*. New York: D. Van Nostrand, 1967.

McBee, Susanna. "Heroes Are Back." *U.S. News and World Report* (April 22, 1985), pages 44ff.

Meilaender, Gilbert. *The Theory and Practice of Virtue*. Notre Dame, IN: University of Notre Dame Press, 1984.

Meilaender, Gilbert. "What Families Are For." *First Things* (October 1990), page 38.

Merton, Thomas. *Time* (March 22, 1982), page 90.

Molloy, John T. "Executive Style, the Inestimable Impact of Image." *Success* (September 1986), page 50.

Murdoch, Iris. *The Sovereignty of the Good*. New York: Ark Paperbacks, 1970.

Nietzsche, Friedrich. *Thus Spoke Zarathustra*. London: Penguin Books, 1988.

Nietzsche, Friedrich. *Twilight of the Idols/The Anti-Christ*. Harmondsworth, Middlesex, England: Penguin Books, 1968.

Nisbet, Robert. *Prejudices*. Cambridge, MA: Harvard University Press, 1982.

Nisbet, Robert. *The Twilight of Authority*. New York: Oxford University Press, 1981.

Novak, Michael. *Ascent of the Mountain, Flight of the Dove*. Harper & Row, 1978.

O'Connor, Flannery. *Mystery and Manners*. New York: Farrar Straus & Giroux, Noonday Press, 1992.

O'Faolain, Sean. *The Vanishing Hero*. New York: Grosset & Dunlap, Universal Library, 1957.

Oliner, Samuel and Pearl. *The Altruistic Personality*. New York: Free Press, 1988.

Pascal, Blaise. *Pascal's Pensees*. New York: E. P. Dutton, 1958.

Patterson and Kim. *The Day America Told the Truth*. New York: Prentice Hall, 1991.

Peters, Thomas, and Robert Waterman. *In Search of Excellence*. New York: Harper & Row, 1982.

Pieper, Joseph. *The Four Cardinal Virtues*. Notre Dame, IN: Notre Dame University Press, 1980.

Pilger, John. *Heroes*. London: Jonathan Cape, 1986.

Postman, Neil. *Amusing Ourselves to Death*. New York: Viking Penguin, 1985.

Postman, Neil. *Conscientious Objections*. New York: Knopf, 1988.

Postman, Neil. "Learning by Story." *Atlantic Monthly* (December 1989), page 129.

Purtil, Richard. *J. R. R. Tolkien, Myth, Morality and Religion*. New York: Harper & Row, 1984.

Raglan, Lord. *The Hero*. Westport, CT: Greenwood Press, 1956.

Reed, Walter. *Meditations on the Hero*. New Haven, CT: Yale University Press, 1978.

Richardson, Donald. *Peace Child*. Ventura, CA: Regal, 1983.

Roche, George. *A World Without Heroes: The Modern Tragedy*. Hillsdale, MI: Hillsdale College Press, 1987.

Root, E. Merrill. *America's Steadfast Dream*. Belmont, MA: Western Islands, 1971.

Sacks, Jonathan. "Reith Lecture Number 3." *Listener* (November 29, 1990), page 17.

Sayers, Dorothy. *Christian Letters to a Post-Christian World*. Grand Rapids, MI: Eerdmans, 1969.

Schaeffer, Francis. *How Shall We Then Live?* Old Tappan, NJ: Revell, 1976.

Shames, Lawrence. *The Hunger for More*. New York: Times Books, 1989.

Sheehan, George. *Running and Being*. New York: Warner Books, 1978.

Sloterdijk, Peter. *Critique of Cynical Reason.* Minneapolis: University of Minnesota Press, 1987.

Sonnenfeld, Jeffrey. *The Hero's Farewell: What Happens When CEOs Retire.* New York: Oxford University Press, 1988.

Stearns, Peter. *Themes in Modern Social History.* Pittsburgh: Carnegie Mellon University Press, 1985.

Stein, Andre. *Quiet Heroes.* New York: New York University Press, 1988.

Stone, Robert. "The Reason for Stories." *Harper's Magazine.* (June 1988), page 75.

Sudjic, Deyan. *Cult Heroes.* New York: Norton, 1990.

Suskind, Ron. "The Power of Political Consultants." *New York Times Magazine* (August 12, 1984), pages 35ff.

Talese, Gay. *Fame and Obscurity.* New York: Laurel, Dell, 1981.

Ten Boom, Corrie. *The Hiding Place.* Old Tappan, NJ: Revell, Spire Books, 1971.

Thurber, James. *The Thurber Carnival.* Harmondsworth, Middlesex, England: Penguin Books, 1977.

Trilling, Lionel. *Sincerity and Authenticity.* Cambridge, MA: Harvard University Press, 1972.

Twain, Mark. *The Adventures of Tom Sawyer.* London: Dean & Son.

Wilder, Amos. *Jesus' Parables and the War of Myths.* Philadelphia: Fortress, 1982.

Yankelovich (poll). *New York Times Magazine* (December 4, 1983), page 120.

AUTHOR

Dick Keyes is the director of the L'Abri Fellowship in Southborough, Massachusetts, a residential study center for students and seekers of the truth of the Christian faith. He holds the B.A. in history from Harvard University and the M.Div. from Westminster Theological Seminary in Philadelphia. He encountered the Christian faith under the teaching of Francis Schaeffer at L'Abri in Switzerland shortly after his college graduation. He has served at L'Abri in London and in Hampshire, England, and as a pastor of International Presbyterian Church in London. He and his wife, Mardi, and their three sons have lived in Southborough for sixteen years.